THE INDEPENDENT VOTER

Independent voters—the 40–50 percent of Americans who reject identification with either of the two major parties or with any party—are increasing in number and impact. Independents are determining the outcome of major elections, upending the long-held categories of political science. Drawing on historical and contemporary data (including survey data, participant observation, interviews, and current writings and scholarship) and providing timely new analysis, the authors argue that independents are an engine for a transformation of US democracy, perhaps even its saviors. Rather than "leaning" to a party or an ideology, independents vary on issues but share a deep distrust of the partisan system. What are the consequences of this distrust? What about shifting trends among Black, Latino, and Asian communities regarding party loyalty? What of young voters who eschew party identification wanting a different kind of political culture? For a wide variety of audiences, this book gives students, scholars, campaign professionals, activists, and media analysts an insight into current voting dynamics and future possibilities.

Thom Reilly is Professor in the School of Public Affairs and Co-director of the Center for an Independent and Sustainable Democracy at Arizona State University.

Jacqueline S. Salit is President of Independent Voting and Co-director of the Center for an Independent and Sustainable Democracy at Arizona State University.

Omar H. Ali is Dean of Lloyd International Honors College and Professor of African-American political history at the University of North Carolina Greensboro.

PRAISE FOR
THE INDEPENDENT VOTER

"This book's exploration of [independent voters] is important and honest. The major media organizations try to marginalize this group as being secretly partisan or not holding any consistent beliefs. These organizations are trying to marginalize independent voters because they know that we're actually the majority, and if we band together, we can take this country back from the extreme partisans they represent."

—Andrew Yang,
from the Foreword

"*The Independent Voter* does a fantastic job chronicling the rise, and power, of the fastest-growing segment of the electorate in the United States. It is clear that more and more Americans are tired of partisan gridlock and want their leaders to be public servants, not party servants. Republicans and Democratic leaders should take note and anyone interested in the future of American democracy should read this book."

—Arnold Schwarzenegger,
former Governor of California

"This work seeks to prove that independent voters do indeed exist and are a powerful force. Thus, anyone interested in elections, voters, and the possibility of reimagining our two-party system should read this book!"

—Cathy J. Cohen,
University of Chicago

"If you are interested in America's independent voters, you must read this book. It analyzes who independent voters are and makes a strong argument about how those not registered with a political party face ballot access challenges in states across the country. This book provocatively grapples with who independent voters are and why they matter."

—Christian Grose,
University of Southern California

"*The Independent Voter* is an important work, both a piece of scholarship and a smoke signal, a cloud on the horizon, a shift in barometric pressure. Reilly, Salit, and Ali paint a picture of an emergence, a political sensibility that simultaneously goes back to the founding of the country and looks forward to a more innovative and free-flowing manner of conducting political life in the 21st century. It's a book about possibility—how ordinary American voters are refusing to play by the partisan rules and are driving the country toward a new culture of self-governance. Read this book if you want to be inspired!"

—John Opdycke,
President of Open Primaries

THE INDEPENDENT VOTER

Thom Reilly
Jacqueline S. Salit
Omar H. Ali

Foreword by: Andrew Yang
Afterword by: Jessie Fields

Routledge
Taylor & Francis Group

NEW YORK AND LONDON

Cover image: Leigh Prather/Shutterstock

First published 2023
by Routledge
605 Third Avenue, New York, NY 10158

and by Routledge
4 Park Square, Milton Park, Abingdon, Oxon, OX14 4RN

Routledge is an imprint of the Taylor & Francis Group, an informa business

Library of Congress Cataloging-in-Publication Data
Names: Reilly, Thom, 1960– author. | Salit, Jacqueline S, author. |
    Ali, Omar H. (Omar Hamid), author.
Title: The independent voter / Thom Reilly, Jacqueline S. Salit,
    Omar H. Ali ; foreword by Andrew Yang ; afterword by Jessie Fields.
Description: New York : Routledge, 2023. | Includes bibliographical
    references and index.
Identifiers: LCCN 2022014082 (print) | LCCN 2022014083 (ebook) |
    ISBN 9781032147338 (Paperback) | ISBN 9781032147345 (Hardback) |
    ISBN 9781003240808 (eBook)
Subjects: LCSH: Party affiliation—United States. | Political parties—
    United States. | Voting—United States.
Classification: LCC JK2261 .R335 2023 (print) | LCC JK2261 (ebook) |
    DDC 324.273—dc23/eng/20220715
LC record available at https://lccn.loc.gov/2022014082
LC ebook record available at https://lccn.loc.gov/2022014083

ISBN: 978-1-032-14734-5 (hbk)
ISBN: 978-1-032-14733-8 (pbk)
ISBN: 978-1-003-24080-8 (ebk)

DOI: 10.4324/9781003240808

Typeset in Bembo
by Apex CoVantage, LLC

CONTENTS

ABOUT THE AUTHORS

Thom Reilly is Professor in the School of Public Affairs and Co-director of the Center for an Independent and Sustainable Democracy at Arizona State University. He is the former chancellor of the Nevada System of Higher Education, chief executive officer for Clark County, Nevada, and head of the child welfare system for Nevada. He received his master's degree and doctorate in public administration from the University of Southern California and a master's in social work at ASU. He is a fellow of the National Academy of Public Administration. His research focuses on public pay and benefits, governance, the independent voter, and child welfare. He is the author of *The Failure of Governance in Bell California: Big-Time Corruption in a Small Town* (Lexington Books, 2016) and *Rethinking Public Sector Compensation: What Ever Happened to the Public Interest?* (M. E. Sharpe, 2012).

Jacqueline S. Salit is President of Independent Voting, a national strategy, communications, and organizing center that works to connect independent voters across the United States and supports their empowerment. Salit is a 30-year veteran of the independent and reform movements, playing vital roles in the third-party presidential campaigns of Ross Perot and Lenora Fulani. She ran the Independence Party segment of Michael Bloomberg's three successful mayoral campaigns in New York. Salit is the author of *Independents Rising* (Palgrave Macmillan, 2012). She co-authored with Thom Reilly a chapter in *Democracy Unchained* (New Press, 2020) and authored the afterword of Omar H. Ali's *In the Balance of Power* (Ohio University Press, 2020). Currently a professor of practice at Arizona State University, she is the co-director of the Center for an Independent and Sustainable Democracy at ASU. Salit is a member of the Dramatist Guild and the author of several plays, including *Shackleton on Ice, Votes, The Society of One-Hit Wonders, Carol and the Grapes of Wrath*, and *BALDWIN/KENNEDY*.

Omar H. Ali is Dean of Lloyd International Honors College and Professor of African-American political history at the University of North Carolina Greensboro. Selected as the Carnegie Foundation North Carolina Professor of the Year, he graduated from the London School of Economics and Political Science and received his PhD in history from Columbia University. He has served as a Fulbright Professor in Bogotá, Colombia, and a library scholar at Harvard University. His research explores the history of African Americans and independent politics, and he is the author of several books, including *In the Balance of Power: Independent Black Politics and Third-Party Movements in the United States* (Ohio University Press, 2008; 2020 revised) and *In the Lion's Mouth: Black Populism in the New South, 1886–1900* (University Press of Mississippi, 2010).

PREFACE

Once outliers, independents or nonaligned voters, can no longer be ignored or marginalized by politicians or political scientists. Millions of independent voters, between 40 and 50 percent of the total electorate, forsaking a party identification and long treated as a sideshow in the circus of US politics, are emerging as a force of their own.[1]

The Independent Voter provides the most in-depth look at this increasingly significant group of US citizens who have chosen not to align with either the Democratic or the Republican party.

This book has been written to reach policymakers, political activists, elected officials, university students, civic and business groups, and concerned individuals of all backgrounds. We hope it serves as a helpful resource for what the authors believe is an overdue reconsideration of the importance of the independent voter in protecting, fortifying, and developing American democracy in the 21st century.

Chapter 1 looks at the independent voter circa the 2020s and explores the demographics, growth, diversity, and rise of the independent voter. Is there a binding ideology or is the modern notion of ideology irrelevant to these disaffected voters? The authors address the two-party bias against outsider forces and how that limits the power of independents. Chapter 2 recounts the political struggles of independents within the broader historical context of the United States since its founding. Although there is nothing in the US Constitution regarding political parties, a bipartisan framework came to dominate the nation. Ordinary citizens have challenged the major parties and their policies through the formation of third parties, organizing independent political networks and creating movements for political reform. Abolitionists of the mid-19th century, the Populists of the late 19th century, and both left-wing and center-right formations in the 20th century are among these independents.

Chapter 3 covers the history of how political scientists have attempted to disapprove the notion of the independent voter, as well as the media's lack of attention to nonaligned voters. For the past 60 years, political scientists have largely discounted the notion of the independent voter. Likewise, the media has almost exclusively viewed US modern politics through the lens of the two-party structure, either ignoring or minimizing the role of the independent voter. Moreover, in Chapter 3, we explore how individuals move in and out of independent status and other contextual factors that impact independent voting over time. Chapter 4 outlines how independents wield power and can act as a bridge to a post-partisan, post-ideological future. Examples are provided on how independents play the field, deciding elections without giving fealty to the party they supported in any momentary cycle.

In Chapter 5, we explore whether independents can serve as a transformative force on the nation's political divide. Can independents propel structural change in the mode of politics that transfers power from the parties to the people? Differences in voter social networks and media consumption among independents, Republicans, and Democrats are explored. Also, we examine the notion that as independent voters grow rapidly in number, their presence in the system is challenging the major parties' hegemony and disrupting ways we have long analyzed and practiced politics and interacted with each other.

The legal and structural barriers hindering independent-voter, independent-party, and independent-candidate participation are addressed in Chapter 6. This includes closed debates, onerous ballot-access requirements, how voter registration laws compel partisanship, and how the courts have yet to accept the voice and legal theories that expand the election process to take into account changes in the electorate.

Chapter 7 contains a series of excerpts from nearly a dozen interviews with independent voters from a range of backgrounds and from around the country. These voters provide an insight into the way they see themselves and the way they are misconceived by the media. Chapter 8 outlines the shared common political opinions, beliefs, and values of independents. What binds them together? Are most independents "in the middle" ideologically, or are they nonideological? Are they low-information voters and how do they compare to nonvoters? This chapter explains the independent-voter mindset, which includes anti-corruption principles, dissatisfaction with the two-party system, greater ballot access/fairness, being a change agent, and the decline of the political parties.

In Chapter 9, we address the challenges of the entrenched and impenetrable two-party system that framers of the US Constitution and other reformers feared most. We outline a series of alternatives and modifications to party-driven democracy, including the possibility of constitutional changes, the passage of updated voting rights legislation, proportional representation/multiparty system, nonpartisan redistricting, open primaries, and nonpartisan and general elections. We note that some of these reforms are being implemented within the context of complete partisan control and use the lens of the early 20th-century progressive

reformer Herbert Croly[2] to assess their impact: the two-party system as undermining the ability of the people to control their destiny by interposing two
authoritarian partisan organizations between the people and their government.

The book concludes with Chapter 10 questioning the ability of the reforms
outlined to succeed in the current environment where the entire electoral system
is under near-complete partisan control. We assert that transformative reforms
will need to embrace evermore daring changes that weaken partisan control,
lessen the role of parties in mediating between the people and their government,
and help citizens develop their civic capabilities.

Finally, this book is a labor of love for the authors. We come from different dis-
ciplines. One (Omar H. Ali) is a historian who has excavated novel and controversial material about the emergence of independent political coalitions between
African Americans and poor white farmers in the post-Civil War era and the
formation of other independent Black and white electoral alliances throughout
the 20th century. A second (Thom Reilly) is a professor of public administration
who has run complex government systems from the local to statewide level. The
third (Jacqueline S. Salit) has been a frontline pioneer in the present-day spheres
of independent politics, whose experience and knowledge have evolved in direct
connection to the rise of this movement-in-the-making. We came together to tell
a story of profound social distress and political possibility and to highlight what
we believe is an emergent force that can put our country on a new and human-
istic path. We have tried to temper our exuberance with data, facts, research,
and the historical record. We have tried to give a balanced view of the various
controversies while not shying away from our clear opinions and analyses. We
hope the book contributes to the political transformations the United States so
desperately needs.

We owe a great deal to several people who assisted with the preparation of
this book and who labored through drafts and offered insightful critiques and
suggestions. Caroline Donnola of Independent Voting was invaluable in helping
organize us. She spent countless hours working on the manuscript and we owe
her a good deal of gratitude for her careful review of our work. David Belmont
supplemented her work with research, statistical analysis, and humor. Christian
Grose at USC provided important insight, comment, and direction on the book.
So, too, did John Opdycke of Open Primaries. Matthew O'Brien, who provided
editing for the book, offered innovative ways to refine our messages. The research
assistance provided by ASU students Jade Bravo, Jason George, Grant Heminger,
and TayLore Reliford was most helpful. Finally, a special thanks for the stories
and insights shared by independent voters that were ably gathered by Independent
Voting's Cathy Stewart and Gwen Mandell.

We appreciate the contribution of the Foreword by Andrew Yang and the
Afterword by Dr. Jessie Fields, fellow visionaries who believe US politics can
become more human and humane.

FOREWORD

It was early 2018, when I publicly announced that I was running for president as a Democrat. It was picked up by only one major publication, and that was only because a friend was a writer. The somewhat dismissive headline? "His 2020 Campaign Message: The Robots Are Coming."

Why did I declare as a Democrat, despite never having run before and having very little connections within the party? Simple—I was a Democrat. I'd always been a Democrat. Most of my friends were Democrats, and the Party had a clear process for selecting their candidate. Also, it seemed like the media would take me a lot more seriously as a member of a major party instead of dismissing me as a fringe candidate.

The lack of media attention continued for quite some time. Despite having been appointed to a few honorary positions in the Obama White House and having served as the president of a national nonprofit, no one thought that I was a serious contender. My team and I continued to work to get the message out and, since the traditional media outlets weren't willing to talk to me or hear out my ideas, my team and I focused on alternative media—primarily, podcasts.

After appearing on a large number of smaller podcasts, we received our first big break in the form of Sam Harris reaching out to have me on his podcast, *Making Sense*.

Sam identifies as a Classical Liberal. He promotes free speech and the open discussion of ideas. He's, for the most part, socially liberal, and he'd rather see Biden in office than Trump.

But, on his podcast, Sam is willing to engage with ideas that fall outside of the current liberal mainstream, bringing on experts who think that the Democrats frequently get things wrong. And he's willing to talk about issues in a way that puts him in the crosshairs of liberals on Twitter quite a bit.

Sam's not alone in this alternative media world. There are many others out there—from Joe Rogan to Bill Maher—who hold liberal beliefs but are willing to engage with people who don't. They're not looking to appease a set ideology but rather to have interesting conversations that challenge their beliefs.

People like Joe, Sam, and Bill speak to an audience that rivals or exceeds the audience of the traditional media. My episode with Joe Rogan received over six million views on YouTube alone—which is a few million more than who tune into the most popular cable newscasts. That's a much wider reach and, if you read the comments section, you know that it's also a much more ideologically diverse audience.

Liberals and conservatives. CNN and MSNBC and Fox. Facebook and Twitter feeds. These all create ideological bubbles. These groups filter out any dissent, create their own language, and alienate anyone who doesn't belong. Which leads to a smaller and smaller bubble, with more and more people being left behind and more and more unwillingness to confront incorrect beliefs.

And so people like Joe and Sam come along and speak to a broader audience, despite facing backlash from these increasingly ideologically extreme bubbles. And being willing to talk to this broader audience is how a relatively unknown entrepreneur ended up on seven debate stages with senators, governors, and former vice presidents, outlasting many of them in the primary.

The two major parties have become too ideologically rigid, extreme, and unwilling to speak to most people where they're at. More and more voters are identifying as independent because most people don't agree with the full set of policies adopted by either party, and they're sick of being attacked publicly for not blindly accepting ideas they disagree with. The Left is canceling comedians for telling jokes, while the Right is calling some of the most conservative members of their caucus RINOs because of single votes that go against party dogma.

Most people out there don't care much about ideology—they care about whether their lives are better or worse. As the parties have lost sight of that, more and more people have started to identify as independents, or nonaligned, or as members of a third party. They want their leaders to work with each other to try things and find solutions to make their lives better. They want leaders who speak the same language as them. They want leaders who are on the same side as them, even if there are some disagreements on policies or beliefs.

After my presidential run, I recognized that our two-party system is failing us. I publicly left the Democratic Party and became an Independent in 2021, starting the Forward Party to advocate for structural reform. The two-party system is unrepresentative, polarizing, and will lead us to anger and ruin. I hadn't thought much about my departing the Democrats, but after it happened it felt like a veil lifted. Partisanship really does influence our thinking in ways most don't realize.

Now that I'm officially an Independent, I've had so many people reach out to let me know that they, too, don't feel at home in any major political party. These Americans have views that aren't represented by Democrats or Republicans.

People who support gay marriage but also limitations on abortion. People who want health care for all while also supporting gun rights.

The one thing in common is that they all want to be able to talk about these things without losing friends and family or feel like they're being condemned.

All of these independent voters have beliefs, but they're not ideological. They believe—I believe—that the United States has room for more than one viewpoint and that what we share as Americans is more important than what we might believe on certain policy issues.

Omar, Thom, and Jacqueline see this group much better than any other people working in this area.

This book's exploration of this group is important and honest. The major media organizations try to marginalize this group as being secretly partisan or not holding any consistent beliefs. These organizations are trying to marginalize independent voters because they know that we're actually the majority, and if we band together, we can take this country back from the extreme partisans they represent.

When you see yourself in this book, I hope you join us in fighting with us to take our country back.

—Andrew Yang

Notes

1 Gallup, Inc., Party Affiliation | "Gallup Historical Trends," *Gallup.Com*, January 29, 2021, retrieved from https://news.gallup.com/poll/15370/party-affiliation.aspx
2 Croly, H. D., *Progressive Democracy*, Macmillan Co., 1914.

INTRODUCTION

Regardless of which party has an advantage in party affiliation, over the past three decades, presidential elections have generally been competitive, and party control of the U.S. House of Representatives and Senate has changed hands numerous times. This is partly because neither party can claim a very high share of core supporters—those who identify with the party—as the largest proportion of Americans identify initially as political independents.

—Jeffrey M. Jones, Gallup, "U.S. Political Party Preferences Shifted Greatly During 2021."[1]

The rise of the independent voter and the weakening of traditional two-party power are among the most explosive phenomena in US politics today. Eight years into the 21st century, independent voters began determining the outcome of presidential elections. They gave their backing to Barack Obama by an eight-point margin in 2008, Donald Trump by a margin of four points in 2016, and Joe Biden by 13 points in 2020; and after one year of his presidency, independent voter support for Biden has dropped dramatically from 44 percent to 29 percent.[2] Dig deeper and these swings cannot be explained by the traditional political categories: liberal, conservative, moderate. In actuality, they cannot be categorized at all, at least not by typical ideological patterns.

Additionally, the voting patterns of independents are not simply voting patterns. The choices made by independents in any given cycle are more akin to the disruptions caused when seismic waves move through the earth's crust—murmurs of profound discontent, signaling deep political shifts. In this way, independent voters are a diffuse civic force, collectively driving what one political analyst aptly called "the politics of otherness."[3]

DOI: 10.4324/9781003240808-1

The authors of this book believe that this unorganized force, an emergent community of voters and nonvoters, a post- and anti-partisan community, has the unrealized power to reshape the politics of the United States. Their size alone makes them formidable. Independents currently constitute either the largest or the second largest group of registered voters in half the states.[4] They are as widespread as the country and as volatile. They count among their legions 44 percent of millennials,[5] 35 percent of Iraq and Afghanistan war veterans,[6] 37 percent of Latinos, and 27 percent of African Americans.[7] While political parties grasp for their votes, the status quo denies their desire for independence. Independents have been largely treated as weak partisans or as those disengaged from the political system altogether.[8] Media, political scientists, and politicians have branded them "leaners," "middle-of-the-roaders," or "closet partisans," even though in reality when independents are followed over multiple elections, they have been found to have no firm partisan loyalties.[9] These labels—echoes of a political drumbeat that is steadily losing its rhythm—distort the reality of dealignment and deflect attention from its causes.

In the last election, independents broke for the Biden/Harris ticket by 14 points, delivering the margins of victory necessary for that ticket to secure the decisive electoral votes of Pennsylvania, Wisconsin, Georgia, and Arizona.[10] In the twin US Senate runoffs in Georgia in January 2021, independents broke for the winners, Raphael Warnock and Jon Ossoff by four points,[11] fueling the narrow victories that set up a 50/50 split in the Senate, allowing the Democrats to control it (when they have party consensus) with the tie-breaking vote of the vice president. Yet those same voters would not declare themselves Democrats. Their chosen identity is independents. President Biden's overall job approval rating has dropped from 57 percent at the start of his presidency to 42 percent after one year. That drop-off has been driven almost entirely by independent voters.[12]

The rise of the independent voter—with no formal name, party affiliation, and common ideological doctrine—is an eruptive force in American politics.[13] They have the power to determine the outcome of elections, disrupt the status quo, and drive structural reform. The question of how independents align, the impact of their choices, and the future of their status as a becoming organized force beg a new kind of analysis. Who are these voters? What does it mean to be independent? What message are they delivering? Why is the pace of their registration growing at rates of 10–14 percent in red and blue states alike?[14] Why do nearly half of all voters in the United States now identify as other than Democrat or Republican?

Does the fact that 51 percent of independents overall and 66 percent of independents aged 18–29 say the two parties are corrupt signify a coming break with the two-party system?[15] Will the ferment in both major political parties lead to splits in which partisan refugees cleave to the mass of independent voters to create a new set of electoral and governing institutions? Given how entrenched the two-party system remains, and how committed that system is to its self-preservation, is it any wonder that there is an existential controversy over whether these voters are a bona fide and distinct sector of the US electorate? All of these questions—and more—are on the table.

Notes

1 Jones, Jeffrey M., "U.S. Political Party Preferences Shifted Greatly During 2021," *Gallup*, January 17, 2022, retrieved from https://news.gallup.com/poll/388781/political-party-preferences-shifted-greatly-during-2021.aspx
2 Ali, Omar H., *In the Balance of Power, Independent Black Politics and Third-Party Movements in the United States*, Ohio University Press, 2020; De Pinto, J., & Backus, F. "How Biden Won the 2020 Election: Exit Poll Analysis," *CBS News*, November 7, 2020, retrieved from www.cbsnews.com/news/election-2020-exit-poll-analysis-how-biden-became-the-projected-winner/; *Cook Political Report*, retrieved from www.cookpolitical.com/analysis/national/national-politics/biden-has-slipped-independents-can-he-win-them-back.
3 Salit, J. "Finding Otherness: A Blueprint for an Independent Conversation About 2020," *Independent Voting*, June 2017, retrieved from https://independentvoting.org/news_post/finding-otherness-blueprint-independent-conversation-2020/
4 Gruber, J., & Opdyke, J. "The Next Great Migration: The Rise of Independent Voters," *openprimaries.org*, 2020, retrieved from https://d3n8a8pro7vhmx.cloudfront.net/openprimaries/pages/4575/attachments/original/1637687269/ROI_Report_R1-1-compressed.pdf?1637687269
5 "Millennials in Adulthood," *Pew Research Center's Social & Demographic Trends Project*, May 30, 2020, retrieved from www.pewresearch.org/social-trends/2014/03/07/millennials-in-adulthood/
6 Statista. "Share of U.S. Iraq and Afghanistan Veterans by Political Party 2020," March 12, 2020, retrieved from www.statista.com/statistics/976355/share-us-iraq-afghanistan-veterans-political-party/
7 "Trends in Party Affiliation Among Demographic Groups," *Pew Research Center—U.S. Politics & Policy*, December 31, 2019, retrieved from www.pewresearch.org/politics/2018/03/20/1-trends-in-party-affiliation-among-demographic-groups/
8 Keith, Bruce E., Magleby, David B., Nelson, Candice J., Orr, Elizabeth, Westlye, Mark C., & Wolfinger, Raymond E., *The Myth of the Independent Voter*, University of California Press, 1992.
9 Abrams, S., & Fiorina, M., *Are Leaning Independents Deluded or Dishonest Weak Partisans?* CISE-ITANES Conference, Roma, Italy, 2011.
10 De Pinto & Backus, 2020; "National Results 2020 *President* Exit Polls," *CNN.com*, 2020, retrieved from https://cnn.com/election/2020/exit-polls/president/national-results.
11 "Georgia 2020 *U.S. Senate Runoff* Exit Polls," *CNN*.com, 2021, retrieved from www.cnn.com/election/2020/exit-polls/senate/georgia
12 *Cook Political Report*, Gallup Inc., 2021.
13 Salit, J., & Reilly, T., "Can Independent Voters Save American Democracy?" In Orr, D. et al. (Eds), *Democracy Unchained: How to Rebuild Government for the People,* The New Press, 2020, pp. 323–336.
14 Gruber & Opdyke, 2020.
15 Salit, 2017.

1

WHO IS THE INDEPENDENT VOTER?

Every society is really governed by hidden laws, by unspoken but profound
assumptions on the part of the people, and ours is no exception."
                                                                    —James Baldwin[1]

In mid-July 2012, two leaders of the independent political movement traveled to
Chicago to meet with a chief strategist for the reelection campaign of President
Barack Obama.[2] The purpose was to finalize months of exchanges exploring how
the campaign could recover its dramatically waning support from independent
voters and assure the president's reelection in November. The meeting was a bust.
The plan fell apart.

The path to Obama's historic victory four years earlier had its share of sur-
prises along the way. Among these was an explosion of popular support from
independent voters. Rising to the occasion in the Democratic presidential primaries, a decisive majority of independent voters attached themselves to the Obama
crusade. Obama's 2004 convention speech decrying the idea of red and blue
America and proposing the ideal of a united country was a clarion call to a new
political culture and a bridge across the racial divide. His opposition to the inva-
sion of Iraq and his status as a political outsider inspired many who saw political elites tilting the playing field in their own direction while undermining the
United States' future.

In mounting succession, in the states that allowed independent voters to
cast ballots in a presidential primary, nonaligned voters lifted up the insurgent
Obama in his challenge to the party's status quo nominee, Hillary Clinton, and
delivered the party's nomination to him. If independents had been excluded
in the open primary states, Clinton would have been the Democratic Party

DOI: 10.4324/9781003240808-2

candidate for president that year.³ Independent voters were Obama's ticket to the nomination.

In the general election, Obama faced Republican John McCain, a career maverick who garnered the GOP nomination after independents rescued his flagging campaign. Obama prevailed, becoming the country's first Black president, besting McCain among independent voters by eight points. The post-partisan Obama was dispatched to the White House. *New York* magazine called him the "first independent President."⁴

It did not take long for the transcendent Obama to fall back to special-interest earth. The financial crisis of 2008 thrust the new president into the arms of the desperate-but-nearly-omnipotent banks. The arrival of the Tea Party, a right-leaning populist revolt absorbed almost instantly by the Republican Party, overheated the environment in Congress. Obama turned over his database of tens of millions of supporters, including independents, to the Democratic National Committee, in effect dissolving the multilateral independent coalition that brought him to power. Upon advice and direction of congressional Democrats, he made a Big Government health-care reform his signature legislative issue rather than digging into the economic chaos and pain that followed in the wake of the Wall Street debacle. Any notion that Obama would champion an overhaul of a political system rife with partisanship and party control fell by the wayside, as did his backing from the national community of independent voters, by then 40 percent of the electorate.

In the 2010 midterm elections, the Democratic Party took a drubbing. Though it's not uncommon for the party holding the White House to lose seats in a midterm, this shift had an ominous feature. Independent voters deserted Obama's party in droves, 56 percent siding with Republicans compared to 37 percent for Democrats.⁵ Obama had been unable to pierce the partisanship embedded in Washington, and he was hemorrhaging support from his anti-partisan base.

These were the circumstances in which the independent leaders began their 2012 reelection conversations with the Obama team. The first discussion took place at a swanky New York hotel bar. Obama's political guru David Axelrod knew the president had a looming problem and designated David Simas, director of opinion research, to follow up. Months of calls and memos followed. The independents offered multiple avenues through which Obama could restore public confidence in his ability to confront the partisan monolith. Certain actions would be required.

Simas was urged to have the president publicly recognize the magnitude of the independent phenomenon, to initiate a restructuring of the Federal Elections Commission from bipartisan club to a regulatory body fully representative of the actual electorate. New facts on the ground required this—namely, that four in every ten voters identified as other than partisan. Reforms of the political and governmental process were therefore pressing. Economic revitalization, by then a core theme of the Obama campaign, had to be linked to a democratic revitalization.

The July day that the independent ambassadors arrived in Chicago to meet with Simas was unusually hot. Axelrod, dressed in running shorts and a T-shirt, greeted them at the door and stopped to chat before he headed out for a jog. Simas, seated behind a large desk mounted with computers, directed his striking, blue-eyed gaze and delivered the news. The Democratic National Committee (DNC) had ruled. There would be no special outreach to independent voters, no acknowledgment that extreme partisanship in the Capitol had to be brought to heel. The conversation was over. The DNC believed they had the election won by focusing solely on the party's base, not the broader and more heretical coalition that had carried Obama to victory four years earlier.

> "I tried to fit you into our world," Simas said in a semi-apology.
> "And we tried to fit you into ours," the independents replied.

Obama went on to win the reelection in 2012. But he lost independent voters by ten points to Republican Mitt Romney. The Democratic Party held the White House but lost what could well have been the key to a durable governing majority. Many believe this shift laid the foundation for the events of 2016, when Donald Trump, waving a banner of insurgency, carried independents by four points.[6] A University of Virginia (UVA) Center for Politics poll found that 15 percent of Americans who had voted for Obama cast ballots for Trump.[7] Many of these were independents. The 2012 election became a case study in how a partisan refusal to acknowledge, understand, and engage with the independent voter and promote a system of independent governance can shift the political landscape in unanticipated and consequential ways.

Independent Voters Create New Realities

It is difficult, if not impossible, to give a satisfying characterization of the independent voter in US politics. The US two-party system—never mentioned in the Constitution but deeply embedded in our political psyches and practices—is firmly a two-sided game. Anything that strays outside of its binary structure or culture is considered suspect, transitory, or inauthentic.

Self-defined independent voters—now between 44 percent and 50 percent of the electorate[8]—have been (and continue to be) antiestablishment in some form or fashion. At the current moment, their antiestablishment spirit is mainly (though not exclusively) evident in their votes for and against candidates of the two major parties. As the *Cook Political Report* observed, "2016 marked the fifth consecutive election in which independents have voted in favor of the party not holding the White House, by an average of 4 percentage points."[9]

Independents remain hard to categorize because they are, by their choice of self-identification, resisting the standard categories of political classification. About 40–50 percent of the US electorate call themselves independents when asked how they self-identify.[10] What's more, many voters in "members-only" or closed primary states register in a party to be eligible to vote in a primary, not because they necessarily align with that party, but, for many, because they want to determine the likely winner of a given race where one or the other major party has close to a monopoly on the final electoral outcome.[11]

Thus, the percentages of self-declared independents—now regularly monitored by Gallup—translate into roughly 80–100 million voting-age Americans who choose to identify themselves as other than partisan. Between 1960 and 2021, the percentage of Americans who classified themselves as independents more than doubled.[12] In the last ten years, the rate of registration of independents in the "party-registration" states has risen by 20 percent.[13] Among new registrants, as of 2021, 60 percent are choosing to be independent of the parties. Currently, in nine states where voters must declare an affiliation or non-affiliation, independents are the largest bloc of voters. In eight more, they are the second largest group. Applying the current rate of growth, it is predicted that nonaligned voters will be the largest or second largest group of voters in all party-registration states by 2035.[14]

Currently, 51 percent of millennials choose the independent label. While the Gen Z numbers are incomplete because they all have yet to reach voting age, it is expected that these new voters will de-align in even larger numbers. The gravitational pull toward independence is accelerating. Today, 37 percent of Latinos are independents, along with 27 percent of African Americans[15] and 45 percent of Iraq and Afghanistan war veterans.[16] As journalist Susan Milligan observed in *US News and World Report* in May 2021, "Independent and unaffiliated voters are having a moment. And this time, it appears that the moment is something more enduring, as those with no major party affiliation have increasing control over the fates of Democrats and Republicans seeking office."

Speaking for Themselves

Strikingly, for all the polling done to uncover and predict the voting patterns of independents, or to assign them an ideological nametag, they are rarely, if ever, asked why they chose to be an independent.

In the fall of 2020, with the COVID-19 epidemic fully underway, Independent Voting[17] conducted an online and telephone survey of 3,500 independents across the nation.[18] Asked to name a reason for being independent, 55 percent said they would "rather vote for the person, not the party." The second highest cohort, 51 percent, said, "The parties are corrupt, plain and simple." Among those 18–29 years old, the number saying the parties are corrupt was 66 percent. Notably, nearly twice as many younger voters as their over-30 counterparts (42 percent to 24 percent) said that their choice to be independent was a way "to protest the two-party system."

These trends underscore a declining faith in the political parties. The noted journalist and social critic Walter Karp, writing in *Indispensable Enemies: The*

Politics of Misrule in America in 1993, prophetically framed the problem: "Control of elected officials means real political power, and party organizations use that power, first and foremost, in order to serve themselves—party organizations are neither malevolent or benevolent; they are self-interested."[19]

Karp further observed:

> In holding elected officials accountable to them, they will see to it that no laws are passed which might weaken the party organization; that no public issues are raised which might strengthen the chances of insurgents and independents; that special privileges are not stripped away from special interests that have been paying the organization heavily for protecting those privileges.[20]

In other words, in Karp's view, which the authors share, the parties—even with their differences—act as protectors of their jointly held if conflict-ridden status quo. To be clear, that is their *function*, not their *dysfunction*. Many who are becoming dissatisfied with this state of affairs are turning elsewhere for political identification. Hence, the rise of the independent voter.

The nearly 50 percent of Americans who call themselves independents span the spectrum in traditional political ideology. Though the media often relate to "independents" as entirely interchangeable with "moderates," and pollsters and politicians will refer to independents as "in the middle," this ideological characterization, indeed any ideological characterization, falls short. The mere fact that a majority of independents cast ballots for Obama, then Romney, then Trump, then Biden in a dozen years casts doubts on the proposition that there is a static ideology at work.

The available data on this complex question is scant, given that the baked-in bias against independents has limited the scope of academic research. Yet, actual political events document a story of boundaries upended, new alliances assembled and disassembled, and a fervent brand of political independence taking shape.

Radical Bellwethers or Disgruntled Centrists or Both?

In 1992, the US political landscape was shaken by the unorthodox presidential candidacy of the iconoclastic billionaire H. Ross Perot. At the time, 32 percent of Americans identified as independent. Already nearly a third of the electorate, their impact outpaced their numbers. Together with the oddball candidate, they acted as a lightning rod for distressed voters from both major parties. Defections from the GOP camp to Perot unseated a sitting president, George H. W. Bush. Defections from the Democrat camp made William Clinton president with the lowest share of the popular vote since 1968.[21]

What was the politic of the Perot coalition? And what role did independents play in that coalition? Exit polling found that independents made up 27 percent of the voting electorate that year. These independents divided their votes among the independent Populist Perot (30 percent), Democrat Clinton (38 percent), and Republican Bush (32 percent).[22] In other words, independents played the field, while providing a hefty chunk of Perot's total. Another overlay adds depth to the picture. Perot, the independent, received support from an ideological mix of voters. Of those who identified as liberals, Perot received 18 percent. Of those who described themselves as moderates, Perot received 21 percent. And for those who considered themselves conservatives, Perot received 18 percent. In summary, Perot voters came from roughly equal percentages of liberals, moderates, and conservatives.[23]

These data reveal two things. Voters spanned the spectrum of traditional ideological categories. At the same time, those voters who cast ballots for Perot did so without a consistent or firm ideology. A vote for Perot was, therefore, not ideologically driven. To paraphrase one political insider on the Perot revolt, Perot's appeal was both as a radical "take our country back" revolutionary and as a proven and capable businessman who knew how to run and manage a large and profitable company.[24]

The question of whether and where independent voters sit on a left/center/right political spectrum has been considered, however incompletely, since 1992. After the 1992 election, the Democratic Leadership Council (DLC) commissioned a report by a star pollster, Stan Greenberg, hoping to understand the appeal of political independence and to press Clinton and the Democratic Party to relate strategically to the Perot voter in the future (see Chapter 4). Greenberg urged the Democrats not to disparage these Americans but to champion their concerns.[25] He and the DLC believed in the potential for a durable majority coalition based on "building support among these disaffected alienated independent voters," as stated by Will Marshall in his remarks at a press conference on the report's findings.[26] The advice was ignored.

By contrast, Republican Congressman Newt Gingrich championed a "Contract with America," which drew on the anti-incumbent, pro-reform fever of the Perot revolt and endorsed key elements of the Perot platform, including term limits and other restraints on party power, galvanizing independent backing for the GOP to take control of the House in the 1994 midterms. However, none of these reforms materialized.

The discussion of whether independents were centrists or radical reformers continued over time. In fact, the precursor to the Reform Party, the Patriot Party[27] established at the start of Perot's second run, deliberately struck the word "centrist" from its founding documents to make the point.[28] Some 17 years later, in May 2011, the Pew Research Center published a report, "Beyond Red vs. Blue," asserting that independents are not moderates but instead combine economic and social attitudes along unorthodox lines.[29] In the *FiveThirtyEight* article titled "The Moderate Middle Is a Myth," Lee Drutman discusses how "Independent voters are all over the ideological map."[30]

The pollster and political consultant Pat Caddell—sometimes described as "the oracle of American politics," who conducted studies in the mid- and late 2010s, among the last he conducted before he died—discovered that independents were not an ideological group but an emergent force for a new political framework beyond what currently existed. In 2017, he took note of an ABC News/*Washington Post* poll where 36 percent identified as independent and 6 percent as "other" while only 55 percent combined identified as either Democrat or Republican. Caddell concluded: The "duopoly is in deep trouble."[31]

In an internal memo to participants attending a national political reform summit in Kansas City that same year, Caddell observed about independents, "Of course, this large plurality of Americans is totally ignored." He went on to cite the results of another series of questions in which respondents were asked to describe President Trump and both major parties as either "in touch" or "out of touch" with the concerns of most people in the United States. Among all respondents, 58 percent said Trump was out of touch, 62 percent said the Republican Party was out of touch, and 67 percent said the Democrats were out of touch. Caddell observed that the most significant finding was regarding the Democratic Party. "Given Trump's generally negative ratings, it is shocking that two-thirds of the electorate finds that the 'opposition' or 'resistance' party is so out of touch," Caddell asserted, concluding that this "illustrates the great opportunity for the politics of 'otherness.'"[32]

Independents' Declining Faith in the Party System

A look at some current national surveys conducted in 2021 put more meat on these nonideological and anti-partisan bones. In July 2021, a national survey by Quinnipiac University found that among independents, 59 percent disapproved of the way Republicans in Congress are handling their jobs and 25 percent approved. In the same survey, 52 percent of independents disapproved of the way Democrats in Congress are handling their jobs and 36 percent approved.[33] Commenting on the astonishing rise of the independent cohort in Nevada, now 34 percent of the state and the largest segment of the electorate, Carson City pollster Don Carlson observed, "Nevadans are increasingly turned off to any formal identification with either major political party because of the growing polarization caused by both."[34]

In the same poll, Quinnipiac also asked independents whether they were satisfied with the way things are going in the nation. Four percent were very satisfied and 29 percent somewhat satisfied. Thirty percent were somewhat dissatisfied, and 35 percent were very dissatisfied. In sum, a third of independents were satisfied with the state of the nation, while two-thirds were dissatisfied. And what of the issue of voting rights in the United States? Thirty-five percent of independents believe that voting rights are well protected while 59 percent believe they are under threat. An ABC News/*Washington Post* poll, conducted June 27–30, 2021, found that 62 percent of independents think passing new laws making it easier for people to vote lawfully is more important than passing new laws making it harder for people to vote fraudulently. A June 22–29, 2021 NPR/*PBS NewsHour*/Marist national poll of registered voters found that 83 percent of independents think voters should be required to show government-issued photo IDs when they vote. A CBS news poll done June 8–13, 2021 indicates that 66 percent of independents nationally think the Founding Fathers would feel things in this country have seriously gotten off track. The ABC News/*Washington Post* poll found that 78 percent of independents think that some people experience discrimination based on their race or ethnicity.

Do these findings fit the American independent neatly into an ideological or partisan category? They do not. This nonconformity, however, is a source of their power. Writing in *RollCall.com*, David Winston, an advisor to Congressional Republicans, commented, "Don't take independents and their concerns for granted . . . the next time you see the media and political partisans selling the idea that elections are 'all about the base,' don't buy it."[35]

Clearly, the rising tide of independent or nonaligned voters is connected to the chaos and power struggles inside and between the two major parties. But what is that connection? What does it say about the state of US politics and the activistic question of whether the diverse Americans who consider themselves independents can lead a transformation of a partisan culture? What practical and conceptual tools are needed to answer these questions?

A Quick Look at Methodology

In 1960, the University of Chicago Press published *The American Voter*, by Angus Campbell, Philip E. Converse, Warren E. Miller, and Donald E. Stokes, which became the gold standard in political science for analyses of the voting public.[36] The book, and its methodology, laid the groundwork for what became the American National Election Studies, the preeminent national polling institution for US elections. The authors concluded that party identification was the main catalyst, cause, and explanation for decision-making at election time.[37]

In the introduction, Campbell, Converse, Miller, and Stokes explain,

> The electoral process is a means of decision making that lies within a broader political order, and in research on voting, it is valuable to have explicitly in view the wider political system in which the electoral process is found.

Further, the data they analyzed from the 1952 and 1956 presidential election cycles "lie within a particular historical setting."[38]

In *The Great Divide*,[39] the economist Joseph Stiglitz characterized the decades directly following World War II as a time when "we had economic growth in which most people shared, with those at the bottom doing proportionately better than those at the top. (It was also the period that saw the country's most rapid economic growth.)" Politically, it was the time of the Montgomery bus boycott and a growing recognition that the call for racial equality had yet to be answered. Culturally, it was the era of "The Family of Man"—a hugely popular photographic exhibit of images curated by the Museum of Modern Art in 1955, which toured the world for eight years, spreading the gospel of humanity's seemingly incandescent common ground.

In this environment, the American voter—and his or her political decision-making and party identification—was first investigated and analyzed on a broad national scale. Not surprisingly, party identification was relatively strong, the distinction between the two major parties was clear, with differences revolving largely around the role of government in the organization and progress of society. There was a political center in government where the parties could meet. Party identification, according to Campbell and his co-authors in 1960, "has a profound impact on behavior."[40]

However, the extent to which researchers and analysts began to codify party identification as the immutable causal factor, not just in voting behavior but in defining the character of the American people, wrenched the authors' findings out of their historical context. The legacy of this conclusion is to view everything and anything that strays outside of party identification as "deviant" (even the election of President Eisenhower was "deviant").[41] But today, with a seething revolt against party identification, it would be impossible to understand this dealignment, including how and why independents are voting as they do, through the lens of party identification rather than the breakdown of a system that relies on it.

Unspoken Voter Suppression

Some of the insights in *The American Voter* have been ignored, and they shouldn't be. In the concluding chapter, "Electoral Behavior and American Politics,"[42] the authors observe:

> The conserving influence of party identification makes it extremely difficult for a third party to rise suddenly and with enough popular support to challenge the existing parties. If the forces on the vote were formed wholly anew in each campaign, new or minor parties would be able to establish themselves fairly easily as serious contenders for power. But these forces are not made anew; . . . the depressing effect of party identification on the opportunity of new parties can scarcely be doubted.

There is considerable wisdom in Campbell et al.'s insight. The key to forestalling a move beyond the domination of the US political system by the two parties—whether toward a third party, third force, or nonpartisan electoral coalition—is to ruthlessly enforce the power of party identification. How is that done? Through a complex matrix of laws, rules, and psychological and social messaging, championing the idea that the two parties combined with a framework of left/right ideology represent the totality of possibility. The academic field of political science and its cheerleaders in the mass media have played a mighty role in policing this arena (see Chapter 3 for an in-depth discussion). Even questions of voting rights and election security post the 2020 presidential election are seen through this lens, such that the public debate over the rules of democracy is a thinly veiled power struggle over which party benefits from any given set of rules. Karp's insight in 1993, that the parties "will see to it that no laws are passed which might weaken the party organization," rings even more true today.[43]

Francis Fukuyama, in a chapter titled "The Necessity of Politics" in *The Origins of Political Order*, points to the ways in which "the *political* job of finding the right regulatory mechanisms to tame capitalism's volatility have not yet been found."[44] Having predicted *The End of History and the Last Man* in his celebrated 1992 work,[45] in which he relished the "victory" of capitalism and liberal democracy, Fukuyama's reversal two decades later is sobering and instructive. He explains the key barriers to achieving that goal as the self-preservationist nature of political institutions:

> Political institutions develop, often slowly and painfully, over time, as human societies strive to organize themselves to master their environments. But political decay occurs when political systems fail to adjust to changing circumstances. There is something like a law of the conservation of institutions. Human beings are rule-following animals by nature; they are born to conform to the social norms they see around them, and they entrench those rules with often transcendent meaning and value. When the surrounding environment changes and new challenges arise, there is often a disjunction between existing institutions and present needs. Those institutions are supported by legions of entrenched stakeholders who oppose any fundamental change.[46]

Even as the parties battle viciously for control of the government, nearly half the country is no longer aligned with the idea that the present-day political parties can effectively and democratically mediate their relationship to the government and "tame capitalism's volatility." The question of which candidate or party a majority of voters cast their ballots for in any given election or cycle, while the outcome might have dramatic and immediate implications, can also be a sign of the underlying decay at work. The decision to identify as an independent in the 21st century is, at least, a statement of noncompliance with the current distribution of power.

In 2020, having swung across the spectrum from Obama to Trump, from the Democrats to the Republicans and back in the midterms, independents broke for the Biden/Harris ticket by 14 points and delivered the winning margins in key battleground states—Arizona, Georgia, Wisconsin, and Pennsylvania.[47] Shortly after the results were in, a Democratic political consultant proclaimed on a national cable news network that Arizona, a red state, now belonged to the Democrats. Did she misspeak? Was she spinning? Or indulging a heedless disregard for recent history?

Notes

1 Baldwin, James, from the essay, "The Discovery of What It Means to Be An American." *James Baldwin: Collected Essays*, The Library of America, 1998, p. 137.
2 The two independents were Harry Kresky, general counsel to Independent Voting (IV), and IV president and one of the authors of this book, Jacqueline S. Salit.
3 Salit, Jacqueline, *Independents Rising: Outsider Movements, Third Parties, and the Struggle for a Post-Partisan America,* Palgrave Macmillan, 2012, p. 7.
4 Heilemann, John, "The New Politics: Barack Obama: Party of One," *New York Magazine*, January 19, 2009.
5 Exit poll results from a survey of 18,132 voters nationwide conducted by Edison Media Research on behalf of the National Election Pool, retrieved from www.washingtonpost.com/wp-srv/special/politics/election-results-2010/exit-poll/
6 Exit poll results, 2016, retrieved from www.cnn.com/election/2016/results/exit-polls
7 See "Conclusion," *UVA Center for Politics Poll,* June 1, 2017, retrieved from https://centerfor-politics.org/crystalball/articles/just-how-many-obama-2012-trump-2016-voters-were-there/
8 Gallup Poll, Party Affiliation, Jan–July 2021, retrieved from https://news.gallup.com/poll/15370/party-affiliation.aspx.
9 Cook, Charlie, "As Is Their Habit, Independents Seem to Be Breaking Against the Incumbent," *The Cook Political Report with Amy Walter,* June 26, 2020.
10 Since state regulations on voter registration vary, and 19 states conduct nonpartisan voter registration, rather than asking voters to declare for a party, surveys that are national in scope use this metric, rather than voter registration data.
11 It's notable that different states take different positions on whether party membership should be a gateway into the voting process. More on these differences later.
12 See the percentage who classify themselves as independents from 1960, retrieved from www.pewresearch.org/politics/interactives/party-id-trend/. From January 21–February 22, 2021, 50 percent classified themselves as independent, retrieved from https://news.gallup.com/poll/15370/party-affiliation.aspx.
13 States have a variety of labels for registering as an independent, from Independent to No Party Preference to Unaffiliated. Each state uses its own nomenclature.
14 "The Next Great Migration: The Rise of Independent Voters," *OpenPrimaries.org,* 2020, p. 13 and Appendix B, pp. 27–56, retrieved from www.openprimaries.org/.
15 "Trends in Party Affiliation Among Demographic Groups," *Pew Research,* March 20, 2018, retrieved from www.pewresearch.org/politics/2018/03/20/1-trends-in-party-affiliation-among-demographic-groups/
16 Craighill, Peyton, "Iraq and Afghan Vets are Conservative. But they're not all Republicans," *Washington Post,* April 1, 2014, retrieved from www.washingtonpost.com/news/the-fix/wp/2014/04/01/iraq-and-afghan-vets-are-conservative-but-theyre-not-all-republicans/
17 Independent Voting is a national organization whose mission is to empower America's independent voters. Visit www.independentvoting.org.
18 "Confronting a New Reality: Independents Speak Out," *Independent Voting,* 2020, retrieved from www.independentvoting.org
19 Karp, Walter, *Indispensable Enemies: The Politics of Misrule in America,* Franklin Square Press, 1993, p. 22.

20 Ibid.

21 "Presidents Elected without a Majority," *Infoplease.com*, retrieved from www.infoplease.com/us/government/elections/presidents-elected-without-a-majority

22 "How Groups Voted in 1992" *Roper Center*, Nov. 3, 1992, retrieved from https://ropercenter.cornell.edu/how-groups-voted-1992, University of Connecticut, Summary of exit polls conducted by Voter Research and Surveys on Election Day.

23 Ibid.

24 Comments made by Fred Newman, an early pioneer of the independent political movement, from Holzman, Lois, & Morss, John, *Postmodern Psychologies, Societal Practice, and Political Life,* Routledge, 2000, pp. 169–170.

25 Broder, David S., "Perot: A Midsummer Night's Dream—or Nightmare," *Washington Post*, July 7, 1993.

26 The Democratic Leadership Council (DLC) held a press conference at the National Press Club in Washington, DC. Al From, the DLC president, led the conference. Stanley Greenberg, a White House pollster, and Will Marshall, president of the Progressive Policy Institute, also spoke to announce the release of a survey of Americans who voted for Ross Perot in the 1992 presidential election. "Ross Perot Voter Survey," *CSPAN Video*, July 7, 1993, retrieved from www.c-span.org/video/?44509-1/ross-perot-voter-survey

27 The Patriot Party, a coalition of Perot voters favoring a move to a national third party, supporters of the independent presidential candidate and reform pioneer Dr. Lenora Fulani, and an amalgam of state-based independent parties, was founded in Virginia in 1994.

28 Salit, Jacqueline, *Independents Rising: Outsider Movements, Third Parties, and the Struggle for a Post-Partisan America,* Palgrave Macmillan, 2012, p. 35.

29 "Beyond Red vs. Blue: The Political Typology," *Pew Research Center*, May 4, 2011, retrieved from www.pewresearch.org/politics/2011/05/04/beyond-red-vs-blue-the-political-typology/

30 Drutman, Lee, "The Moderate Middle is a Myth," *FiveThirtyEight*, September 24, 2019.

31 Balz, Dan, & Clement, Scott, "Nearing 100 Days Trump's Approval at Record Lows But his Base is Holding," *The Washington Post*, April 23, 2017, retrieved from www.washingtonpost.com/politics/nearing-100-days-trumps-approval-at-record-lows-but-his-base-is-holding/2017/04/22/a513a466-26b4-11e7-b503-9d616bd5a305_story.html

32 Internal memo from Pat Caddell to participants who attended "Unrig the System," a summit held in Kansas City in April 2017 hosted by the Bridge Alliance, the Independent Voter Project, The Centrist Project, Represent.Us, FairVote, and Level the Playing Field.

33 "Quinnipiac University National Survey," August 4, 2021, retrieved from https://poll.qu.edu/poll-release?releaseid=3814.

34 Hickey, Pat, "Declaration of Independents—Nevada's New Voters," July 22, 2021, *Reno Gazette Journal*.

35 Winston, David, "Election Day 2022 will be Independents' Day," July 14, 2021, retrieved from www.rollcall.com/2021/07/14/election-day-2022-will-be-independents-day/

36 Campbell, Angus, Converse, Philip E., Miller, Warren E., & Stokes, Donald E., *The American Voter* (unabridged edition), University of Chicago Press, 1960.

37 Ibid., p. 137.

38 Ibid., pp. 3–4.

39 Joseph Stiglitz, *The Great Divide: Unequal Societies and What We Can Do About Them*, Norton, 2015, p. 421.

40 Campbell, Converse, Miller, & Stokes, 1960, p. 137.

41 Campbell, Converse, Miller, & Stokes, 1960, pp. 537–538.

42   Campbell, Converse, Miller, & Stokes, 1960, p. 553.
43   Karp, Walter, *Indispensable Enemies: The Politics of Misrule in America*, Franklin Square Press, 1993, p. 22.
44   Fukuyama, Francis, 2011, p. 7.
45   Fukuyama, Francis, *The End of History and the Last Man*, Free Press, 1992.
46   Fukuyama, Francis, 2011, p. 7.
47   CNN Exit Polls, 2020, retrieved from www.cnn.com/election/2020/exit-polls/president/national-results; CNN Exit Polls on battleground states, 2020, Arizona, retrieved from www.cnn.com/election/2020/exit-polls/president/arizona; Georgia, retrieved from www.cnn.com/election/2020/exit-polls/president/georgia; Wisconsin, retrieved from www.cnn.com/election/2020/exit-polls/president/wisconsin; Pennsylvania, retrieved from www.cnn.com/election/2020/exit-polls/president/pennsylvania

2

INDEPENDENTS IN AMERICAN HISTORY

So long as we confine our conception of *the political* to activity that is openly declared we are driven to conclude that subordinate groups essentially lack a political life or that what political life they do have is restricted to those exceptional moments of popular explosion. To do so is to miss the immense political terrain that lies between quiescence and revolt.

—James C. Scott, *Domination and the Arts of Resistance:*
Hidden Transcripts[1]

On a mid-summer afternoon in June 1889, near the county seat of Sumter, South Carolina, delegates of the Colored Farmers Alliance representing more than 20 counties welcomed a delegation of poor white farmers. At the gathering—a barbecue, picnic, and rally, all at once—people shared food, stories, and songs. Speeches were given, friends connected, and new acquaintances were made. It was a scene repeated across the South in what was an emerging region-wide movement of farmers, sharecroppers, and agrarian workers.

Among the speakers addressing the crowd was one of the Colored Alliance's most prominent leaders, George Washington Murray. Born into slavery, and a witness to the ravages of the Civil War, he experienced both the promise of Reconstruction and its crushing collapse. However, today was a new day. While speaking from the veranda of an old house, leaning into the audience, he declared "a new era has dawned in which white and colored farmers [will] pull together for the good of South Carolina."[2] While the white delegates of the Southern Farmers Alliance—a parallel organization to the Colored Alliance—made their way through the crowd, which now numbered in the hundreds, the band playing on the veranda noticed the men and graciously decided to play a round of "Dixie."

DOI: 10.4324/9781003240808-3

Despite their differences, placing some of these Black and white Southerners on opposites sides of the battlefield less than a generation earlier, they each shared the experience of being poor. African Americans had welcomed fellow white farmers into a coalition to advance their shared economic interests. In turn, the white Alliancemen passed a resolution expressing their gratitude to their hosts. It was a good day, full of goodwill. But this coming together, like other efforts to unite poor and working people across the "color line"—a line crafted and reinforced by those benefiting most from such divisions—would come to a fiery end.[3]

In 1877, with the collapse of Reconstruction—the federal effort to rebuild the infrastructure of the South and democratize the region following Emancipation—the old plantation class reasserted its political and economic hegemony. It did so across the region via the Democratic Party, which was explicit in advocating white supremacy. Meanwhile, small-scale farmers, as well as sharecroppers and agricultural workers, had begun gathering in fields, churches, and town halls in their respective communities. They came together to find ways of maximizing their resources in the face of growing poverty and debt. Their efforts initially focused on economic uplift, including sharing their resources and labor. Soon, however, it became evident that without engaging the electoral arena—by running their own candidates and mobilizing voters—their efforts to collectivize and maximize their labor in planting, harvesting, and selling their crops in the context of falling global market prices and little access to capital (which were invariably attached to excessive interest rates) could only take them so far.[4]

In this context, some began to plow new ground, plant seeds of cooperation across the color line, and imagine a world free of their impoverishment and political dependency. Among those, like George Washington Murray, who envisioned a new kind of South, was the Rev. Walter A. Pattillo in neighboring North Carolina. Pattillo, embodying the past and future possibilities, was the son of a white planter and an enslaved Black woman. He, too, was looking for ways forward and would build on the history of independent and third-party politics. This history included the formation of the Liberty Party in 1840 as part of the abolitionist movement to end slavery; the Republican Party of the 1850s, which advocated "free soil" in the nation's westward expansion over Native American lands turned US "territories," and which served as a political vehicle for industrialists in the Northeast who were opposed to the expansion of slavery; and, following the Civil War, the Greenback Labor Party, which fielded antimonopoly candidates in a period of growing industrial labor struggle.

Pattillo, like Murray, had come of age during Reconstruction, which saw the enactment of the 13th, 14th, and 15th Amendments to the US Constitution that respectively made slavery illegal, extended citizenship to African Americans, and gave the right to vote to Black men 21 years of age and older. Poor whites also gained from the advances made during the early years of Reconstruction. For the first time, poor white people were given access to education through the introduction of public education in the region and the possibility of purchasing land.

Prior to the Civil War, literacy was discouraged among poor whites, let alone African Americans, fearing alliance-making between what was the majority of the Southern population; meanwhile, land was not allowed to be purchased in small portions, favoring planters over small farmers, which changed only through Congress' intervention. For the poor, the franchise, access to land, and an education were game changers. Maybe their world could be made anew?

Having the opportunity to learn to read and write, Pattillo pursued multiple courses of action in the 1870s and early 1880s. He did so as a farmer, minister, and "lecturer" for the Colored Farmers Alliance. Like Murray, he joined the Colored Farmers Alliance, first established in Texas by a group of two dozen Black farmers and one white farmer, Richard M. Humphrey, an Irish-American small cotton farmer and former Confederate soldier. Like other Colored Alliance lecturers throughout the South, Pattillo fanned out across the countryside to organize and recruit fellow farmers, sharecroppers, and agrarian workers. But by the late 1880s, Pattillo began to see the limits of his and other poor communities' efforts to uplift themselves without engaging the electoral arena. Soon, he emerged as an independent political leader in what would later be called the Populist movement. In the late summer of 1889, he lent himself to the burgeoning efforts to bring together poor and working people in his state to create a third party. That party, which became the People's Party, would ultimately form a Black and independent alliance by running shared candidates via the Republican Party (the party most African Americans supported) and white independents (comprising disaffected voters of the Democratic Party) via the People's, or Populist, Party.

Meanwhile, Jim Crow—the legal disfranchisement and segregation of African Americans starting in Mississippi and followed by South Carolina—was on the rise. By convention, African Americans were discriminated against first, with the codification of racial slavery, followed by scientific racism with the rationalization of Black inferiority in the face of Enlightenment ideals of liberty. But as it later became clear, Jim Crow was largely a political reaction to Black and independent alliance-making, which faced waves of violence in the terrifying form of public lynching. The journalist Ida B. Wells had begun recording growing incidents of violence across the South in her study *Southern Horrors: Lynch Law in All Its Phases*, first published in 1892.[5] Despite the violence and divisive tactics employed by the Democratic Party and its paramilitary adjuncts (such as the Red Shirts and soon the Ku Klux Klan), the Populists won a majority of seats in the North Carolina state legislature. Across the South, the Populists elected more than two dozen people to Congress, two governors, and in 1892 James B. Weaver, the Populist candidate for US President, won nearly 9 percent of the vote.

The local victories, however, were short-lived. White terrorism toward Black people and their white allies, combined with the enactment of segregationist laws, ensured that no alliance-making would continue, at least not in the immediate future. By the turn of the new century, Blacks and whites were legally segregated, physically set apart, with Black voters disenfranchised through local statutes, and ultimately state constitutions, including grandfather clauses, "white primaries," and literacy tests, among other voter-suppression measures.

The Democratic Party's reaction to the Black and independent alliance had taken an especially violent form in Wilmington, North Carolina, where Black and white allies had been elected and worked in shared governance. The bloody coup of November 10, 1898, in the port city, where the fusion government was overthrown, foreshadowed the violence inflicted on Black people in years to come in other areas of the South. In Grimes County, eastern Texas, where another Black and independent alliance had succeeded, Black Populist leaders were assassinated in open fields and near the county courthouse in broad daylight.[6] However, the so-called Wilmington Riot, a full-blown massacre of Black people, was so brutal that it took three generations for the descendants of both its victims and perpetrators to begin to revisit the destruction and trauma it brought to their respective communities.[7]

And yet, the rise and suppression of the Populist movement would also point to a thread in American history: the power of people mobilizing against the ruling parties and the parties' inability to fully contain them. New movements were in the making.

Independents as Catalysts of Reform

The history of independent movement-making and third parties to challenge one or both of the dominant parties to enact reforms dates to the early 19th century. While there is nothing in the US Constitution about political parties, the Founding Fathers expressed a deep distrust in partisan formations. In 1796, George Washington famously warned in his farewell address against "the baneful effects of the spirit of party."[8] For Washington, partisanship was divisive and ultimately corrosive to the republic—and he wasn't alone in his thinking. As the political theorist Robert Dahl wrote in *On Democracy*, "Political 'factions' and partisan organizations were generally viewed as dangerous, divisive . . . and injurious to the public good."[9] Yet a two-party system emerged, first in the form of the Federalists and Democratic-Republicans (Anti-Federalists), followed by the Democrats and Whigs, and then by the mid-19th century, the Democrats and Republicans, the dominant two parties we've had in the United States since. Some argue that a bipartisan system creates a degree of stability in the United States. The question, however, is for whom? Who benefits from bipartisan rule? It's a question that independent voters—of all backgrounds—have asked over and again.[10]

The year 1854 marked a turning point for Republicans—at the time, a force made up of independent voters—and, as it turns out, the nation as a whole. Building on networks established by the anti-slavery Liberty Party, dating to the 1840s, and in conjunction with Northeastern industrialists who opposed the expansion of slave labor in the new western territories, the Republican Party captured a plurality of Congressional seats that year.[11] By doing so, it supplanted the Whigs as the other dominant party in the United States. Since then, the Democratic Party (whose origins in the 1820s lay in the extension of suffrage to poor white males, while maintaining the exclusion of women and people of color) and the Republican Party have maintained a bipartisan monopoly. As the political scientist David Gillespie describes, "The American polity has become a *duopoly*: a system in which the electoral route to power has been jointly engineered by Democrats and Republicans to underwrite their hegemony. They have done it by gravely disadvantaging outside challengers."[12]

Not since Abraham Lincoln's election as president in 1860 has a third-party candidate won the presidency—not even close. After all, those who make the rules rule; and the major parties, starting in the early 20th century, made the rules, regulations, and laws to ensure their duopoly, shielding them from structural political reforms that would truly democratize our elections (as will be discussed in later chapters). In turn, independent voters, sometimes tactically using third parties as vehicles, at other times leveraging their vote for insurgent candidates in the major parties, have been the force of challenge and change.

But just as independents pose a threat to bipartisan rule, the dominant parties have sought to co-opt such challenges in order to stifle, if not suffocate, their dissent. Historically, when the parties have been unable to do so, even when they have partially or nominally adopted certain demands, they resort to tactics to marginalize or destroy them. This is particularly true when the electoral challenges have come from movements for labor rights, women's rights, and Black civil and political rights.[13] For the dominant political parties, the question of how much to concede to the outsiders, the independents, is ever-present. For the parties, their survival is paramount.

Twentieth-Century Reforms and the Rise of Regulation

While the independent political movement of Black and white Populists of the late 19th century was destroyed, the democratic impulse that propelled the movement was not. Other movements arose, as would other third parties. Some third parties were more narrowly dissenting from one or the other major parties, such as the Progressive Party, also known as the "Bull Moose Party," formed in 1912 by former US President Theodore Roosevelt after he lost the Republican presidential nomination (this in an era before presidential primaries were instituted). Other third parties grew out of independent movements, such as the pro-labor Socialist Party, which elected more than 1,200 people to public office in the opening decades of the 20th century, including nearly 80 mayors and two congressmen.

In 1920, the women's suffrage movement—an independent movement beginning in 1848—succeeded in passing the 19th Amendment to the US Constitution, extending the right to vote to women. (Some states, such as Wyoming, had enacted the right to vote for women earlier.) One of the movement's key organizations, the National Women's Party, led by feminist firebrands Alice Paul and Lucy Burns, who drew inspiration from the suffragists in England, grew out of years of on-the-ground mobilization, protests, and lobbying. Also in 1920, the Socialist candidate running for US President, Eugene V. Debs, this time running from jail, received nearly one million votes. Four years later, the independent Progressive Party's US presidential candidate, "Fighting Bob" La Follette, a senator from Wisconsin, received nearly five million votes. In each of these cases, independent voting was as much to win elections as to demonstrate growing opposition to bipartisan monopolies and their policies.[14]

The 1929 stock market crash—precipitated by low wages, large debt, a struggling agricultural sector, bank loans that could not be liquidated, and excessive speculation—and the Great Depression that followed would fuel mass movements for reform. Unemployed councils, the Congress of Industrial Organizations, and the Black-led Sharecroppers Union (reminiscent of the Colored Farmers Alliance and making some of the very same demands regarding cotton-picking wages) sprang up around the country. Each of these labor and agrarian organizing efforts, in turn, fueled support for independent political parties: In Wisconsin, La Follette's Progressive Party reemerged as a significant force; in Minnesota, the Farmer–Labor Party came to power; in Alabama, the Communist Party effectively mobilized tenant farmers; and in New York, the American Labor Party elected three congressmen.

But with widespread unrest and the rise of independent political forces came a shift in the method of bipartisan control: Regulation of the electoral process itself became paramount. Soon the hyper-regulation of the electoral process would entrench the Democratic and Republican parties.[15] With the economic collapse of the 1930s and the need for massive government intervention to create a safety net for tens of millions of impoverished citizens, the dominant parties became increasingly centralized in their structure. During this period the parties transformed the federal government from a kind of coordinating body to a highly centralized regulatory body providing welfare to both ordinary people and corporate America. Regulation would become *the* way for businesses to improve their competitive edge, maximize profits, and support the parties and candidacies that supported them.

Threatened by the growing support for these independent organizations and parties, the Democratic Party, in particular, pivoted to make key concessions. Notably, in 1935, President Franklin D. Roosevelt—promising a New Deal for the American people—and Congress enacted laws that gave labor unions the right to organize, limited the workday to eight hours, established a minimum wage, protected child labor, and guaranteed Social Security and unemployment insurance. In the South, African Americans remained victims of discrimination when state bodies were charged with carrying out federal mandates, especially regarding loans and agrarian subsidies. Nevertheless, the overarching commitment from government to support poor and working people (under independent political pressure) resulted in African Americans, in particular, breaking with the party of Lincoln and joining the Democratic Party, albeit mostly in the North where Jim Crow had not eviscerated Black voting. Along with organized labor, Black voters would form the vital backbone of the Democratic Party's New Deal coalition.

But there were tensions within the New Deal coalition. Two notable splits, one from the left, the other from the right, emerged in the years following World War II. In 1948, one of Roosevelt's former vice presidents, Henry Wallace, ran for president on the Progressive Party (same name, but different from La Follette's Progressive Party). Meanwhile, the "Dixiecrat" segregationist Strom Thurmond broke away from the Democratic Party with the States' Rights Democratic Party. Both Wallace and Thurmond received more than one million votes. Wallace eventually returned to the Democratic Party and Thurmond joined the Republican Party. So as African Americans moved into the Democratic Party, white Southerners began allying with the Republicans.

Just as FDR had been pressed to adopt a number of the positions taken by independent forces, specifically his pro-labor opponents, Democratic Party standard-bearer Harry S. Truman would likewise be forced to adopt positions taken by independents to his left. However, once elected to office, the new president joined the Wisconsin Republican Senator Joseph McCarthy in attacking these independents. Under the banner of the anti-communist Red Scare, a litany of state election laws were enacted to keep such "outsiders" off the ballot. By the end of the 1950s, these discriminatory and undemocratic rules and regulations devised by elected officials of the dominant parties prevented most independent candidates and parties from even participating in elections. Still, the demand for voting rights for the disenfranchised would not subside. Activists organized boycotts, sit-ins, and other forms of protest in what became the Civil Rights Movement. The Congress for Racial Equality, the National Association for the Advancement of Colored People, the Southern Christian Leadership Conference, the Student Non-Violent Coordinating Committee, and the Black churches, long a source of leadership training and activism, took up the cause of democracy and inclusion. Each, in their own way, challenged the unconstitutionality of Jim Crow and mobilized grassroots support on the streets, in the countryside, and in the hearts and minds of those who witnessed the courageous efforts of the movement's foot soldiers and compelling leaders. The Democratic Party struggled to navigate this new reality.

One expression of this independent political pressure took place in the late summer of 1964, when independent Black organizers Victoria Grey, Annie Levine, E. W. Steptoe, and Fannie Lou Hammer led the Mississippi Freedom Democratic Party to challenge the seating of the all-white "regular state party" at the

Democratic Party's national nominating convention. Appearing on national television while offering testimony of the beatings she faced for trying to register to vote, Hammer asked,

> Is this America, the land of the free and the home of the brave where we have to sleep with our telephones off of the hooks because our lives be threatened daily because we want to live as decent human beings, in America?[16]

The Mississippi Freedom Democratic Party was eventually awarded two at-large delegates in a compromise orchestrated by Senator Hubert Humphrey of Minnesota. Four years later he would lose the presidential election to the Republican nominee, Richard Nixon, when the Democratic governor of Alabama, George Wallace—who famously declared "Segregation now, segregation tomorrow, segregation forever!"—ran on the American Independent Party line and received six million votes from Southern white Democrats, denying the presidency to the northern, too-liberal Humphrey.

As in the 1930s, the Democratic Party-dominated bipartisan federal government in the 1960s was pushed to pass key legislation. This time, it was in support of civil and political rights, namely the 1964 Civil Rights Act and the 1965 Voting Rights Act. But a new generation of activists would demand further reforms.

Post-Civil Rights Independent Political Activism

Inspired by the Civil Rights Movement, several statewide independent political parties formed in the late 1960s. La Raza Unida in the Southwest, the Puerto Rican Young Lords in Chicago and New York City, and the Black Panther Party, in Oakland, California, with chapters across most Northern cities, took more militant stances than Civil Rights activists. Theirs was more revolutionary than reform-minded, more culturally nationalist than integrationist in character—each inspired by revolutionary movements in Africa, Asia, and Latin America. Meanwhile, other independent parties grew out of the anti-war movement in response to the war in Vietnam. These included California's Peace and Freedom Party, Vermont's Liberty Union Party—where Congressman Bernie Sanders began his political career—and the Wisconsin Labor–Farm Party.

But each of these parties, whether reform or revolutionary in their goals, either came under attack or its leaders were co-opted. With the exception of Peace and Freedom, one of only two left-wing political parties in the country with permanent ballot status (the other one being the Workers World Party in Michigan), the Young Lords and the Black Panthers were violently suppressed by the police. Leaders, like Black Panther Fred Hampton, were murdered or others, famously Angela Davis, were imprisoned with state intervention, as it was later revealed through the FBI's COINTELPRO projects. The Liberty Union and Labor–Farm parties, meanwhile, faded away. Peace and Freedom had a small resurgence, decades later, but also faded away. Still others eventually gave up the independent ghost and allied with the Democratic Party.

As the sociologist Phyllis Goldberg eloquently writes,

> Dr. Martin Luther King, Jr., who was considering an independent presidential run just before his murder in 1968, and Malcolm X, in his "the ballot or the bullet" speech a few years earlier, recognized that the problematic relationship of the African American people to the Democratic Party was a central issue in working out a strategy for the exercise of Black power.[17]

As a result, African-American leaders decided to gather and try to chart out an electoral course for the Black community as a whole. In 1972, following a Black convention tradition going back to the first half of the 19th century, African Americans gathered for the National Black Political Convention in Gary, Indiana. There, Richard Hatcher, the city's mayor who was hosting the convention, spoke of a third path beyond either trying to elect more Black people via the Democratic Party or forming an all-Black party. He imagined the coming together of a multiracial third party that could mobilize broadly. In the end, however, the convention opted to elect more African Americans to office under the banner of the Democratic Party while a small number of convention attendees decided to form an all-Black party. The future remained murky.[18]

By the late 1970s, some began looking to new strategies to create something independent of the major parties. One was the product of the Labor Community Alliance for Change—a coalition of grassroots activists and organizers, rank-and-file trade unionists, and progressive elected officials. In 1979, the New Alliance Party was formed as a Black-led, multiracial progressive party, attracting Black and Latino elected officials who were being marginalized by the Democratic Party machine. Independent politics became their weapon of choice to push back on their own party bosses. Soon, the New Alliance Party went national. Running multiple presidential campaigns, its leading figure, developmental psychologist and educator Dr. Lenora Fulani, became the first woman and the first African American to appear on the ballot in all 50 states in 1988. She accomplished this only after getting more than 1.2 million signatures and winning 11 lawsuits against state election boards. Following the explosive impact of Rev. Jesse Jackson's two presidential campaigns, Fulani's 1988 campaign was run under the banner "Two Roads Are Better Than One"—that is, vote for Jackson in the Democratic Primary and use the independent road if he is denied the nomination. The Fulani campaign became something of a model for the 1992 emergence of Texas billionaire H. Ross Perot, who received nearly 20 million votes running as an independent. (He had consulted Fulani's legal team to learn how to get on the ballot, given the complicated and convoluted set of rules and regulations making it extremely difficult, logistically and financially, to do so.)

Other parties had come on the scene, including the Libertarian Party (1971), with additional ones emerging over the next two decades, including the Independence Party (1991), Constitution Party (1992), Reform Party (1995), Working Families Party (1998), and Green Party (2001). Some had grown out of particular independent reform movements (e.g., the Reform Party), while others served as adjuncts of either the Democratic or Republican parties (the Working Families Party). But increasing numbers of Americans had begun to feel a kind of independent/anti-party sentiment, in part because of the hyper-partisanship that was beginning to take hold in the nation.

Independent political challenges would be curtailed by limiting access to the ballot, subsidizing party primaries with public funds while they exclude nonaligned voters (lest we forget that political parties are private entities), and creating voting districts through gerrymandering where politicians chose their constituents before their constituents chose them. The days of outright political violence were largely past—that is, the "paramilitary politics" of the late 19th century, as the historian Steven Hahn describes, or the kind of violence directed toward the Black Panthers by the FBI and police. It was a crude and brutal way of suppressing the voices of Americans. Bipartisan rule took a more sophisticated form as the parties evolved their ways of staying in power.[19]

Bipartisan Rule Through Electoral Regulation

Despite their differences, at the end of the day, Democrats and Republicans lock arms in protecting their two-party system. They do so by taking deliberate and concerted measures to ensure their stability and their shared control of the governmental process through control of the electoral process via regulation, bolstered by a culture of bipartisanship. The mass media is largely complicit.

Additionally, over the course of the 20th century, campaign finance laws were written and rewritten, largely as a function of two-party rivalry and as a means to curb the influence of certain special interests but always with an eye toward repressing the rise of independents. Reapportionment and redistricting were implemented by bipartisan legislatures. Moreover, bipartisanism, as opposed to nonpartisanism, filtered the conduct of elections and was institutionalized, for example, with the Federal Election Commission (FEC) in 1975, and then with the pseudo-governmental Commission on Presidential Debates (CPD) in 1987. The two parties took more direct control of the election process, the legislative process, and thereby the policy-making process.

To be sure, bipartisan political control in the United States has stymied the further expansion of democracy in the United States. Among African American voters in particular, the experience of feeling trapped and being beholden to the Democratic Party within the bipartisan system is especially poignant. In a September 1, 2020, op-ed titled "The Future of Black Politics" in *the New York Times*, Black Lives Movement leader Jessica Byrd described the BLM Black National Convention held on August 28, 2020, and notes the focus of the convention being on ordinary Black people, including the poor, women, trans, and queer, stating, "For Black voters the feeling of being used without being listened to is pronounced." This is another way of expressing how African-American voters are being taken for granted by the Democratic Party. As the Black Census Project notes,

> Nationally, Black voters are a key part of the American electorate, making up about 11 percent of registered voters overall and 19 percent of voters who are registered as Democrats or say that they lean Democratic, and about 2 percent of the Republican party base.[20]

However, 57 percent of respondents to their national survey described being unfavorable or indifferent to the Democratic Party.[21] Their analysis draws out tensions between generations of Black voters: Young Black voters in swing states said they were reluctant to cast ballots because both their grandparents and parents did so religiously while receiving little in return.

The University of Chicago political scientist Cathy Cohen's GenForward national surveys underscore the feeling of younger African Americans regarding why they are increasingly politically independent. When asked the question "Would you say you consider yourself an Independent more because you are FOR a mix of political views associated with both major political parties or is it more because you are AGAINST what both the major political parties represent?" About 66 percent said they are against what the two major parties represent—notably, 21 points more than what white youth state.[22] Despite older Black leaders urging the need to "get out the vote," this survey data suggests that simply voting is not enough for younger African Americans, who largely assert that neither major party represents their desires and wants. Indeed, a deep anti-partisan sentiment has become increasingly apparent.[23]

At a National Action Network rally on September 5, 2020, the Rev. Al Sharpton, representing an older Black generation voter sentiment, spoke passionately about the importance of voting. But the question of what (little) the Black community has gotten out of voting for the Democratic Party was not addressed. As the Harlem-based African-American physician and independent political leader Dr. Jessie Fields, who was at the rally, notes,

> There is a conflict here which I think [independents] can address by expanding voting rights and political reform. The heart and soul of the fight for expanding voting rights is to enfranchise independent nonparty Blacks and other people of color and this is the most threatening and the most potentially transformative freeing of the Black community which the

Democratic Party will fight tooth and nail against and which also threatens the Republican party establishment in terms of the maintenance of the two party control.[24]

Bipartisan control over the electoral process (via rules and regulations, which, in turn feeds bipartisan culture) is the way the two parties come together in opposition to the "outsiders." As Jessica Byrd's op-ed goes on to discuss, through the campaigns she worked on and in the formation of the Electoral Justice Project of the Black Lives Matter movement,

We knew that for more of us to participate in elections, we would need more than new faces. We needed a new process. . . . The solution, as we see it, is not in traditional party politics. . . . Parties want our votes while promising little and delivering less. That is because the electoral system was designed as binary.[25]

Taking Stock

So many have forged the path, plowed the fields, harvested, and either expanded or failed in making what the United States remains: a limited democracy with so much more promise. Independent voters have been catalysts for the expansion of democracy as part of social, economic, and political reforms—at times succeeding, mostly failing, but throughout shaping what was to come. For the Black and white Populists that included key reforms, such as the direct election of US senators and many aspects of New Deal-era policies, notably the subsidization of farmers (albeit unequally distributed to Black farmers).

Frederick Douglass, who joined the Liberty Party in the late 1840s after initially being skeptical of engaging electoral politics, given how complicit it was in the institution of slavery, declared, "Those who profess to favor freedom and yet depreciate agitation, are people who want crops without ploughing the ground. . . . Power concedes nothing without a demand. It never did and it never will."[26] Rev. Walter Pattillo grew the independent movement with the Colored Alliance, helped to form the People's Party, and supported the fusion tactic with Republicans to advance the needs of poor and working communities but went into obscurity following the turn of the century. Meanwhile, George Washington Murray was elected to Congress, pushing back against Jim Crow in South Carolina and serving as the last elected Black congressman from the state for nearly a century.

As the Anglo-Irish historian Benedict Anderson (not to be confused with Benedict Arnold, the Revolutionary War figure who fought on both sides of the war) noted, the nation is an "imagined community."[27] Insofar as the United States of America has been an invention, independents have been its revolutionary driving force, reimagining it over and again through their political action.

Notes

1 Scott, James C., *Domination and the Arts of Resistance: Hidden Transcripts*, Yale University Press, 1992, p. 199.
2 Ali, Omar H., *In the Lion's Mouth: Black Populism in the New South, 1886–1900*, University Press of Mississippi, 2010, p. 126.
3 DuBois, W. E. B., *The Souls of Black Folk*, A.C. McClurg & Co., 1903; Ali, Omar H., *In the Lion's Mouth: Black Populism in the New South, 1886–1900*, University Press of Mississippi, 2010.
4 Foner, Eric, *Reconstruction: America's Unfinished Revolution, 1863–1877*, Harper-Collins, 2014.
5 Jones Royster, Jaqueline, ed., *Southern Horrors and Other Writings: The Anti-Lynching Campaign of Ida B. Wells, 1892–1900*, second edition, Bedford St. Martin's Press, 2016.
6 Ali Omar H., *In the Lion's Mouth: Black Populism in the New South*, University Press of Mississippi, 2010.
7 Cecelski, David S., & Tyson, Timothy B., eds. *Democracy Betrayed: The Wilmington Riot of 1898 and its Legacy*, The University of North Carolina Press, 1998.
8 "George Washington's Farewell Address," *Independent Chronicle*, September 26, 1796. See the Avalon Project at Yale Law School, retrieved from https://avalon.law.yale.edu/18th_century/washing.asp.
9 Dahl, Robert A., *On Democracy*, Yale University Press, 2000, p. 87.
10 Gillespie, J. David, *Challengers to Duopoloy: Why Third Parties Matter in American Two-Party Politics*, The University of South Carolina Press, 2012.
11 Among the other third parties of the era were the American (Know-Nothings) and Constitutional Union parties; see Donald J. Green, *Third Party Matters: Politics, Presidents, and Third Parties in American History*, Praeger, 2010.
12 Gillespie, J. David, *Challengers to Duopoloy: Why Third Parties Matter in American Two-Party Politics*, The University of South Carolina Press, 2012, p. ix.
13 Other issues in years to come included environmentalism, lowering the voting age—a direct result of the anti-war movement—advancing LGBTQ rights, disabilities rights, along with long-standing issues from the far-right, such as nativism or its more recent anti-immigrant resurgence.
14 Goldberg, Phyllis, "The Independent Tradition Gives Birth to America's Premier Black Independent, Lenora B. Fulani," *When Democracy is on the Job, America Works*, 1992.
15 See Rosenstone, Steven J., Roy L. Behr, & Lazarus, Edwad H., *Third Parties in America: Citizen Response to Major Party Failure*, second edition, Princeton University Press, 1996.
16 "Fannie Lou Hammer: Testimony at the Democratic National Convention," *The American Yawp Reader*, Stanford University Press, retrieved from www.americanyawp.com/reader/27-the-sixties/fannie-lou-hamer-testimony-at-the-democratic-national-convention-1964/
17 Goldberg, Phyllis, "The Independent Tradition Gives Birth to America's Premier Black Independent, Lenora B. Fulani," *When Democracy is on the Job, America Works*, 1992.
18 Moore, Leonard N., *The Defeat of Black Power: Civil Rights and the National Black Political Convention of 1972*, Louisiana State University Press, 2018.
19 Hahn, Stephen, *A Nation Under Our Feet: Black Political Struggles in the Rural South from Slavery to the Great Migration*, Harvard University Press, 2005.
20 "More Black than Blue: Politics and Power in the 2019 Census," *Black Futures Lab, Black-Census.org*, 4, retrieved from https://blackcensus.org/wp-content/uploads/2019/06/Digital-More-Black-Than-Blue.pdf
21 Ibid.

22 GenForward Survey, "Institutions and Polarization," (02/23–03/10/2018), retrieved from https://genforwardsurvey.com/survey-search/?query=independent&survey=83 &question=Q40C; see also Cohen, Cathy J., *Democracy Remixed: Black Youth and the Future of American Politics*, Oxford University Press, 2011.

23 See Ali, Omar H., Orosco, Stephanie, Rodman, Brittany et al., "College Independents Poll: The Emergence of a Non-Partisan Politics?" *Office of Research and Economic Development*, The University of North Carolina at Greensboro, 2013, retrieved from https://research.uncg.edu/wp-content/uploads/2013/08/College-Independents-Poll-2012-uploaded082313.pdf

24 From e-mail correspondence from Jessie Fields to David Cherry, Omar H. Ali, and Jacqueline S. Salit on September 6, 2020.

25 Byrd, Jessica, "The Future of Black Politics," *The New York Times*, September 1, 2020; an op-ed by Keeanga Yamahtta titled "The End of Black Politics" from June 2020 also makes the case for a de-alignment of younger Black voters from the Democratic and Republican parties.

26 Douglass, Frederick, "West Indian Emancipation Address (August 4, 1857)," In Blassingame, John W. (Ed), *The Frederick Douglass Papers*, ser. 1, vol. 1 (1855–63), Yale University Press, 1985.

27 Anderson, Benedict, *Imagined Communities: Reflections on the Origin and Spread of Nationalism,* second edition, 1983.

3

INDEPENDENT VOTERS OR SHADOW PARTISANS?

> We do not know nearly as much about this critical group of voters as many pundits think. The electoral movements of this poorly understood category underlie the unstable majorities of our time.
>
> —Morris Fiorina, 2016[1]

The democratic ideal of an independent, "free-thinking" citizen evaluating the many political choices arranged before them and making intelligent, informed decisions has held a place of distinction throughout the history of American political thought. But not in US academic scholarship. For the past 60 years, research and analysis by political scientists has largely discounted or attempted to disprove this notion of "independence." Modern US politics has largely been viewed through the lens of a two-party power structure: Democrats and Republicans. Political and other social scientists have been extremely skeptical and dismissive of the independent voter, concluding they were uninformed and uninvolved and/or labeling the independents as leaners, disengaged, disaffected, and/or shadow partisans. With a few exceptions, most academics studying American politics are simply unable to conceive of a voter who doesn't choose to identify with one of the major parties.[2]

The American National Election Studies (ANES) Surveys

The root concept of independent voters as a different political species goes back to the work of Angus Campbell and his colleagues, who first published *The American Voter* in 1960.[3] Analyzing data produced by the American National Election Studies (ANES),[4] the authors describe the identity of party affiliation as a central

DOI: 10.4324/9781003240808-4

characteristic explaining voting behavior and other political attitudes and behaviors. The surveys that *The American Voter* analyzed have been considered by many to be the gold standard in the field. *The American Voter* authors acknowledged that some kind of "independent" existed, but they introduced a bias about their significance in the political arena by describing the independent as having little interest in campaigns and outcomes and suggesting their choice between competing candidates as being uninformed.

The real key to understanding the independent voter, and the literature regarding that voter, lies in examining the survey questions classifying respondents. Most of what we know about independents comes from survey data. And most surveys predispose the majority of independents as leaners toward either of the two political parties. Beginning in the second half of the 20th century, when individuals identified themselves as an independent, researchers and pollsters began to introduce a follow-up question on whether they prefer one party over the other if they had to vote then and there. Most independents indicated a lean toward one of the two major political parties' candidates. Political scientists have labeled these individuals as "independent leaners" and have argued that the number of pure independents is actually quite small—below 10 percent and this percentage has remained constant since the 1950s.[5] They have introduced a narrative that these "leaners" really are partisans rather than independent and that many people who like to think of themselves as independent-minded and free of party influence are not. Samara Klar, an associate professor at the University of Arizona School of Government and Public Policy and co-author of the book *Independent Politics*,[6] explained it this way: "More often than not, we can count on leaners to vote for that party, support the party's positions, and sometimes even donate money to the party's candidate. What's more, leaners consistently support their party from election to election."[7] Others have been more unequivocal asserting that "leaners are partisans"[8]; or as Ruy Teixeira, senior fellow at the Center for American Progress, contends, the "greatest myth in American politics: that independents are actually independent. They are not. As numerous studies have shown, the overwhelming majority of Americans who say there are 'independent' lean toward one party or the other."[9]

Mischaracterizing Independent Voters as Leaners

The counterargument is that a lot is unknown about the voting patterns over time of the independent voter, and no conclusive evidence exists that independent leaners vote in a partisan manner consistently. Furthermore, it can be argued that the two major parties—Republicans and Democrats—don't want competition in the political process and go to great lengths to use outdated laws to make sure that most voters have only two choices. According to Reed Galen, co-founder of the Lincoln Project,

As the two parties' duopoly formed at the ballot box, they used their official authority to restrict and prevent political outsiders from fully participating in national and local elections. Across the country, these limitations and barriers to entry remain strong as Republicans and Democrats use arcane rules and outdated laws to make sure most voters only have two choices— and not particularly good choices at that.[10]

One of the authors of this book, Omar H. Ali, professor of history at the University of North Carolina Greensboro and author of *In the Balance of Power, Independent Black Politics and Third-Party Movements in the United States*, makes this analogy. Noting the conventional wisdom among political scientists that independents are really partisans in disguise, he "likens that to a desperately hungry person who is offered a rotten tomato or an overripe banana." They're going to choose one or another, "because those are the only real options they have."[11]

The introduction of the follow-up survey questions by political scientists and pollsters allowed for a narrative that has effectively discounted the very existence of independents. Increasingly, others have begun to question the accuracy of this position based on the framing of the question, given the context of voting in the United States—a highly constricted two-party system in which voting for a non-major-party candidate almost always means voting for someone who will not win; so if one wants to vote for a winning candidate, one is compelled to vote for a major-party candidate. There is growing evidence that a sizable number of independents move in and out of independent status in ways that impact independent voting over time. Morris Fiorina, professor of political science at Stanford University, senior fellow at the Hoover Institution, and former chairman of the board of the ANES, contends that following independent leaners over several elections is key to understanding their voting patterns.[12] Along with his colleague Samuel J. Abrams, they conducted such an analysis and found that, following independent leaners across multiple elections, "their partisan stability is closer to pure independents than weak partisans."[13] They further noted "classifying all leaners as weak partisans' mis-characterizes the partisanship of Americans and overestimates the rate of party voting."[14]

As documented in prior chapters, independent voters, or those who do not identify as Republicans or Democrats, made up more than two-fifths of the electorate in 2021.[15] Eight years into the 21st century, these voters began influencing the outcome of presidential elections. Independents helped elect Barack Obama in 2008, by eight percentage points.[16] In 2016, they changed course and backed Donald Trump by a four-point margin.[17] Then in the fall of 2020, they broke for Joe Biden and Kamala Harris by 13 percentage points—delivering the margins of victory necessary for that ticket to secure the decisive electoral votes of Pennsylvania, Wisconsin, Georgia, and Arizona.[18] In the January 2021 Senate runoffs in Georgia, independents broke for the winners, Raphael Warnock and

Jon Ossoff, by four points, fueling the narrow victories that have delivered control of the Senate to the Democratic Party.[19] And now less than a year into his presidency, Biden's downturn in his approval rating has come disproportionately from independents.[20] The volatile voting patterns of independents during the last several presidential elections seem to contradict the conventional wisdom being advanced by political scientists that most independents are partisans and vote as particular partisans. If this were the case, we would be seeing consistent partisan support for the presidential candidates.

Practically, every other voting demographic has remained fairly constant over the last several presidential elections. If you want to identify the anomaly, look at the voting patterns of independents—a group of unpredictable voters with no formal name, no party affiliation, and no common ideological doctrine. According to Fiorina, "We do not know nearly as much about this critical group of voters as many pundits think. The electoral movements of this poorly understood category underlie the unstable majorities of our time."[21]

Conventional wisdom about independents as leaners may be significantly overstated or simply wrong. When former Governor Arnold Schwarzenegger was asked for his thoughts about political scientists' claims concerning independents, he stated:

> I don't understand if someone says that he sees the color green and they say "Well really the person doesn't really see green, they're seeing purple." I mean I don't see what gives them the right to redefine what the people's wish is. So I don't know . . . so I don't know what the reason behind it is. But to me, if someone says, "I am now getting out of the Republican Party to declare myself an independent, or if I'm getting out of the Democratic Party and declaring myself independent," to me, I take it at face value. If they say they're independent, they're independent. To me it's the freedom to go either way. Don't count on me. Don't count on me anymore. I'm outta here.[22]

Furthermore, there needs to be a better understanding about the reasons for the dramatic and enduring exodus of voters from the two parties. The continuing flight of millions of voters from identifying with the Republican or Democratic parties and the distrust of traditional two-party power are among the most volatile phenomena in US politics today. Dismissing the significance of the largest voting bloc in the nation is viewed by many as shortsighted.[23] Even highly partisan former Majority Leader Harry Reid noted:

> I have tremendous affection for the two parties. But our system has become so filled with tribalism, it's hard for me to comprehend. I know there is tremendous dissatisfaction, which is causing many people, many young people, to not be party-affiliated. . . . We, as party members, like to wear

that Democratic badge wherever we go. But you better start reaching out to independents and treat them as independents.[24]

The History of Classifying the Independent Voter

Let's examine in more detail how we got here. Since the 1960 study, national and regional surveys for the most part have included analysis of the views of independent voters in comparison to voters who identify themselves with parties. These surveys through almost five decades document a growing number of independents. The Pew Research Center is perhaps the most oft-cited source. The Pew Research Center, in the lead up to the 2010 mid-term elections, began classifying independents, regardless of lean, into five groups: Shadow Democrats, Doubting Democrats, Shadow Republicans, Disaffected Republicans, and Disengaged Independents. Pew determines self-identification through periodic telephone polls of Americans nationwide. Its research during recent years consistently states that the number of political independents continues to grow, noting that both parties have lost ground among the public. Nonetheless, as is obvious from the categories Pew created, the frame of reference continues to be the parties.

Independent voters now make up the largest segment of the American electorate, with Gallup showing upwards of 50 percent of registered voters in January of 2021 identifying as independents.[25] This is the highest percentage on record in Gallup's decades-long history of polling. Gallup attributes the rise of political independence in the United States to increasing frustration with government and the bipartisan control over politics.

Likewise, ANES shows independents ranging from 14 percent to 38 percent of respondents, depending on how a researcher classifies "leaners." Independents who identify as leaners are individuals who responded "Independent" to the initial party identification question and then responded to the follow-up question by indicating they consider themselves closer to one party or another. The ANES data clearly demonstrates the major uptick in use of the independent label at the end of the 1960s. Both the overall number and the number of "true" independents roughly doubles from the late 1950s. ANES periodically asks Americans in surveys, "Generally speaking, do you usually think of yourself as a Republican, a Democrat, an Independent, or what?" It also asks those who chose a partisan label whether they consider themselves a strong Democrat or Republican, and they ask those who chose the independent label whether they see themselves closer to the Democratic or Republican Party or neither. Thus, the idea of independents as "true" independents (those who do not lean to either party) is distinguished from "leaners," who many consider "closet partisans."[26]

After the convulsions of the 1960s, from the Civil Rights Movement to the Vietnam War and beyond, voter attitudes about the two major political parties began to shift. The divisions between civil rights advocates and many segregationist Southerners in the Democratic Party shaped voters' perspectives about their party. Likewise, opposition to the Vietnam War provoked divisions among partisans in both parties. And the subsequent regional shift over the following decades, whereby Republicans became dominant in most Southern states for the first time in history, shifted voter affiliations yet further. Another seminal event was the inclusion of 18- to 21-year-olds in the electorate for the first time in 1972 with the 26th Amendment to the US Constitution and this age group's growing disenchantment with their parties. Since this age cohort was the most likely to differ from the major parties in their views about civil rights and the Vietnam War, this amplified the disaffiliation from parties. All of these political convulsions produced the first notable "bubble" of independents in national and regional polling. According to the authors of *The American Voter Revisited*, 2008, "The effects of the civil rights revolution, the Vietnam War, and Watergate were manifest among people who were informed about politics and care for real political issues. Hence, they could not be considered Independents of *The American Voter* type."[27]

While the literature of the past 50 years consistently describes a growth trend of voters self-identifying as independents, it is also accompanied by a robust debate about the real meaning of this trend. At its heart, this debate is fueled by skepticism among many authors that voters who claim the independent label are "really" independent. While some skeptics acknowledge that this trend must have some significance, they cling to the notion that most people who claim to be independent are really "undercover" or "closet" partisans. In this view, few voters are truly independent. This view that independents are masking their true partisanship is shared by a wide array of popular commentators, especially in the media and among political actors.[28] In 2019, PEW found that the overwhelming number of independents continue to lean toward one or the other major parties "with 17% . . . Democratic-leaning independents, while 13% lean toward the Republican Party. Just 7% of Americans decline to lean toward a party."[29] These suppositions are widely debated among academics and in the popular press.[30] They figure that most voters must have a partisan mindset, as the authors usually do. This view is also reinforced by many academics who demonstrate in their research that voters who claim to be independent are really behaving like partisans, and in some cases "leaners . . . vote in a more partisan manner than weak partisans."[31]

The surge of independents appearing in the early 1970s fueled this debate. David Broder's 1972 book, *The Party's Over*, pointed to the possible end of parties or at least their significance in shaping American politics.[32] However, this speculation was soon pushed aside by research that indicated that partisanship was alive and well.

In the 1980s, after the Republican Party won the presidency and the US Senate, much of the post-partisan thinking had disappeared and a new crop of literature returned to the notion that parties shape voters. This period also corresponds to the rise of increasingly sophisticated analyses of voting behavior, supported by the growth in polling in general. Most of this research claimed that many self-identifying independents are actually partisans who consistently act in partisan ways and hold consistently partisan views.

Then, in 1992, the book *The Myth of the Independent Voter* was published. Its author Bruce Keith and his colleagues used a variety of datasets to demonstrate that the independent mindset mirrors the mindset of their partisan fellow citizens.[33] Unfortunately for Keith et al., Ross Perot launched his explosive independent presidential campaign just as the book came out, demonstrating a clash between the more conservative views of the academy and the more radical impulses of tens of millions of American voters.

Since the publication of Keith et al.'s study,[34] voter behavior research has focused on determining the stability of partisanship rather than examining the theoretical assumptions made about independent voters.[35] Before Keith, the body of literature on independent voters was notably different. It described a political system where independent voters were not necessarily partisans and that declining importance of partisan identities would eventually lead to American politics evolving beyond a two-party system.[36] Campbell et al.[37] argued that this will occur because independents are fundamentally different than partisans, given that they are less politically engaged than their partisan counterparts.

Another skeptical view suggests that independent voters could be even more partisan, in a sense, than "mainstream" partisans. This idea stems from anecdotal evidence of people refusing to identify with a party because they do not see the party they used to identify with as "partisan enough." There is a misconception that these voters are embracing an independent status because they want their party to pursue a more moderate agenda or to move to the middle instead of catering to the extreme. In fact, there is evidence that they are abandoning their party labels for the exact opposite reason: They see the party as moving too far from its core values.

Regardless of their true independence, the question persists whether independents play a significant role in elections. In other words, who cares how someone self-identifies? The questions that usually motivate political actors and often reflect the media's view as well are, Do they vote Democratic or Republican? Are political independents the swing voters that ultimately decide many elections? If they are truly straddling the parties, or willing to choose than abandon one for the other, as the evidence shows, they are some of the most influential voters in the electorate. Or, lacking the motivation of partisanship, are they less involved in elections and thus less influential than partisan voters?

Linda Killian's 2012 work best represents the research into these questions. In *The Swing Vote: The Untapped Power of Independents,*[38] she dives into an exploration of voters who, in her analysis, contributed a significant margin of victory for Barack Obama in key states in 2008, and Republican Congressional candidates in 2010. She found that people increasingly see a disconnect between the priorities of elected officials and those of voters. She supports this perspective with reference to polls showing confidence in government at an all-time low.[39]

Killian's presumption is that voters who are disenchanted with parties are a growing bloc and therefore most likely to ignore normal partisan signals and evaluate candidates based on their likelihood to seek compromise and moderate solutions. She recommends that candidates increasingly reach out to swing voters, who are up for grabs in any election. Others similarly see party independence as a function of conflicting pressures on the voter, combined with a more pragmatic, less ideological disposition. Independent voters are also more likely to consider the country's economic conditions, while partisan-identified voters use the cues of party and ideology.[40]

One aspect to understanding the potential influence of independent voters in any given election is data about whether independent turnout is the same or lower than partisan voters. Here the use of the "unaffiliated voter" designation, referring to the voter's registration status, is most often cited. In this case, independents have a much lower turnout. However, it has been argued that this is likely a result of legal and institutional barriers preventing those voters from participating in the election in the same fashion as partisan voters. (Chapter 6 addresses the legal and structural barriers hindering independent voter participation.) Both political parties maintain their duo-monopoly status via federal and varying state election laws to ensure that third parties have little or no chance of challenging the two-party apparatus and continue to keep independent voters marginalized. In other cases, authors who broaden the concept of independent to consider those not registered as unaffiliated still assume that independent voter participation is lower than that of others. Also, given the rise of partisanship, candidates turn to mobilizing their party base in order to win elections.

Methodological Problems With Studies Indicating Independents Are Leaners

Several scholars have disputed the findings that most independents are leaners and suggest that there is no conclusive evidence for this position.[41] Others have argued that responses to survey question probes asking independents if they lean toward the Democratic or Republican Party are significantly contaminated by short-term electoral elements operating in the campaign, such as the candidates and specific issues[42]. Fiorina contends that researchers consistently cite a handful of studies that find that leaners are partisans and they "fail to deal with a serious methodological objection . . . reverse causation or, in contemporary social-science argot, endogeneity."[43] Retrocausality, or backwards causation, is a concept of cause and effect in which an effect precedes its cause in time and so a later event affects an earlier one.[44] An endogeneity problem arises when there is a factor that is related to your Y variable that is also related to your X variable, and you do not have that factor in your model.[45]

Abrams and Fiorina put it this way:

> In consequence it has become common practice to classify leaning independents as partisans, leaving only pure independents in the middle party ID category. This is a rather remarkable practice that should require thoroughly compelling evidence to justify. An independent leaner has explicitly said "no" to the stem question about partisan identity (do you think of yourself . . . ?). We can think of no other case in political science where analysts change a respondent's explicit response to a survey item on the basis of information from other items—*especially one generally used as the dependent variable*. We believe such strong conclusions are premature. Citizens who classify themselves as independent leaners in one election are less likely to classify themselves the same way in the next election than are weak identifiers.[46]

If most independents are truly partisans, how does one explain the shifting support of independents during the last several presidential elections? As noted earlier, Abrams and Fiorina's panel studies following "independent leaners" over multiple elections found they have no firm partisan loyalties.[47]

Fiorina elaborates on this point:

> Clearly independents are a heterogeneous category. Some are closet partisans. Some are ideological centrists. Some are cross-pressured, preferring one party on some issues but a different party on other issues. Some are unhappy with both parties but one more than the other, and some are, quite simply, clueless. But whatever they are, they are an important component of the electoral instability that characterizes the contemporary era. Their critical contribution to contemporary elections lies in their volatility.[48]

Similarly, professors C. Michael Bitzer, Christopher Cooper, Whitney Manzo, and Susan Roberts researched down-ballot voters in North Carolina and found that unaffiliated voters were not simply shadow partisans, but varied from Democrats and Republicans in terms of demographics, political behavior, and political attitudes.[49]

In 2015, the Morrison Institute for Public Policy conducted a study of Arizona independents. A statewide poll of 2,000 voters was supplemented by focus groups with 33 voters to delve into the growth of independents, who first became a plurality of Arizona registered voters in March 2014. The Morrison study found that nearly half of independents had changed their registration from another party. Independent respondents were significantly more likely than Democrats or Republicans to describe themselves as moderates, but, even so, nearly one-quarter of independents considered themselves to be liberal or conservative. When asked about specific issues, however, the range of opinions of independents was quite diverse, and sometimes appeared similar to voters of one or the other of the major parties. Independents demonstrated their mindset by responding at the lowest rate to the question, "I prefer to vote along party lines." The independent perspective was best summed up by one focus group participant: "We're not a party. We're a mindset."[50]

Americans Embarrassed By Their Political Party?

Samara Klar at the University of Arizona and Yanna Krupnikov at Stony Brook University have recently added some important research that furthers our understanding of the independent voter. They explored the social significance of the growth in people refusing to identify themselves with a political party and suggested that independents and partisans differ psychologically.[51] They do not dispute the notion that independents may be "closet partisans" (they call them "undercover partisans"); but they do dispute the bias that independents are not politically engaged, stating that "engagement levels are comparable across independents and partisans."[52] Nonetheless, they contend that the refusal to publicly identify with a party must be revealing something important. And they believe the predictors of independent political engagement differ substantially from partisans. Their research attempts to identify what independent self-identification reveals and what constitutes the differential predictors of engagement.[53]

Dispelling the notion that independence is an indicator of political disengagement, Klar and Krupnikov answer the question why voters refuse to identify as partisans, even if they display other attitudes and behaviors that mirror partisans. The answer lies in the perception voters have of how others will view them if they identify as partisans. They assert that many Americans are embarrassed by their political party and do not wish to be associated with either side. Instead, they intentionally mask their party preference, especially in social situations.[54]

Finally, Klar and Krupnikov turn to the influence of media and social messages on a voter's decision to identify as an independent. As negative reporting about partisan conflict and negative associations with partisan views are shared with voters, they are more likely to identify as independent. Thus, partisan conflict drives independents away from partisan self-identification, even if they otherwise hold fairly consistent views with one of the major political parties.[55] This research reinforces a widespread view that the growing perception of polarization in the public arena is turning voters away from the political system and perhaps fueling the rise of independents.

Political Polarization

The extent of literature devoted to studying political polarization has been wide-ranging in recent years. A lively debate ensues among authors about whether and how much the public is truly polarized. Questions persist about whether the public is polarizing, and thus driving polarization among political elites, or whether incentives to polarize among the political elite are driving growing polarization in the public. It may very well be a dialectical interplay between the public and the political elite, creating a kind of feedback loop. Some authors contend that the public is not nearly as polarized as political elites. Others have studied the extent to which perception of polarization belies a greater consensus in the public. That is, do people believe they are polarized more than they are?

The 2014 Pew Research Center study *Political Polarization in the American Public* is one of the most in-depth treatments of the topic. It is based on a survey of 10,000 adults nationwide, and it concluded that "partisan antipathy is deeper and more extensive—than at any point in the last two decades."[56] In each party, negative views of the opposing party are twice as large as they were a generation ago. A variety of measures of partisan antipathy, including sorting by residence, choice of friends, and marriage, indicate that partisan animus has turned into social animus. However, Pew notes, "These sentiments are not shared by all—or even most— Americans . . . [In fact], more believe their representatives in government should meet halfway to resolve contentious disputes rather than hold out for more of what they want."[57] Pew considers the implications of this distance between partisans and moderates regarding their political behavior. Could this majority view be leading to rejection of the parties altogether, and thus a factor in the growth of independents? Pew doesn't draw that conclusion, but states "many of those in the center remain on the edges of the political playing field, relatively distant and disengaged."[58]

Some of the most intriguing research on polarization finds a greater perception of polarization in the public than exists in fact.[59] The proportion of the public that describes important differences between the two major parties has risen by 30 percentage points in the past half century.[60] Fiorina, in his 2017 book *Unstable Majorities: Polarization, Party Sorting and Political Stalemate*,[61] suggests that the answer to the question "Has the American electorate polarized?" is no, according to the data; however, the US public believes the answer is yes.[62] He suggests that this perception in the public also varies depending on where they fall along the continuum of partisanship and political engagement.

In short, the political polarization research dances around the possibility that public perceptions of growing polarization are contributing to the increase in independent self-identification, but none address it head-on. Most of the research is concerned with finding the causes of polarization, rather than studying the consequences. Perhaps, perceptions of polarization and demonstrated polarization among political elites are significant factors driving the rise of independents.[63]

Recognizing and Respecting Independents for Who They Say They Are

As discussed, conventional wisdom by political scientists and other academics contends that most independents are partisans, and that the number of true independents is fairly inconsequential, given their numbers are less than 10 percent of the total voting population. These studies are based on follow-up probes of surveys that ask those who identify as independents whether they lean toward one of the two major parties. However, as outlined in this chapter, there are serious concerns about the accuracy of this position. At a minimum, this position is overstated. At most, the position is simply wrong. There is a lot that still needs to be learned about this emerging group of voters. Most studies that find leaners are partisans simply do not account for a sizable number of independents who move in and out of independent status. They also do not account for their voting patterns over time. Many voters who identify as independent leaners in one election are less likely to identify themselves in the same manner in the next election. Their identification may depend on specific candidates or issues on the ballot. When independents are followed over multiple elections, they have been found to have no firm partisan loyalties. Voting patterns of independents over the past several presidential elections confirm the unpredictable and volatile nature of this bloc. Additionally, methodological concerns have been raised with these studies around their failure to deal with reverse causation or endogeneity. Finally, giving self-identified independents effectively a binary choice on whether they lean toward one or another of the major two parties, or remain independent in the face of an election where the likely outcome will be the candidate of one or the other major party, is a subject of controversy and needs to be reevaluated.

What we do know is that US voters are abandoning the two major parties in a dramatic fashion. Public disgust with both parties is rising. Party loyalty is breaking down at an accelerated pace, and voters are choosing to reject the Democrat and Republican labels and identify as independent. We do know that independents encompass voters who are on both ends of the political spectrum and those "in the middle." They have no party platform or playbook to refer to when going to the voting booth. And they are unpredictable. Or are they? Are there common shared values that bind them together? Anti-incumbency? Anti-corruption? Pro-reform? (We will explore these shared values in Chapter 8.)

The bottom line is that we have much to learn about this group of voters. Traditional ways of measuring voter identification do not capture the independent voter. At this moment, when concerns about the state of US democracy are high, it is critical to recognize and respect independents for who they say they are and not rely on the conventional categories into which they have been fit.

Notes

1 Fiorina, M., "Independents: The Marginal Members of an Electoral Coalition," *Hoover Institution*, 2016, retrieved from www.hoover.org/research/independents-marginal-members-electoral-coalition
2 Salit, J., & Reilly, T., "Can Independent Voters Save American Democracy? Why 42 Percent of American Voters are Independent and How They Can Transform our Political System," In *Democracy Unchained: How to Rebuild Government for the People*, New Press, 2020, pp. 323–335.
3 Campbell, A., Converse, P. E., Miller, W. E., & Stokes, D. E., *The American Voter*, Wiley, 1960.

4 Data Center, ANES | American National Election Studies, 2021, retrieved from https://electionstudies.org/data-center/

5 Sides, J. Three Myths about Political Independents, *The Monkey Cage*, 2013, retrieved from https://themonkeycage.org/2009/12/three_myths_about_political_in/; Political Independents: Who They Are, What They Think, *Pew Research Center—U.S. Politics & Policy*, 2019, retrieved from www.pewresearch.org/politics/2019/03/14/political-independents-who-they-are-what-they-think/; Mayer, W. G., *The Swing Voter in American Politics*, Brookings Institution Press, 2008.

6 Klar, S., & Krupnikov, Y., *Independent Politics: How American Disdain for Parties Leads to Political Inaction*, Cambridge University Press, 2016.

7 Klar, S., & Krupnikov, Y., "9 Media Myths About Independent Voters, Debunked," *Vox*, 2016, retrieved from www.vox.com/2016/1/22/10814522/independents-voters-facts-myths

8 Petrocik, J. R., "Measuring Party Support: Leaners are Not Independents," *Electoral Studies*, 2009, pp. 562–572.

9 Teixiera,R.,"TheGreatIllusion,"*TheNewRepublic,*2012,retrievedfromhttps://newrepublic.com/article/100799/swing-vote-untapped-power-independents-linda-killian

10 Galen, R., "How Republicans and Democrats Prevent Independent Candidates from Getting on the Ballot," *NBC News*, 2018, retrieved from www.nbcnews.com/think/opinion/how-republicans-democrats-prevent-independent-candidates-getting-ballot-ncna866466

11 Milligan, S., "Independents Exercise Increasing Control Over Democratic, Republican Candidates," *USNews*, 2021, retrieved from www.usnews.com/news/the-report/articles/2021-05-21/independents-exercise-increasing-control-over-democratic-republican-candidates

12 Fiorina, M. P., *Unstable Majorities: Polarization, Party Sorting, and Political Stalemate*, Hoover Institution Press, 2017.

13 Ibid, p. 119.

14 Abrams, S., & Fiorina, M., *Are Leaning Independents Deluded or Dishonest Weak Partisans?* 2011, retrieved from https://cise.luiss.it/cise/wp-content/uploads/2011/10/Are-Leaners-Partisans.pdf

15 Gallup, Inc., Party Affiliation | "Gallup Historical Trends," *Gallup.Com*, 2021, retrieved from https://news.gallup.com/poll/15370/party-affiliation.aspx

16 Local Exit Polls—Election Center 2008 – Elections & Politics from CNN.com, *CNN.com*, 2008, retrieved from https://edition.cnn.com/ELECTION/2008/results/polls/#USP00p1

17 "2016 Election Results: Exit Polls," *CNN.com*, 2016, retrieved from https://edition.cnn.com/election/2016/results/exit-polls

18 "National Results 2020 *President* Exit Polls," *CNN.com*, 2020, retrieved from https://edition.cnn.com/election/2020/exit-polls/president/national-results

19 "Georgia 2020 *U.S. Senate Runoff* Exit Polls, *CNN.com*, 2020, retrieved from https://edition.cnn.com/election/2020/exit-polls/senate-runoff/georgia

20 Todd, C., Murray, M., & Kamisar, B., Biden's Silver Lining Amid Poll Slide: Time is Still on his Side, *NBC News*, 2021, retrieved from www.nbcnews.com/politics/meet-the-press/biden-s-silver-lining-amid-poll-slide-time-still-his-n1277430; Niedzwiadek, N., "Florida Poll: 53 Percent Disapprove of Biden's Job Performance," 2021, Politico PRO; Kane, P., "Democrats' Problem is not Focusing on Issues Most Important to Independents, *Washington Post*, 2021, retrieved from www.washingtonpost.com/powerpost/democrats-midterm-independents/2021/10/23/4271ad96-335f-11ec-a1e5-07223c50280a_story.html

21 Fiorina, M., 2016.

22 Jackie Salit, Personal Communication, January 10, 2019.

23 Salit, J., & Reilly, T., 2020, pp. 323–335.

24 Thom Reilly & Jackie Salit, Personal Communication, March 14, 2019.

25 Gallup, Inc., 2021.

26 Data Center, 2021.

27 Lewis-Beck, M., Jacoby, W., Norpoth, H., & Weisberg, H., *The American Voter, Revisited*, The University of Michigan Press, 2011, p. 129.

28 de Neufville, R., "Do Independent Voters Matter?," *Big Think*, 2018, retrieved from http://bigthink.com/politeia/do-independent-voters-matter; Jacobs, T., "'Independent' Voters Are Generally Not, Pacific Standard," 2017, retrieved from https://psmag. com/news/independent-voters-are-generally-not-3560; Sabato, L., "The Myth of the Independent Voter Revisited," *Center for Politics*, 2009; Trountine, P., & Roberts, J., "Why Indie Voters Don't Make California Purple," *The Huffington Post*, 2011, retrieved from www.huffpost.com/entry/why-indie-voters-dont-mak_b_255393; Sommers, S., "Just How Independent Are Independent Voters?," *The Huffington Post*, 2012, retrieved from www.huffpost.com/entry/just-how-independent-are-_b_1777512; Drum, K., "Most Independent Voters Aren't, Really," *Mother Jones*, 2014, retrieved from www.motherjones.com/kevin-drum/2014/04/most-independent-voters-arent-really/; Hankin, S., "The Myth of the 'Independent' Voter," *Republic 3.0*, 2014; Walter, A., "The Myth of the Independent Voter," *The Cook Political Report*, January 15, 2014; Enten, H., "Americans Aren't Becoming More Politically Independent, They Just Like Saying They Are," *FiveThirtyEight*, 2015, retrieved from https://fivethirtyeight.com/features/americans-arent-becoming-more-politically-independent-they-just-like-saying-they-are/; Bump, P., "The Growing Myth of the 'Independent' Voter," *The Washington Post*, 2016, retrieved from www.washingtonpost.com/news/the-fix/wp/2016/01/11/independents-outnumber-democrats-and-republicans-but-theyre-not-very-independent/; Holland, J., "What Everyone Gets Wrong About Independent Voters," *The Nation*, 2016, retrieved from www.thenation.com/article/archive/what-everyone-gets-wrong-about-independent-voters/; Malone, C., "New Hampshire's Independent Voter Myth," *FiveThirtyEight*, 2016, retrieved from https://fivethirtyeight.com/features/new-hampshires-independent-voter-myth/

29 "Political Independents: Who They Are, What They Think," *Pew Research*, 2019, retrieved from www.pewresearch.org/politics/2019/03/14/political-independents-who-they-are-what-they-think/

30 Eris, D., "Debunking the Myth of the Myth of the Independent Voter," *Independent Voter Network*, 2010, retrieved from https://ivn.us/2010/11/24/debunking-myth-myth-independent-voter/; Killian, L., *The Swing Vote: The Untapped Power of Independents*, St. Martin's Press, 2012; Klar, S., & Krupnikov, Y., "9 Media Myths About Independent Voters, Debunked," *Vox*, 2016.

31 Campbell et al., 1960, p. 130.

32 Broder, D. S., *The Party's Over: The Failure of Politics in America*, first edition, Harper & Row, 1972.

33 Keith, B. E., Magleby, D. B., Nelson, C. J., Orr, E., Westlye, M. C., & Wolfinger, R. E., *The Myth of the Independent Voter*, University of California Press, 1992.

34 Keith et al., 1992.

35 Lewis-Beck, M., et al. 2011; Weisberg, H. F., 1993, *The Public Opinion Quarterly*, pp. 428–30.

36 Campbell, A., Converse, P., Miller, W., & Stokes, D., *The American Voter*, J. Wiley & Sons, 1960; Franklin, C. H., "Issue Preferences, Socialization, and the Evolution of Party Identification," 1984, *American Journal of Political Science*, 28, no. 3, pp. 459–78; Jennings, M. K., & Markus, G. B., "Partisan Orientations over the Long Haul: Results from the Three-Wave Political Socialization Panel Study," 1984, *American Political Science Review*, 78, no. 4, pp. 1000–18; Key, V. O., "A Theory of Critical Elections." February 1, 1955, *The Journal of Politics*, 17, no. 1, pp. 3–18; Page, B., & Jones, C., "Reciprocal Effects of Party Preferences, Party Loyalties, and the Vote," 1979, *American Political Science Review*, pp. 1071–89; Smith, E. R. A. N., *The Unchanging American Voter*, University of California Press, 1989; Weisberg, H., F., "A Multidimensional Conceptualization of Party Identification," 1980, *Political Behavior*, pp. 33–60.

37 Campbell et al., 1960.

38 Ibid.

39 Reilly, T., Whitsett, A., Garcia, J., Hart, W., McWhorter, P., Reiss, B., Grose, C., Cornelius, M., & Giamaros, S., *Gamechangers: Independents Voters May Rewrite the Political Playbook*, Morrison Institute, 2017.

40 Ibid; Killian, 2012.

41 Abrams & Fiorina, 2011; Jackson, J., "Issues, Party Choices, and Presidential Votes," 1975, *American Journal of Political Science*, pp. 161–85; Fiorina, M., "An Outline for a Model of Party Choice," 1977, *American Journal of Political Science*, pp. 601–25; Fiorina, 2016; Page & Jones, 1979, pp. 1071–89.

42 Abrams & Fiorina, 2011; Brody, R., "Change and Stability in the Components of Partisan Identification," 1978, Paper Prepared for the NES Conference on Party Identification; Brody, R., *Stability and Change in Party Identification: Presidential to Off-Years.*, In Paul M. Sniderman, Richard A. Brody, and Philip E. Tetlock (Eds), *Reasoning and Choice,* 1991, Cambridge University Press, pp. 179–205; Brody, R., & Rothenberg, L., "The Instability of Partisanship: An Analysis of the 1980 Presidential Election," 1988, *British Journal of Political Science*, pp. 445–65; Miller, W. E., "Party Identification, Realignment and Party Voting: Back to Basics," *American Political Science Review*, pp. 557–68, 1991.

43 Fiorina, 2016, p. 5.

44 Wikipedia Contributors, "Retrocausality," *Wikipedia*, 2021b.

45 Wikipedia Contributors, "Endogeneity (econometrics)," *Wikipedia*, 2021a.

46 Abrams & Fiorina, 2011, p. 5.

47 Ibid.

48 Fiorina, 2016, p. 10.

49 Bitzer, C., Cooper, C., Manzo, W., & Roberts, S., "The Rise of the Unaffiliated Voter in North Carolina". Prepared for Presentation at the State of the Parties 2020 and Beyond Virtual Conference. Ray. C. Bliss Institute of Applied Politics, University of Akron, November 4–5, 2021.

50 McFadden, E., Daugherty, D., Hedberg, E., & Garcia, J., "Who is Arizona's Independent Voter?," *Morrison Institute for Public Policy*. Arizona State University, 2015.

51 Klar & Krupikov, 2016.

52 Klar, S., "Partisanship in a Social Setting." *American Journal of Political Science*, 58, no. 3, pp. 687–704.

53 Ibid.

54 Klar & Krupikov, 2016.

55 Ibid.

56 "Political Polarization in the American Public," *Pew Research Center—U.S. Politics & Policy*, 2014.

57 Ibid.

58 Ibid.

59 Vedantem, S., "Partisanship is the New Racism," *Psychology Today*, 2011; Van Boven, L., Judd, C. M., & Sherman, D. K., "Political Polarization Projection: Social Projection of Partisan Attitude Extremity and Attitudinal Processes," 2012, *Journal of Personality and Social Psychology*, pp. 84–100; Barber, M., & McCarty, N., "Causes and Consequences of Polarization," In *Task Force on Negotiating Agreement*, American Political Science Association, 2013; Fiorina, 2016; Levendusky, M., & Malhotra, N., "(Mis) Perceptions of Partisan Polarization in the American Public," 2016, *Public Opinion Quarterly*, pp. 378–91.

60 Fiorina, 2016.

61 Fiorina, M. P., *Unstable Majorities: Polarization, Party Sorting, and Political Stalemate*, Hoover Institution Press, 2017.

62 Ibid.

63 Reilly et al., 2017.

4

INDEPENDENTS AND THEIR
USES OF POWER

Can the nation's citizens rise to the further challenge? Will twenty-first century historians remember Americans as angry but helpless in facing Washington's dug-in interests and the increasing inadequacy of the party system? Or
will the public, responding to the mysterious chords of ancient insurgencies
and shrugging off the unnerving precedents of earlier great-power declines,
somehow keep punching toward another national renewal—a broad political
and governmental update of the first American Revolution.
                                          —Kevin Phillips, *Arrogant Capital*[1]

It would be difficult to pinpoint the exact moment at the tail end of the 20th
century when the political tables began to turn, when, as Phillips remarks in the
quote, the "increasing inadequacy of the party system" began to show, when the
consent of the governed grew uneasy, and the governed became restless. One
could mark the sweeping effort to impose term limits on members of Congress
that began in 1990 as the starting gun.[2] Or the insurgent presidential bid by Rev.
Jesse Jackson in 1984 as one inflection point. Or the two-for-one combo in 1988
of Jackson's second run in the Democratic primary followed by Dr. Lenora Fulani's independent "Two Roads Are Better Than One" campaign.[3] Both rose out
of an anguish with how the political establishment related to African Americans,
a sense that this community of voters was being taken for granted by the Democratic Party that was unable to fulfill the promise of a Great Society, unwilling to
fight a genuine War on Poverty, and slow to acknowledge the reality of systemic
racism.[4]

Would one point to the 1992 independent presidential campaign of Ross Perot
as the moment when 20 million Americans abandoned the two major parties and
lifted up an independent alternative, asking the country to take back control of

DOI: 10.4324/9781003240808-5

the government from special interests? What about conservative commentator Pat Buchanan's bolt from the Republican Party in 2000? Or consumer advocate Ralph Nader's run in 2000, which inflamed Democrats who believed Nader had cost Al Gore the election? Were these events simply run-of-the-mill protests from the sidelines, without historical staying power? Or were they each in their own way canaries in the coal mine, warnings of fissures in a two-party system that had ruthlessly hardened its control of politics and policy at great cost to the country?

And what of the swings by independent voters—the 40–50 percent who choose to identify themselves as outside the categories demanded by the party system? First, lifting the insurgent Obama and rejecting the establishment's offering of Hillary Clinton? Delivering the presidency to Obama by eight points over John McCain? Upending the Democrats' control of the House two years later? Backing the independent socialist Bernie Sanders in the revolution of 2016, followed by support for Donald Trump by a four-point margin in that year's general election?

Are these the actions of a citizenry that is "angry but helpless," as Kevin Phillips, the Republican-turned-independent, asked in the 1995 preface to his scorching indictment of the Washington elite?[5] Or are these events an activistic prelude to what Phillips called an "update of the first American Revolution," one in which partisan control over government is wrested from the hands of the party system and a new form of democratic practice evolves to take its place?[6]

Any effort to remake the US party system of politics and government will be a tortuous one, filled with losses and betrayals. Those in power do not concede easily to any form of power-sharing. Of the periodic major-party co-optation of the reform/restructuring process, Phillips observed in 1995:

> What we have seen instead is the pretense of pseudo-revolution in which the winners make a great deal of noise about change, but the principal reality is that one set of politicians hustling money from special interests and doing their bidding in legislation has simply been changed for another.[7]

The study of politics is the study of power in society—who has it, who doesn't, how it is distributed, and why. In our American duopoly, we are consumed (if not obsessed) with power plays between Democrats and Republicans, which party controls the political agenda, the presidency, Congress, governorships, and state legislatures. We have become painfully aware that our duopoly has often produced political power that, when unchecked, prevents needed reforms and skews resources and policies away from the common good. It perpetuates inequality and undermines our democracy. As American existential psychologist Rollo May warned in his book *Power and Innocence* (1972), power is the ability to not only cause change but also to prevent it.[8]

However, while power is often defined only in negative terms, and as a form of domination, it can also be a positive force for individual and collective capacity to act for change. Political philosopher, author, and Holocaust survivor Hannah Arendt in her book *On Violence* (1970) defines power as "the ability not just to act, but to act in concert."[9] While Talcott Parsons, one of the most influential figures in sociology in the 20th century, suggests in his 1963 article "On the Concept of Political Power" that power is a "mechanism operating to bring about changes . . . in the process of social interaction."[10] Independents, even while denied access to the ballot box and with limited ability to hold office, wield power differently, often by working collectively with citizens and groups and seizing the moment.

Throughout the turn of this century, and the attendant attempts to create an independent force of some kind, the presence and activity of the independent voter has been a constant. What role, or roles, have independents played in the journey so far? Here we propose three main arenas to note: Independents get change started; independents are a bridge to a post-partisan, post-ideological future; and independents play the field.

Independents Get Change Started

The year was 1993. Bill Clinton had been elected president with 43 percent of the popular vote. The incumbent president, George H. W. Bush, had been turned out of office after one term. And a Texas billionaire with no history in politics or government, Ross Perot, had mesmerized the country with his independent presidential bid and stood on the debate stage with Clinton and Bush, garnering nearly 20 million votes.

The Democratic Party held the White House and a majority in Congress, but the party was worried. Clinton had taken office without a clear majority and his mandate to govern was thin. Internally, the party was restive and divided, echoes of the Jesse Jackson Rainbow movement still reverberating against the party's turn toward Clintonian centrism. Looking to the future—not merely the next election but the prospect of creating a durable electoral majority—the DLC commissioned a study of the Perot voter. "These voters hold the key to the future of American politics, and there are widespread misconceptions about them," announced Al From, president of the DLC, at the Washington, DC press conference on July 7, 1993, where the results of the study were released. From argued that the arrival of the independent voter in the mold of the Perot uprising offered a "rare chance to realign US politics around a new Democratic governing majority."[11] What was the profile of these Americans? Will Marshall, president of the Progressive Policy Institute, which ran the study, had this answer: "The Perot voters don't want centrism, they want change."[12] Further, Marshall observed, "In their view, breaking the gridlock means standing outside the old, polarized debate, offering ideas that break the intellectual gridlock between left and right, and don't simply take sides in that debate." Any strategy to engage with these voters, he said, "has to speak to the deep alienation that these voters feel towards politics as usual, towards the two parties, and towards the government."[13]

These findings must have been conflicting for the DLC. They were promoting a brand of Democratic Party politics built around an idea of centrism, not rebellion or rejection of the status quo. Nonetheless, at the time they believed, or urged, that Clinton could make sufficient inroads with these voters to buttress his weak coalition. That would mean grasping a new reality. Stanley Greenberg, who conducted the survey, saw that new reality in stark terms. "I believe we will find [it is] an enduring phenomenon." Greenberg saw

> the depth of the alienation of these voters from both political parties, from the political institutions of this country, from the system as a whole, which leaves them estranged from this process, watchful of the process, wanting change, but also deeply, deeply skeptical.

Their independence, he said, "is a fact of political life of which all the parties and leaders of this country are going to have to take into account."[14]

Greenberg estimated that roughly half of Perot's 20 million votes came from independents and that the Perot voter was younger than the overall electorate. "They are out here as independents for a reason. They believe [they were] failed by the political process of the past number of decades, and they're looking for something new."[15]

To his credit, Greenberg searched for an in-depth insight into the mindset of this independent uprising, the "underlying thematic dimensions." Even he seemed surprised by the results. He described Perot voters as "quite libertarian," including that they were identical to Clinton voters on the question of abortion. Perot voters, he said, were "uncomfortable" with the politics of the Republican coalition and disagreed sharply with the positions of the Christian Coalition. They had "strong support for tolerance." Greenberg asserted that these independents were antiestablishment, populist, and harboring an emotional dimension that "ordinary people [are] forgotten in the process." Perot voters were "distinguished on being for radically changing government." Political reform, curbing special interests, and restoring public trust were key. They wanted a government that "would act creatively and efficiently to try to help ordinary people."[16]

The DLC had their work cut out for them. Vice President Al Gore's "Re-Invent Government" project received a dismal response, its 384 recommendations failing to touch the "underlying themes" animating the independent voter. Ultimately, though, the Clinton camp knew that its most important aim was negative, not positive. It was to prevent the independent explosion from being able to "congeal into a permanent third force."[17]

Perot ran again in 1996, this time representing the coming-into-existence Reform Party. Reform held the nation's first ever all-independents primary, fought back when Perot was excluded from the presidential debates that had allowed him in 1992, and continued to champion the values and themes that Greenberg had discerned in his study. The second campaign further instilled the multiracial dimension of the independent movement. Lenora Fulani, the history-making African-American independent presidential candidate in 1988, led her followers into the fledgling Reform Party. A popular figure from the start, Fulani and the Black Reformers Network hosted a gathering on the eve of the Reform Party's founding convention in Kansas City in 1997.[18] Three hundred delegates—the majority white—from all corners of the Perot movement attended. When Fulani announced that history was being made because it was the first time that Black people were present at the founding of a major national political party, the delegates rose to their feet and cheered.

Independents had gotten something started. They had shaped a new political movement with a cross-ideological recognition of the need to build something new. The Reform Party itself was short-lived. But the mark that it made, the visibility it gave to independent voters, the challenge those voters made to the status quo, and the arrival of the idea that there was something other than rigid party loyalty and brittle ideologies were all the early successes of a movement still struggling to be born.

Notably, for all of its potential to spark what Phillips called an "update of the first American Revolution," the left was AWOL, even hostile at times, decrying the Perot voter as neofascist.[19] Commenting on this, the renowned left-wing journalists Alexander Cockburn and Andrew Kopkind wrote in *The Nation* magazine:

> The electoral system in America is now being convulsed by the broadest, fiercest voter insurgency in perhaps 140 years, and the left is watching from the sidelines . . . The two formerly major parties are a shambles, institutions of government and the press despised, political authority disdained, and every measure of popular anger overflowing. And yet those who have long expected this transformative moment to come, have organized and struggled for its arrival, are—if they are realistic—confronted primarily by their own irrelevance to this historic hour.[20]

Independents Are a Bridge to a Post-Partisan, Post-Ideological Future

The year was 2001. Not long after Michael Bloomberg formally announced his intention to run for mayor of New York City, a small group of strategists and stakeholders gathered around a conference table at his campaign headquarters in Manhattan. Bloomberg was running as a fusion candidate. "Fusion" is the practice of candidates having the right to run on more than one party line, which is legal in only six states, an arrangement allowing voters to choose which party line they prefer to cast their ballot on. It is a sophisticated, though sometimes corruptible, mechanism that gives voters a way to choose a candidate for public office while signaling to the candidate their expectations for his or her manner of governing.

At the head of the table was David Garth, the media guru considered responsible "for the central role of television in modern American politics."[21] Garth—an imposing figure with a legendary track record of molding the images of politicians and public figures, staging political upsets, and arranging key endorsements behind the scenes—would quarterback strategy and messaging for the campaign.

Bloomberg had charted a fusion course to run as the nominee of both the Republican Party, by then a minor force in the Big Apple, and the Independence Party of New York City (IPNYC), a relative newcomer to the city's brass knuckles political scene. With long-standing roots in the Black and progressive communities, IPNYC was an unorthodox by-product of the 1992 Perot explosion. The melding of these political brands, infused with the biography and deep pockets of Bloomberg himself, would naturally fall to Garth. The meeting was to be the moment that Garth would map out his strategy.

Garth was clear and directive. The Republican Party line gave Bloomberg access to outer-borough blue-collar conservatives and business-class blueblood liberals. The Independence Party, according to Garth, had one essential function: to give New York Democrats a way to support Bloomberg without having to vote for the Republican Party. Garth was emphatic on this point. No one could become the mayor of New York City without getting significant numbers of votes from Democrats, who had a five-to-one registration advantage over Republicans.

Missing from Garth's equation was that the universe of registered voters in New York City included close to one million independent voters.[22] Independence Party representatives at the conference table that day loudly objected to Garth's algorithm.[23] Of course, the ballot line gave Democrats a place to go, a shield against the Republican brand, they agreed. But let's not forget, they argued, that there are one million independent voters out there who want to know that Mike is as concerned to win their support as he is to offer safe passage to Democrats. Garth was unmoved. The meeting was adjourned. And a second meeting never happened.

There was, of course, much drama to come in that 2001 campaign, all unforeseen. The conflicts that surfaced at the small vignette presided over by Garth would, for a time, fade into the background. On September 11, Al-Qaeda suicide bombers attacked the World Trade Center. Three thousand New Yorkers perished as two hijacked commercial airliners crashed into the Twin Towers. All campaigning was suspended as police, firefighters, and the National Guard sifted through the rubble for bodies and the nation went into shock.

The mood and dynamics of the mayoral contest were recast. Where would it lead? No one knew. Suddenly, one's party label seemed less important than the quality of the leadership. Would the presumption that the Democratic Party had the upper hand in this election continue to hold? Who could best unite the city and govern under these harrowing circumstances? The idea that party ideology and party loyalty could dictate terms seemed inadequate at a moment when tectonic plates were shifting.

Still, New York is a political town with gnawing racial divisions that invariably surface, even in turbulent times such as the months following September 11, 2001. The Democratic primary, originally scheduled for 9/11, had pit two main contenders against one another: Mark Green, the white liberal icon and darling of the government elite; and Fernando Ferrer, the Puerto Rican Borough President of the Bronx. In spite of his liberal credo, Green supporters had distributed racially offensive leaflets designed to deter white conservative Democrats from backing Ferrer. A firestorm erupted in the midst of the rescheduled primary. Green won the nomination, but the bonds of loyalty to the Democratic Party in the communities of color were substantially frayed. Bloomberg and the Independence Party were there to pick up the pieces.

Going into Election Day, the race was too close to call. Late in the evening, the results were tabulated. Bloomberg had won the election by 35,000 votes, the narrowest mayoral margin in 96 years.[24] Nearly 60,000 New Yorkers, led by independent voters, had pulled the lever for Bloomberg on the Independence Party line. Bloomberg won 60 percent of independent voters overall. He also polled 25 percent of the Black vote, a sharp rebuke to the Democratic Party, giving a glimpse of the power of a Black and independent electoral coalition. The independent platform, with its militant message for nonpartisan governance, had put Bloomberg over the top. He was not only mayor of the most important American city; he was a socially progressive business leader, a billionaire, buoyed by the infrastructure and message of an upstart start-up, engineered to empower political independents and install a form of nonpartisan governance.

Bloomberg made good on his promise to the IPNYC to speak directly to the concerns of the city's one million independents. He pushed ahead, using his mayoral authority to put on the ballot a citywide referendum proposing to shift municipal elections from the control of party machines to a nonpartisan system giving greater power to the voters. The measure was denounced by virtually every important institution in the city, from major-party organizations to the unions to *the New York Times*. It was defeated in 2003 by a wide margin, with both Bloomberg and the independents vowing to bring the issue back around when the time was right. In 2005, the IPNYC helped Bloomberg garner 47 percent of the Black vote in his reelection campaign. In 2009, the independents delivered his margin of victory again.

The idea of reforming the primaries, the rights of independent voters, and the fundamental unfairness of political parties competing for power in a competition that they controlled grew in stature during the Bloomberg years. Within a decade, open primaries and the voting power of independents would enter the national conversation and make their way into the mainstream of reform agendas.

Independents were kingmakers. Bloomberg would not have won the mayor-alty for three terms without them. But more importantly, they were showing they could be a bridge to a post-partisan, post-ideological political world.

Playing the Field

It was October 2016. Pollster Pat Caddell asked voters a handful of weeks before the presidential election whether they agreed or disagreed with this statement: "The real struggle for America is not between Democrats and Republicans but between mainstream America and the ruling political elites."[25] Sixty-seven percent agreed, 24 percent disagreed.

A few weeks later Donald Trump was elected president of the United States. More than 42 million independents cast ballots in that race—31 percent of the total electorate, the highest proportion since the advent of polling. Forty-six percent backed Trump, 42 percent backed Clinton, and 12 percent supported a third-party or independent candidate or declined to respond to the exit poll.[26] The independent vote, only eight years earlier a vital component of the Obama coalition, had swung to the other side of the spectrum.

In the swing states of Florida, Pennsylvania, Michigan, North Carolina, and Wisconsin, independents provided Trump with his margin of victory over Clinton. These data offer a reverse reflection mirror on what had occurred in the primary season, just a few months earlier. Challenging Clinton in the Democratic presidential primaries, the socialist Bernie Sanders carried Wisconsin, winning 72 percent of independents, and Michigan, with 71 percent of independents. Though Sanders lost Pennsylvania to Clinton, he carried independents there with 72 percent.[27] Voters in general, and independents in particular, were responding, not to an ideological or partisan cleavage but to something else: the accelerating trend that was leaving mainstream America behind in the globalized world run by "the ruling political elites."

While self-identified independents were significant, the minor parties struggled to impact. The combined support for the top three independent candidates—Gary Johnson (Libertarian Party), Jill Stein (Green Party), and Evan McMullin (Independent)—was at 15 percent a month before the election, but then the vote for minor candidates deflated. Johnson ultimately polled 3 percent, Stein 1 percent, and McMullin (only on the ballot in 11 states) polled 22 percent in Utah (his home state) but barely registered elsewhere.[28]

When Barack Obama captured the White House in 2008, he brought with him a new formula for winning national elections. The formula was movement + party infrastructure. Obama's voters included a newly politicized influx of Americans who saw him as an outsider who could lift up the body politic and fix what was wrong with an overly partisan and special interest-controlled government. The Democratic Party was compelled by a Black-led, multiracial, and independent constituency to mobilize its vast infrastructure on behalf of Obama. While his

2012 campaign was a far cry from his 2008 movement/campaign and, as noted in Chapter 2, sacrificed its original coalition at the behest of the DNC, there was enough of an echo to power him to a second term. America did not want to expel its first Black president from the White House.

Coming in to the 2016 presidential cycle, the Democratic Party was seemingly blind to the political chemistry that had produced the Obama win. Party infrastructure + a reliance on identity politics, quarterbacked by Hillary Clinton—a symbol, many felt, for the global elite—could not withstand the growing pressure to disrupt the status quo. In contrast, Trump and the Republican National Committee deployed the Obama formula: party infrastructure + movement. Taking his cues from Sanders's popularity with independent voters in the Democratic primaries, Trump rode into the White House with an antiestablishment message. Its nationalist and racist tones were a part of the message. But as Robert Merry observed in his essay "Removing Trump Won't Solve America's Crisis": "When a man as uncouth and reckless as Trump becomes president by running against the nation's elites, it's a strong signal the elites are the problem."[29] The independent vote, swinging as it did between Obama and Trump, is best understood as a call to challenge the elites. That Trump was an imperfect, even duplicitous, standard bearer for that call was not the issue. He was the available messenger.

If the voter revolt throughout 2016 was both ardent and conflicted, it revealed much about the breakdown in political stability, including the public's belief in that stability.[30] The brilliant novelist and social critic Arundhati Roy described the pandemic that arrived three years later as "a sudden moment of rupture that exposed the inequalities of the world."[31] The 2016 election cycle in the United States was such a rupture.

California Dreamin'

In chaotic times, strange bedfellow events are more likely to occur, as the political center does not hold, and the unexpected becomes commonplace. California provided one graphic example. The same year that Donald Trump won the presidency, there was an election for US Senate in California. California had enacted a Top Two nonpartisan election system in 2010, the net effect of which in 2016 was to send two progressive women of color to the final round of voting. Of the two Senate candidates on the ballot in the November election, one was Loretta Sanchez, a Mexican-American Congresswoman from the 47th Congressional District. The other was Kamala Harris, a Black and South-Asian woman who had been California's attorney general and is now vice president of the United States. Both are daughters of immigrant families and staunch advocates for women's rights. Some three million Californians voted for Trump at the top of the ticket and then for either Sanchez or Harris. Trump lost the state, Harris won the Senate seat. The decision by millions of voters to combine those seemingly incompatible choices is a story about the breakdown of the ideological divide.

In 2020, independents reversed course by a large margin. Rejecting the outcome of 2016, independents favored the Biden/Harris ticket by 13 points, a swing of 17 points from the previous presidential cycle.[32] Independents delivered the winning margin to Biden in the critical states of Arizona, Georgia, Pennsylvania, and Wisconsin. The disruptors decided, apparently, to put Trump's brand of disruption on hold.

Still, the lopsided vote among independents in 2020 is not an endorsement or a sign of allegiance to the Democratic Party. A broad and diverse electoral majority sought by Bill Clinton, abandoned by Barack Obama, and lost by Donald Trump has not held. Independents are playing the field.

Notes

1   Phillips, Kevin P., *Arrogant Capital: Washington, Wall Street, and the Frustration of American Politics,* Hachette, 1995, p. XVI.
2   In 1990, a Colorado voter initiative to impose term limits on members of Congress passed with 71 percent of the vote. Initiative and Referendum Institute at the University of Southern California, retrieved from www.iandrinstitute.org/docs/Colorado.pdf. Over the next few years, 27 additional states passed congressional term limits through initiative and referendum. In May 1995, the US Supreme Court ruled in *U.S. Term Limits, Inc. v. Thornton,* 514 U.S. 779 (1995) that states can't impose term limits on their federal representatives or senators.
3   In 1988, Dr. Lenora B. Fulani was the first woman and first African American in US history to appear on the ballot in all 50 states.
4   "The Great Society," *History.com,* retrieved from www.history.com/topics/1960s/great-society
5   Phillips, Kevin P., 1995.
6   Ibid.
7   Ibid.
8   May, Rollo, *Power and Innocence,* W.W. Horton & Company, 1972.
9   Arendt, Hannah, *On Violence,* Harvest Books, 1970.
10 Parsons, Talcott, "On the Concept of Political Power," 1963, *Proceedings of the American Philosophical Society,* pp. 107 and 232–62.
11 "The Ross Perot Voter Survey" covered by C-SPAN, presented by Al From, DLC president, Stanley Greenberg, a White House pollster, and Will Marshal, president of the Progressive Policy Institute, July 7, 1993, retrieved from www.c-span.org/video/?44509-1/ross-perot-voter-survey
12 Ibid.
13 Ibid.
14 Ibid.
15 Ibid.
16 Ibid.
17 From, Al and Marshall, Will, "The Road to Realignment: Democrats and Perot Voters," *Democratic Leadership Council,* 1993 (out of print).
18 The Reform Party's Black Reformers Network, "Unity and Diversity," October 31, 1997, Kansas City, Missouri, retrieved from www.youtube.com/watch?v=zwSHPZJlrxg
19 Tomasky, Michael, the *Village Voice,* May 26, 1992. As referenced by Gregory Curtis, "Threat or Menace," *Texas Monthly,* August 1992.
20 Cockburn, Alexander, & Kopkind, Andrew, "The Democrats, Perot, and the Left," *The Nation Magazine,* 1992.

21 Roberts, Sam, "David Garth, 84, Dies; Consultant Was an Innovator of Political TV Ads," *The New York Times*, December 15, 2014, as quoted by Democratic Party strategist Robert Shrum.
22 This included members of the IPNYC as well as nonaligned independents.
23 Jacqueline S. Salit, one author of this book, was one. Cathy Stewart, chief organizer of the city branch of the Independence Party, was the other.
24 Source: New York City Board of Elections, General Election Vote, November 6, 2001.
25 Caddell, Pat, "Patrick Caddell: The Real Election Surprise? The Uprising of the American People," *Fox News*, November 7, 2016, retrieved from www.foxnews.com/opinion/patrick-caddell-the-real-election-surprise-the-uprising-of-the-american-people
26 Exit polls, 2016, retrieved from www.cnn.com/election/2016/results/exit-polls;
27 Exit polls, 2016, Wisconsin, retrieved from www.cnn.com/election/2016/primaries/polls/WI/Dem; Michigan, retrieved from www.cnn.com/election/2016/primaries/polls/mi/Dem; Pennsylvania, retrieved from www.cnn.com/election/2016/primaries/polls/pa/Dem
28 Merline, John, "Trump Leads Clinton by One Point Going into Debate in IBD TIPP Tracking Poll," *Investors.com*, October 19, 2016, retrieved from www.investors.com/politics/trump-leads-clinton-by-one-point-going-into-debate-in-ibdtipp-tracking-poll/
29 Merry, Robert, "Removing Trump Won't Solve America's Crisis," *The American Conservative*, May 18, 2017, retrieved from www.theamericanconservative.com/articles/removing-trump-wont-solve-americas-crisis/
30 Stein, Jeff, "The Bernie Voters who Defected to Trump, Explained by a Political Scientist," *Vox.com*, August 24, 2017, retrieved from www.vox.com/policy-and-politics/2017/8/24/16194086/bernie-trump-voters-study
31 From an interview with Bilal Qureshi at the Edinburgh International Book Festival on August 31, 2020, retrieved from www.youtube.com/watch?v=iOcRil4AjeQ
32 Exit polls, 2020, retrieved from www.cnn.com/election/2020/exit-polls/president/national-results.

5

CAN INDEPENDENTS BE KEY TO BRIDGING THE POLITICAL DIVIDE?

> Where I live and who my friends are and what media I consume all shape what
> I see, which then shapes decisions I make about what media I consume and
> where to live and who to be friends with.
>
> —Eli Pariser, 2020[1]

It was just a handful of days after the 2016 presidential election. Donald Trump had won the White House. Hillary Clinton had conceded with the words, "We have seen that our nation is more deeply divided than we thought." A portion of independent voters, who as a group had carried Barack Obama to the presidency eight years earlier by eight points, had shifted their support toward Trump, leaving any analysts willing to look at that shift scratching their heads. How to explain this seeming anomaly?

Two experts on the independent voter sat in the green room at the PBS station in Phoenix.[2] They'd been invited by the host of *Arizona Horizon*, Ted Simons, to discuss the results of a new study by the Morrison Institute at Arizona State University, which pointed to the role that independent voters were playing at a micro-level to ameliorate the political divide. As they waited for their cue to enter the soundstage and join Simons for the live broadcast, they talked quietly together about how important the results of the study could turn out to be.

Once on set, Simons, who had previously disclosed that he was an independent voter on a prior show with one of these guests, dove right in.

The conversation was pointed and fast-paced from the start. "As independent voters increasingly make up a larger share of the electorate, many times they are not addressed in research or in the media." The ASU study intended to make up for that deficit. What was the importance of the findings? The study offered

DOI: 10.4324/9781003240808-6

an incredible new landscape of how to think about breaking down the political divide in this country. Independents talk to Democrats and Republicans, and have them as friends. Often it's the case that Democrats just have friends who are Democrats and Republicans have friends who are Republicans.

The study showed the various ways that independents—who rely on a broader and more diverse set of news and media sources—could break down silos, change conversations, bring in excluded information, and moderate the tensions of the divide.

The conversation broadened to the implications of the findings given the results of the election. Independents had been 31 percent of the total voters, the largest share since exit polling had begun. This was now a massive constituency in US politics. Could the micro-level findings of the Morrison Institute study apply to this emergent national force? And what of the question of ideology? What of the assumption that independents are not politically in the middle? After questioning by Simons, the Arizona 2016 data was reviewed. Trump had won the state with 48.1 percent of the vote, nearly 5 points less than Republican Mitt Romney had polled four years earlier. Senator John McCain had won reelection with 53.7 percent. The notoriously abusive and negligent Sheriff Joe Arpaio in Maricopa County was defeated by an 11-point margin. An increase in the minimum wage had passed with 58.3 percent of the vote. A referendum to legalize marijuana had narrowly failed. Did these add up to an ideologically and party-line defined Arizona electorate? Hardly. More to the point, the Arizona story, born out by the 2020 election in which Joe Biden carried independents by 14 points and Democrat Mark Kelly defeated the Republican incumbent for a US Senate seat, the electorate was in a state of motion. Driving that motion, in many respects, were the volatile independents who wanted to break open the silos.

Gracious as always, Simons thanked his guests for coming on the show. As they exited the studio onto Central Avenue in downtown Phoenix, enjoying November's temperate weather, they paused to take stock. They smiled and shook hands to say goodbye, agreeing that it was more than possible that these small measures of positive and human interactivity, led by independents, could play a part in healing a divided political culture.

Media Bias and Hyper-Partisanship

The last several decades have seen not just an increasingly polarized electorate in the United States but the proliferation of a hyper-partisan media.[3] The co-occurrence of the two phenomena signals a disturbing connection between bias and hyper-partisanship. In US politics, if one party supports a bill or an issue, the other immediately is almost certainly against it. And increasingly there is a hyper-partisan nature to the news media. As individuals are fed information they agree with, they begin to affirm their own beliefs and not consider opposing viewpoints. Psychologists refer to this as "confirmation bias." Failure to consider different viewpoints is exemplified by social media, and current technologies using algorithms funnel voters to see news sources that cater to only their political biases—in turn, reinforcing those biases. Thus, we are currently living in an era of hyper-partisanship in which the goal becomes winning, no matter what, rather than which party can formulate policies that will benefit its voters the most.

The motivations of independents in political interaction is more nebulous, whereas the partisans aim to convince, regarding their candidate or position, or to dissuade, regarding the opposition candidate or position.[4] Independents are seen as the target of that influence, not as influencers between partisans. However, new research shows that even with political polarization, independents may play an important mediating and moderating role in healing the political divide.

Voters today are just as shaped by news as the news is shaped for them. In a cafeteria-style format, we consume news from a personalized menu that, in addition to informing us, satisfies our appetite for reinforcing our individual beliefs. This is compounded by the reality that when we do talk about politics, we tend to talk about it with family and friends who think as we do. As a result, liberal, moderate, and conservative voters virtually live in alternative realities depending on their personal point of view, preferred news sources, and social networks.[5] Sociologists have long established the influence our networks of media consumption and friends have on our political opinions.[6] In recent decades, the rise of 24-hour cable news and online media sources has produced a "long tail" economic model of media.[7] In this new media economic model, individuals can find sources of news interpreting current events in any way to fit an individual's worldview. Contrast this with the older media model, constrained by analog limitations (only three television networks, radio, and local newspapers) as well as the Federal Communication Commission's fairness doctrine (revoked in 1987).[8] The traditional model was forced to present current events to appeal to the broadest possible audience, in a work week-structured format, with news programs interspersed with entertainment programming, and with a manifest to present different sides of controversial issues.[9]

Defining Media Bias

While public and academic concern over the impacts of biased media have increased in the wake of the past two presidential elections, media bias itself remains conceptually under-theorized.[10] Despite lacking a clear conceptual definition of bias, social scientists have attempted to establish the existence and pervasiveness of media bias in the United States and globally over the last several decades.[11] Along the way, various explanatory models of bias have emerged.[12] Some models view bias as the result of structural conditions, considering the amount of formal power the state has to influence media,[13] while other models focus on the media elites, journalists, and editors who may intentionally or unintentionally frame factual news stories in a way that reflects their own ideological positions.[14]

Recently, economists have developed models of bias, theorizing that it may be more driven by consumer demand than allowed for in previous models.[15] They argue that media companies must fight to both keep existing consumers and attract new consumers in an increasingly saturated media marketplace, making the consumption patterns and political views of consumers theoretically impor-tant to understanding bias.[16] Economic explanations are especially compelling when considering bias in the contemporary media landscape.[17]

The contemporary media landscape is starkly different from the traditional media model as discussed earlier. Practically, this has impacted both the form and substance of news programs: They adhered to a specific "work week" schedule where news programs aired at only specific times and were interspersed with entertainment programming *and* presented all sides of controversial issues.[18] Today, hyper-partisan media sources have resulted in the creation of websites like FactCheck.org[19] aimed at dispelling myths and providing the general public with straightforward analysis of political issues, thereby highlighting the pervasiveness of bias, the media consumer awareness of bias, and the desire of at least some consumers to access accurate accounts of newsworthy events.[20]

The disagreements over how to best conceptualize and operationalize bias have consequences, particularly regarding the difficulty in clearly illustrating the impact of consuming biased media on voter beliefs and behaviors.[21] If consumers are unwitting, passive recipients of biased coverage, it is possible that consuming media will change their views or voting behavior. However, if consumers drive media bias by intentionally seeking media that reflects their views, consuming biased media will likely reinforce existing views and behaviors.[22]

Empirical research shows mixed results that make it difficult to clearly discern if consuming biased media has an impact on political beliefs or overall political engagement. Some research findings indicate that media can shape political views, either on specific issues or on general political views more broadly,[23] although changes induced by media messaging are not necessarily stable over time.[24] Other research findings indicate that consumers choose media that reinforces their exist-ing views, especially when their views score high on political extremity,[25] with some research indicating that increased exposure to media coverage of politics makes people more likely to vote but does not sway their choice in candidates.[26]

Independent Voters as Conscientious Consumers

Some economists argue that the relationship between partisanship and media choices may be more complex than it initially appears, highlighting a need to distinguish between "biased consumers," who seek out information that confirms preexisting views, and "conscientious consumers," who seek out media with the least overt bias that will give them the most factually accurate overview of a particular issue.[27] Yi Xiang from the University of Hong Kong Science and Technology and Miklos Sarvary from INSEAD[28] argue that increases in biased media sources will have little effect on conscientious consumers who tend to compensate for this increase by drawing on a greater number of unique sources in order to construct a more balanced picture of current political events.

While Xiang and Sarvary[29] introduce the idea that consumer goals in choosing media may be an important factor to consider, the distinction between "biased" and "conscientious consumers" is not well theorized. However, the distinction between consumer types is helpful when considering independent voters as a distinct group that have been largely absent from studies on the effects of media bias. Unlike partisans, who are, by definition, biased toward one of the two major parties, independents as a group are not formally committed to a particular party and, therefore, theoretically more likely to be "conscientious consumers." Furthermore, given that independents are generally considered to hold moderate or centrist views rather than extremist views, they may be less inclined to selective exposure to media that reinforces their political views.[30]

Media Usage and Party Identification

Pew Research has been a leader in examining media usage across various demographics. Its 2016 report[31] showed a heavy reliance on TV news, followed by online, radio, and finally print; this pattern inverted by age for TV and online news with those under 50 more reliant on news from online sources than from TV.[32] These results mirrored an earlier survey, which examined information from the 2016 presidential campaign.[33] These surveys focused on ideology and did not examine how these results varied for party identification. They also illuminated other studies focusing on partisan differences between Democrats and Republicans. (Those studies did not include independents as a group.)

In 2014, Pew reported a striking difference between how conservatives and liberals get information about government and politics through the news media, social media, and interactions with those close to them.[34] It examined the ideological spectrum (liberal to conservative) finding consistent conservatives clustered around one news source, Fox News Channel (FNC), and consistent liberals relied on an array of news sources. Its study examines the ideological spectrum, leaving the decisions of political spectrum (Republican to Democrat) to the reader; Pew does not classify moderates in the study, just the extremes. There is, however, an implied assumption that independents lie in the ideological middle, even politically, as if registering no preference translates to

moderate ideology. Simon Zschirnt[35] from Texas A&M is among the researchers who explain:

> Democratic self-identification is not necessarily the polar opposite of
> Republican self-identification and vice versa and political independence is
> not necessarily the midpoint of a Democratic-Republican continuum . . .
> Voters may be both Independents [sic] and party supporters or, just as likely,
> identify as neither. Thus, rather than being correlated in a coherent man-
> ner, attitudes toward Democrats, Republicans, and Independents [sic] are
> largely unrelated . . . these groups systematically differ in the extent to
> which their members construct their partisan identity as a reaction against
> opposing partisan identities.[36]

PEW Research Center conducted a follow-up survey in late 2019 as part of
their Election News Pathways Project[37] and found similar use of media sources
by Republicans and Democrats. Fox News (16 percent) and CNN (12 percent)
were named by the largest number of US adults as their primary news sources.
Six other news outlets were named by at least 2 percent of the population: ABC
News, CBS News, MSNBC, NBC, NPR, and *the New York Times*. The remaining 51 percent of the population surveyed named a variety of media sources,
resulting in a long tail of more than 50 other news outlets.

Pew's examinations of media usage offer a missed opportunity to examine
the habits of independents as a group, alongside partisans instead of as opposed
to partisans. In 2016, it published a study of social media platforms only, which
included independents but did not report how media consumption varied with
party identification.[38]

Media connections and outlets such as Twitter and Facebook create a new
and unpredictable atmosphere for understanding voter behavior, particularly of
independents. The landscape of social networking and social media outlets, acting
as news sources, has created new opportunities for innovative campaign strategies,
as exemplified by the Trump campaigns.[39] The ability to drive coverage and direct
the conversation across the breadth of media could be possible only with the aid
of social networking sites where hyper-targeting of users is a regular feature.[40] On
its own, Twitter has altered the understanding of political communication, resulting in higher levels of partisanship and less communication of nuanced policy,
combined with higher levels of controversial grandstanding.[41]

Social Networks and Political Engagement

Social networks impact political engagement in multiple ways. Structurally, networks provide important access to information and political elites while simultaneously creating a social context that encourages engagement through peer
influence.[42] For these reasons, being connected to others who are politically

engaged makes one more likely to be politically engaged themselves.[43] Networks also facilitate interactions between people. Over time, individuals can develop a strong partisan identity in which their relationship to a political party becomes a vitally important part of their social identity that is reinforced through these interactions with others who share their views.[44],

Political networks, however, tend to be relatively homogenous. While this is unsurprising, given that networked individuals are often similar because of structural conditions,[45] recent research on political discussions reveals that ideological homogeneity is produced and maintained through networked interactions. Partisan identity, strengthened through interactions with their co-partisans, makes individuals more reluctant to discuss politics with those who hold different partisan identity (out-partisans).[46] This reduces cross-cutting discussions that increase tolerance[47] and make it easier for individuals to accurately assess the veracity of information,[48] both of which are important skills in an increasingly polarized world where "fake news" abounds. The propensity individuals have for avoiding interactions with out-partisans raises questions about the structural and interactional role of independent voters, who may serve as an important moderating force in an increasingly polarized political climate.[49]

One answer to this issue may lie in broader research on the role of outsiders in homogenous networks. Ronald Burt of the University of Chicago[50] argues that individuals are inclined to seek out and build ties with others who share similar views and values. Over time, groups become increasingly homogenous, and ties to external groups weaken eventually becoming non-existent. The result is a collection of groups that are relatively isolated. Despite the boundaries between groups, there are individuals in each group who remain closer to the periphery. These individuals are more likely to have ties with members of other groups and, as such, are more likely to be open-minded and open to new and innovative ideas than individuals who are located at the center of a group.[51] Those on the periphery can play an important role in conveying new insights and challenging established ideas within a group.[52] Applying Burt (2004)[53] and Christian Fuchs's (2009)[54] study from the University of Westminster theories to political networks, independent voters who are ideologically situated in the space between Democrats and Republicans may play an important role in moderating political views of partisans. This is especially true if independents have a lower level of polarization and a more expansive social network[55] and is consistent with Sharon Meraz's of the University of Illinois at Chicago (2012)[56] research showing that political moderates have less group cohesion and fewer linkages to partisan networks.[57]

Networks and Partisan Strength

Individuals relate to their party identity, with the strength of that identity as a qualifier, by adjusting their social interactions either on social media platforms or in their personal circle of friends, collectively known as networks.[58] As far as party identification and engagement, strength of partisanship is the primary factor; the more a person identifies with their choice, the more engaged they are in civil society.[59] It is difficult to tease out the choices independents would make, if nonpartisan electoral choices were available, especially since much of the time during the lead up to any election is spent pointing out the futility of voting for any choice other than a major-party candidate, and after the election those who voted for alternative candidates are invariably blamed by supporters of the losing candidate.[60]

As social network users "unfriend"[61] those who disagree with them, an echo chamber effect evolves.[62] Kyle Heatherly of the Indiana University, Bloomington and Yanquin Lu of Bowling Green State University[63] showed how stronger relationships between a voter's level of polarization against the opposition party and for "their" party implies less conversation between those who disagree. The discomfiting nature of discussing politics in highly polarized context may mean that independents "have fewer discussion partners when they think that the important matters of the day are political matters."[64] It follows that independents should have a lower level of polarization and a more expansive social network but may not be engaged in larger numbers of cross-cutting conversations.[65] The strength of personal influence, which increases with polarization in tight networks of partisans,[66] is not as well examined for independents, which are usually removed, as a group, from research focusing on strength of party identification and influence.

Media Consumption, Networks, and Voter Type

With the majority of research on networks of media consumption and influence treating independents as partisans, a study by one of the authors of this book, Thom Reilly of Arizona State University, and Eric Hedberg from NORC,[67] focused on the need to understand the role of independents as a distinct group, in political behavior, social networks, and media consumption. The study sought to answer the following research questions:

1   What does media use look like for independents, as opposed to partisans?
2   Do independents influence the patterns of media use of partisans?

In their study, they considered the social influences of independent voters on the media consumption of partisans. By comparing the answers to these questions between the two major parties and independents, they wanted to gain insights into what possibly shapes the worldview of voters who sometimes live in very different worlds.

The authors collected data from a lengthy survey of more than 1,300 Arizona-registered voters. The survey instrument asked respondents about their political persuasion, sources of news, and interactions with their own personal networks.

Respondents were asked to self-identify on the ANES seven-point political spectrum:[68]

1 Strong Democrat
2 Democrat
3 Independent, leans Democrat
4 Independent
5 Independent, leans Republican
6 Republican
7 Strong Republican

However, unlike the recommendation in Keith et al. (1992),[69] when collapsing into three groups this study classified leaners—respondents who selected options 3, 4, or 5—as independent, thus treating them as independents instead of partisans. Considering the more recent work of Klar[70] and, to a lesser extent, Zschirnt,[71] which showed the importance of the independent identity, classifying them as partisans seems counterproductive in examining their influence on partisans.[72]

The Reilly and Hedberg study, focusing on independents, with "true" and "leaners" combined, aimed to add to the body of knowledge on the media habits of independents and whether there is an influence on partisans who interact with them through social networks, online or otherwise. Furthermore, the authors sought to determine whether independents act as a bridge between polarized partisans with a network, online and physical, spanning those different versions of reality without the same polarizing force for disagreement.

The survey instrument also named several media sources and asked whether the respondent used the media source, was aware of the media source but did not use it, or was unaware of the media source. The survey, using established methodology,[73] then asked the respondent to name up to five friends, whether those individuals know each other, and the political persuasion of their network members.[74] The survey included established measures of political persuasion of opinions on a variety of issues and assessed where each broadly classified political group (Democrats, Republicans, and independents) seeks information and news in Arizona, replicating Pew's research and prior academic work.[75] In addition to media consumption, the study enumerated details about individual personal networks. Independents should have more variety in their personal networks concerning media consumption and political affiliations. Independents may also have less cohesive networks, given the variety of opinions. This study used well-established methodologies for the measures of networks.[76]

To measure media use, political news sources were scored on a continuum of "left" to "right" based on the use differences between strong Republicans and Democrats. An amended version of Pew Research Center's *News Use Across Social Media Platforms 2016*[77] survey was used for the analysis. The scored

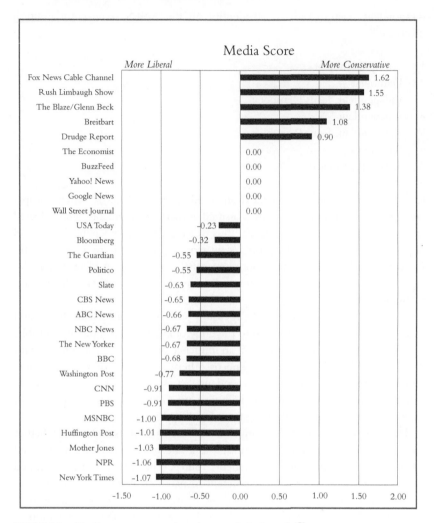

FIGURE 5.1 Media source scores based on statistical model[79]

Source: Hedberg, E.; Reilly, T.; Daugherty, D.; & Garcia, J. *Voters, Media & Social Networks.* Morrison Institute for Public Policy, Arizona State University, (April, 2017).

sources *as seen in Figure 5.1* range between *the New York Times* on the left (or Democratic) spectrum to Fox News on the right (or Republican). There was no content analysis regarding news media in this study, with media sources identified as the ones that respondents viewed most often.[78]

As the average score of individual media moved "right," the number of media sources decreased dramatically. For instance, *as presented in Figure 5.2* nearly eight in ten Arizona Republicans use Fox News as their primary news source. No other news source for Republicans ranked above 54 percent. Arizona Democrats and independents,

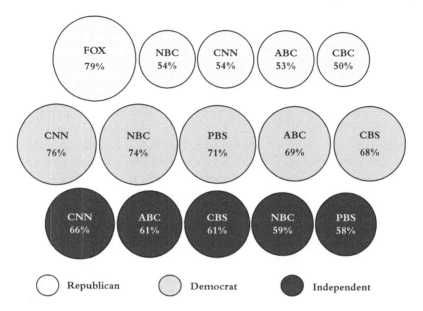

FIGURE 5.2   Top media sources by parties[81]

Source: Hedberg, E.; Reilly, T.; Daugherty, D.; & Garcia, J. *Voters, Media & Social Networks*. Morrison Institute for Public Policy, Arizona State University, (April, 2017).

meanwhile, were more similar in using a variety of TV news sources, such as CNN, NBC, PBS, ABC, and CBS. Independents, due to their internet preferences, relied less on TV news. Republican and Democratic voters prefer more traditional media outlets (48 percent television, 9 percent radio, and 8 percent printed source) and are less likely to use the internet (35 percent) than independents. The internet is the prime news source for younger voters (54 percent) and independents (46 percent).[80]

Consistent with previous theoretical understandings of homogeneity in networks,[82] and empirical work on both moderates and independents,[83] more independents reported having friends who are Democrats than Republicans and more Republican friends than Democrats. The results of the network density analysis offer some additional insight into how independents fit into partisan networks structurally and in the context of interactions. As network density increases for partisans, so too does partisanship. The inverse is true for independents: As network density increases for independents, their networks are less likely to contain other independents. As such, independents with high network density are more likely to be closely tied to those who are committed partisans and may serve as an important source of diverse opinions in a way that is theoretically consistent with previous literature on homogeneity in networks.[84]

In terms of interactions, independents were equally likely to frequently discuss politics with Democrats, Republicans, and other independents. While both

Democrats and Republicans were more likely to have frequent political discussions with their respective co-partisans, members of both partisan groups are more likely to engage in frequent political discussions with independents than with out-partisans. This lends support to the argument that partisans are less inclined to avoid disagreement in discussions than they are inclined to avoid engaging with those who identify with the opposing party.[85] Theoretically, this makes independents an important tie for partisans. Without partisans, their social networks are far more ideologically homogenous. The benefits of cross-cutting conversations, including increased tolerance,[86] ability to accurately assess whether information about politics is true,[87] and decreased likelihood of relying on partisanship for voting decisions,[88] are more likely to occur as a result of conversations between partisans and independents than conversations between Democrats and Republicans, given that the former conversations are more likely to occur frequently than the latter.[89]

In addition to being more frequent discussion partners than out-partisans, independents were less likely to end friendships over disagreements than either Democrats or Republicans. Young Democrats are the group most likely to end a friendship over a political dispute. This is particularly interesting because Democrats as a group (17 percent) are much less likely than Republicans as a group (27 percent) to frequently talk about politics with independent friends. While this is not definitive evidence that cross-cutting conversations with independents increase tolerance for different views,[90] it does offer some support for the idea that interactions with those who belong to different groups may be less invested in protecting the ideological homogeneity of their networks by terminating relationships over disagreements.[91]

The results combining media usage and friend networks are even more interesting, suggesting independents are at ease discussing news with Democratic and Republican voters, expanding the reach of news through social networks by sharing news that partisans might not get otherwise. The statewide study found Arizona Republicans talk politics with independent friends at the same frequency as they talk with their Republican friends. However, Republicans largely forgo such dialogue with Democratic friends. In these politically polarized times, Democrats do likewise.

The study found that while Republicans with Republican friends score the most conservative media use, Republicans with independent friends score average on the media-use scale, suggesting a moderating role by independent voters.

However, the final analysis illustrating that diverse social networks can moderate media consumption (especially for Republicans) offers some hope. While algorithms and content filters may make it less likely that people are exposed to diverse news sources online, diverse networks may be able to counteract the effects of technology. Who we interact with profoundly shapes how we think and, as importantly, how we feel. Our own logic seems to follow the evidence that we choose to look at based on how we feel. That is, a fact is not simply a fact;

it is subject to our interpretation based on our choices of where we go for information and the ways in which we receive seemingly "neutral" information. As Cristian Vaccari[92] of the University of Loughborough noted, personal communication with social contacts can increase receptiveness to new ideas. As technology becomes more ubiquitous and online news sources more popular, independents may play an increasingly important role in broadening partisan media consumption patterns that are shaped by algorithms.[93]

Scholars have long recognized the influences of media and friendship spheres on individual political beliefs. Reilly and Hedberg's research suggests social networks may provide a conduit for communication shared between various voters regarding elements of news and issues that otherwise might have been omitted or ignored by their individual media of choice. Even with political polarization, connectivity through social networks—especially independent voters, who have less cohesive networks and are at ease interacting with both Republicans and Democrats—may provide an indirect moderation, if not expansion, of media news sources.

Independents may very well be the key to bridging the political divide.

Notes

1 Molla, Ranji, *Social Media is Making a Bad Political Situation Worse*, November 19, 2020, retrieved from www.vox.com/recode/21534345/polarization-election-social-media-filter-bubble

2 The two experts were Dr. Thom Reilly and Jacqueline S. Salit, both co-authors of this book. Reilly, Executive Director of Morrison at the time, had designed a study which examined the media sources and social networks of a broad sample of Arizonans.

3 Abramowitz, A. I., & Saunders K. L., "Is Polarization a Myth?" 2008, *Journal of Politics* 70, no. 2, pp. 542–55; Barnidge, M., & Peacock, C., "A Third Wave of Selective Exposure Research? The Challenges Posed by Hyperpartisan News on Social Media," 2019, *Media and communication* 7, no. 3, pp. 4–7; Fiorina, P. M., Abrams, S. J., & Pope, J., *Culture War?: The Myth of a Polarized America*, Pearson Longman, 2005; Lockhart, M., Hill, S. J., Merolla, J., Romero, M., & Kousser, T., "America's Electorate is Increasingly Polarized Along Partisan Lines About Voting by Mail during the COVID-19 Crisis," 2020, *Proceedings of the National Academy of Sciences* 117, no. 40, 24640–642, retrieved from https://doi.org/10.1073/pnas.200802311; Osmundsen, M., Petersen, M. B., & Bor, A., "How Partisan Polarization Drives the Spread of Fake News," *Brookings*, May 13, 2021, retrieved from www.brookings.edu/techstream/how-partisan-polarization-drives-the-spread-of-fake-news/

4 Huckfeldt, R., & Sprague, J. "Discussant Effects on Vote Choice: Intimacy, Structure, and Interdependence," 1991, *Journal of Politics* 53, no. 1, pp. 122–58, retrieved from www.jstor.org/stable/2131724; Huckfeldt, R., & Sprague, J., "Networks in Context: The Social Flow of Political Information," 1987, *American Political Science Review* 81, no. 4, pp. 1197–216, retrieved from doi:10.2307/196258

5 Hedberg, E., Reilly, T., Daugherty, D., & Garcia, J., *Voters, Media & Social Networks*, Morrison Institute for Public Policy, Arizona State University, (April, 2017).

6 Friedkin, N. E., & Johnsen, E. C., "Social Influence and Opinions," 1990, *Journal of Mathematical Sociology* 3–4, pp. 193–206, retrieved from doi:10.1080/00222 50X.1990.9990069

7 Anderson, C., *The Long Tail: How Endless Choice is Creating Unlimited Demand*, Business Books, 2007; Webster, J. G., & Ksiazek, T. B., "The Dynamics of Audience Fragmentation: Public Attention in an Age of Digital Media," 2012, *Journal of Communication* 62, no. 1, pp. 39–56, retrieved from doi:10.1111/j.1460-2466.2011.01616

8 Wikipedia Contributors, "FCC Fairness Doctrine," *Wikipedia*, September 30, 2021, retrieved from https://en.wikipedia.org/wiki/FCC_fairness_doctrine

9 Hall, T., & Phillips, J.C., "The Fairness Doctrine in Light of Hostile Media Perception," June 22, 2011, *CommLaw Conspectus—Journal of Communications Law and Policy* 19, no. 2, pp. 395–422.

10 Eberl, J., Boomgaarden, H. G., & Wagner, M., "One Bias Fits All?: Three Types of Bias and their Effect on Party Preferences," 2017, *Communication Research* 44, no. 8, pp. 1125–48; Entman, R., "Framing Bias: Media in the Distribution of Power," 2007, *Journal of Communication* 57, pp. 163–73; Gunther, R., Beck, P. A., & Nisbet, E. C., "'Fake News' and the Defection of 2012 Obama Voters in the 2016 Presidential Election," 2019, *Electoral Studies* 61, pp. 1–80.

11 Eberl, J. et al., 2017; Rothman, S., *The mass Media in Liberal Democratic Societies*, Paragon House, 1992; Starr, P., *The Creation of the Media*, first edition, Basic Books, 2004.

12 Here, the authors recognize that all written materials come from particular perspectives. In this way, all accounts are biased. What we are discussing here are self-conscious, intentional ways in which events and particular data are presented to sway readers/viewers to think in particular ways. There is a rich history to discussions on this matter in the history and philosophy of science as well as communication studies and sociology, in which epistemology (how we know what we know) and ontology (what there is to know) are explored and deconstructed. Postmodernism, in general, challenges the assumption that "facts" can be separated from the context in which those facts are identified and discussed.

13 Cline, A. R., "Bias." In Eadie, W. (Ed), *21st Century Communications*, Sage, 2009, pp. 479–486.

14 Bennett, W. L., *News: The Politics of Illusion*, Pearson/Longman, 2004.

15 Mullainathan, S., & Shleifer, A., "The Market for News," 2005, *American Economic Review* 95, pp. 1031–53.

16 Baron, B. P., "Persistent Media Bias," 2006, *Journal of Public Economics* 90, pp. 1–36; Gentzkow, M., & Shapiro, J. M., "Competition and Truth in the Market for News," 2008, *Journal for Economic Perspectives* 22, pp. 133–54; Mullainathan, S., & Shleifer, A., 2005; Vigna, S. D., & Kaplan, E., "The Fox News Effect: Media Bias and Voting," 2007, *Quarterly Journal of Economics* 122, no. 3, pp. 1187–243.

17 Vigna, S. D., & Kaplan. E., 2007; Webster, J. G., & Ksiazek, T. B., 2012.

18 Anderson, C., 2007.

19 Retrieved from www.factcheck.org/

20 Reedy, J., Wells, C., & Gastil, J., "How Voters Become Misinformed: The Emergence and Consequences of False Factual Beliefs," 2014, *Social Science Quarterly* 95, no. 5, pp. 1399–418.

21 Gans, H., *Deciding What's the News*, Vintage Books, 1980; Groseclose, T., *Left Turn: How Media Bias Distorts the American Mind*, St. Martin's Press, 2011.

22 Groseclose, T., 2011; Vigna & Kaplan, 2007.

23 Reedy et al., 2014; Tsfati, Y., Stroud, N. J., & Chotiner, A., Exposure to Ideological News and Perceived Opinion Climate: Testing the Media Effects Component of Spiral-of-Science in a Fragmented Media Landscape, 2014, *International Journal of Press/Politics* 19, no. 1, pp. 3–23.

24 Kalla, J., & Broockman, D., "The Minimal Persuasive Effects of Campaign Contact in General Elections: Evidence from 49 Field Experiments," 2017, *American Political Science Review* 112, no. 1, pp. 148–66.

25 Barnidge, M., Gunther, A. C., Kim, J., Hong, Y., Perryman, M., Tay, S. K., & Knisely, S., "Politically Motivated Selective Exposure and Perceived Media Bias," 2020, *Communication Research* 47, no. 1, pp. 82–103; Gentzkow, M., & Shapiro, J. M., 2008; Knobloch-Westerwick, S., & Meng, J., "Looking the Other Way: Selective Exposure to Attitude-Consistent and Counterattitudinal Political Information," 2009, *Communication Research* 36, no. 3, pp. 426–48; Vigna & Kaplan, 2007.
26 Gerber, A., Karlan, D., & Bergan, D., "Does Media Matter?: A Field Experiment Measuring the Effect of Newspapers on Voting Behavior and Political Opinions," 2009, *American Economic Journal: Applied Economics* 2, no. 1, pp. 35–52.
27 Xiang, Y., & Sarvary, M., "News Consumption and Media Bias," 2007, *Marketing Science* 26, no. 5, pp. 611–628.
28 Ibid.
29 Ibid.
30 Barnidge, M. et al., 2020.
31 Mitchell, A., Gottfried, J., Barthel, M., & Shearer, E., "The Modern News Consumer," *Pew Research Center's Journalism Project*, July 7, 2016, retrieved from www.pewresearch.org/journalism/2016/07/07/the-modern-news-consumer/
32 Ibid., p. 4.
33 Gottfried, J., Barthel, M., Shearer, E., & Mitchell, A., "The 2016 Presidential Campaign—A News Event That's Hard to Miss," *Pew Research Center's Journalism Project*, February 4, 2016, retrieved from www.pewresearch.org/journalism/2016/02/04/the-2016-presidential-campaign-a-news-event-thats-hard-to-miss/
34 Mitchell, A., Gottfried, J., Kiley, J., & Matsa, K. E., "Political Polarization & Media Habits," *Pew Research Center's Journalism Project*, October 21, 2014, retrieved from www.pewresearch.org/journalism/2014/10/21/political-polarization-media-habits/
35 Zschirnt, S., "The Origins & Meaning of Liberal/Conservative Self-Identifications Revisited," 2011, *Political Behavior* 33, no. 4, pp. 685–701, retrieved from doi:10.1007/s11109-010-9145-6
36 Ibid, p. 688; Alvarez, R. M., "The Puzzle of Party Identification: Dimensionality of an Important Concept," 1990, *American Politics Quarterly* 18, pp. 467–91; Kamieniecki, S., "The Dimensionality of Partisan Strength and Political Independence," 1988, *Political Behavior* 10, no. 4, pp. 364–76, retrieved from doi:10.1007/BF00990809; Weisberg, H. F., "A Multidimensional Conceptualization of Party Identification," 1980, *Political Behavior* 2, no. 1, pp. 33–60.
37 Mitchell, A., Jurkowitz, M., Oliphant, J. B., & Shearer, E., *How Americans Navigated the News in 2020*, 2020, retrieved from www.pewresearch.org/topic/news-habits-media/media-society/american-news-pathways-2020-project/
38 Gottfried, J., & Shearer, E., "News Use Across Social Media Platforms," *Pew Research Center's Journalism Project*, May 26, 2016, retireved from www.pewresearch.org/journalism/2016/05/26/news-use-across-social-media-platforms-2016/
39 Barthel, M., "Liberal Democrats Most likely to Have Learned About Election from Facebook," *Pew Research*, 2016, retrieved from www.pewresearch.org/fact-tank/2016/05/12/liberal-democrats-most-likely-to-have-learned-about-election-from-facebook/; Fingas, J., "Engadget is Now a Part of Verizon Media," *Engaget.Com*, 2021, retrieved from www.engadget.com/donald-trump-social-network-211532975.html; McGraw, M., Nguyen, T., & Lima, C., "Team Trump Quietly Launches New Social Media Platform," *Politico*, July 1, 2021, retrieved from www.politico.com/news/2021/07/01/gettr-trump-social-media-platform-497606; Montanaro, D., "NPR Cookie Consent and Choices," *NPR*, March 24, 2021, retrieved from https://choice.npr.org/index.html?origin=www.npr.org/2021/03/24/980436658/trump-teases-starting-his-own-social-media-platform-heres-why-itd-be-tough; Oates, S., & Moe, Wendy W., "Donald Trump and the 'Oxygen of Publicity': Branding, Social

Media, and Mass Media in the 2016 Presidential Primary Elections," *SSRN*, August 25, 2016, retrieved from https://papers.ssrn.com/sol3/papers.cfm?abstract_id=2830195.

40 Alashri, S., Kandala, S. S., Bajaj, V., Ravi, R., Smith, K. L., & Desouza, K. C., "An Analysis of Sentiments on Facebook during the 2016 US Presidential Election." In Kumar, R., Caverlee, J., & Tong, H. (Eds), *Proceedings of the 2016 IEEE/ACM International Conference on Advances in Social Networks Analysis and Mining,* ASONAM 2016, pp. 795–802, [7752329], Institute of Electrical and Electronics Engineers Inc., retrieved from https://doi.org/10.1109/ASONAM.2016.7752329; Bovet, A., Morone, F., & Makse, H. A., "Validation of Twitter Opinion Trends with National Polling," *ArXiv. Org.*, October 5, 2016, retrieved from https://arxiv.org/abs/1610.01587; Chin, C., "Social Media and Political Campaigns," 2021, *Georgetown Public Policy Review*, retrieved from www.gpprspring.com/social-media-political-campaigns#test-copy-of-retweets-hashtags-and-political-campaigns; Hassell, A., & Weeks, B. E., "Partisan Provocation: The Role of Partisan News Use and Emotional Responses in Political Information Sharing in Social Media," 2016, *Human Communication Research* 42, pp. 641–61, retrieved from doi:10.1111/hcre.12092; Heidhues, P., & Koszegi, B., "Naivete-based Discrimination," 2016, *Quarterly Journal of Economics, qjw042*, retrieved from https://doi-org.ezproxy1.lib.asu.edu/10.1093/qje/qjw042; Hoffmann, F., Inderst, R., & Ottaviani, M., "Hypertargeting, Limited Attention, and Privacy: Implications for Marketing and Campaigning (Working paper)," 2014, retrieved February 27, 2017, from www.novasbe.unl.pt/images/novasbe/files/INOVA_Seminars/Roman_inderst.PDF; Kulshrestha, J., Eslami, M., Messias, J., Zafar, M. B., Ghosh, S., Gummadi, K. P., & Karahalios, K., "Quantifying Search Bias: Investigating Sources of Bias for Political Searches in Social Media," *Proceedings of the 2017 ACM Conference on Computer Supported Cooperative Work and Social Computing*, pp. 417–432, 2017, retrieved from https://doi.org/10.1145/2998181.2998321; Lee, J., & Lim, Y., "Gendered Campaign Tweets: The Cases of Hillary Clinton and Donald Trump," 2016, *Public Relations Review* 42, no. 5, pp. 849–55, retrieved from doi:http://dx.doi.org.ezproxy1.lib.asu.edu/10.1016/j.pubrev.2016.07.004; Levendusky, M. S., & Malhorta, N., "(Mis)perceptions of Partisan Polarization in the American Public," 2016, *Public Opinion Quarterly* 80(Special issue), pp. 378–91, retrieved from doi:10.1093/poq/nfv045; Swan, J., & Fischer, S., "Scoop: Trump in Talks with Upstart Apps About New Social Network," *Axios*, March 24, 2021, retrieved from www.axios.com/trump-social-media-platform-freespace-a77d7dfc-3288-48bf-bc7e-8942da24bdbd.html

41 Alashri, S. et al., 2016; Jones, J., & Trice, M., "Social Media Effects: Hijacking Democracy and Civility in Civic Engagement," *PubMed Central (PMC)*, 2020, retrieved from www.ncbi.nlm.nih.gov/pmc/articles/PMC7343248/; Russel, A., *U. S. senators on Twitter: Party polarization in 140 characters (Doctoral dissertation).* University of Texas at Austin. Austin: UT Electronic Theses and Dissertations, 2014, retrieved December 15, 2016, from http://hdl.handle.net.ezproxy1.lib.asu.edu/2152/28543; Smith, E. A., "The Diverse Impacts of Politically Diverse Networks: Party Systems, Political Disagreement, and the Timing of Vote Decisions," 2015, *International Journal of Public Opinion Research* 27, no. 4, pp. 482–96, retrieved from doi:10.1093/ijpor/edv018; Trubowitz, P., "Trump's Foreign Policy Speech was an Attempt to Woo Independent Voters for the General Election, Not Placate Foreign Leaders [Blog post]," April 28, 2015, retrieved from blogs.lse.ac.uk: http://blogs.lse.ac.uk/usappblog/2016/04/28/trumps-foreign-policy-speech-was-an-attempt-to-woo-independent-voters-for-the-general-election-not-placate-foreign-leaders/

42 Ayala, L. J., "Trained for Democracy: The Differing Effects of Voluntary and Involuntary Organizations on Political Participation," 2000, *Political Research Quarterly* 43, pp. 99–115; Leighley, J. E., "Group Membership and the Mobilization of Political Participation," 1996, *Journal of Politics* 58, no. 2, pp. 447–463; McClurg, S. D., "Social

Networks and Political Participation: The Role of Social Interaction in Explaining Political Participation," 2003, *Political Research Quarterly* 56, pp. 448–64; Rolfe, M., *Voter Turnout: A Social Theory of Political Participation*, Cambridge University Press, 2012; Siegel, D. A., "Social Networks and Collective Action," 2009, *American Journal of Political Science* 53, no. 1, pp. 122–138; Verba, S., Schlozman, K. L., & Brady, H. E., *Voice and Equality: Civic Voluntarism in American Politics*, Harvard University Press, 1995.

43 Gerber, A. S., Green, D. P., & Larimer, C. W., "Social Pressure and Voter Turnout: Evidence from a Large-Scale Field Experiment," 2008, *American Political Science Review* 102, no. 1, pp. 33–48; Ioanides, Y. M., *From Neighborhoods to Nations: The Economics of Social Interaction*, Princeton University Press, 2013; Pacheco, J. S., "Political Socialization in Context: The Effect of Political Competition on Youth Voter Turnout," 2008, *Political Behavior* 30, pp. 415–36.

44 Ellis, C., & Stimson, J., *Ideology in America*, Cambridge University Press, 2012; Greene, Steven, "Social Identity Theory and Party Identification," 2004, *Social Science Quarterly* 85, no. 1, pp. 136–54; Hanson, K., O'Dwyer, E., & Lyons, E., "The Individual and the Nation: A Qualitative Analysis of US Liberal and Conservative Identity Content," 2019, *Journal of Social and Political Psychology* 7, no. 1, pp. 378–401.

45 Burt, R. S., "Structural Holes and Good Ideas," 2004, *American Journal of Sociology* 110, no. 2, pp. 349–99; Fuchs, C., "Information and Communication Technologies and Society: A Contribution to the Critique of the Political Economy of the Internet," 2009, *European Journal of Communication* 24, no. 1, pp. 69–87.

46 Ellis & Stimson, 2012; Hanson et al., 2019; Settle, J. E., & Carlson, T. N., "Opting Out of Political Discussions," 2019, *Political Communication* 36, no. 3, pp. 476–96, 2019.

47 Pattie, C. J., & Johnston, R. J., "It's Good to Talk: Talk, Disagreement and Tolerance," 2008, *British Journal of Political Science* 38, pp. 677–98.

48 Garrett, R. K., Weeks, B. E., & Neo, R. L., "Driving a Wedge between Evidence and Beliefs: How online Ideological News Exposure Promotes Political Misperceptions," 2016, *Journal of Computer-Mediated Communication* 21, no. 5, pp. 331–48.

49 Reilly, T., & Hedberg, E., "Social Networks of Independents and Partisans: Are Independents a Moderating Force?" 2022, *Politics & Policy* 50, no. 2, pp. 225–243.

50 Burt, 2004.

51 Burt, 2004; Fuchs, 2009.

52 Burt, 2004; Fuchs, 2009.

53 Burt, 2004.

54 Fuchs, 2009.

55 Foos, F., & de Rooij, E. A., "All in the Family: Partisan Disagreement and Electoral Mobilization in Intimate Networks—A Spillover Experiment," 2016, *American Journal of Political Science*, pp. 1–16. doi:10.1111/ajps.12270

56 Meraz, S., "The Democratic Contribution of Weakly Tied Political Networks: Moderate Political Blogs as Bridges to Heterogenous Information Pools," 2012, *Social Science Computer Review* 31, no. 2, pp. 191–207. doi:10.1177/0894439312451879

57 Reilly & Hedberg, 2022.

58 Baker, K. J., "Why People Are Unfriending Newly Public Trump Supporters (Blog post)," *BuzzFeedNEWS*, November 9, 2016, retrieved from www.buzzfeed.com/katiejmbaker/why-people-are-unfriending-newly-public-trump-supporters?utm_term=.gvae03pRA#.hgGm5WXQw; Hassell & Weeks, 2016; Klar, S., "Partisanship in a Social Setting," 2014, *American Journal of Political Science* 58, no. 3, pp. 687–704, retrieved from doi:10.1111/ajps.12087

59 Beck, P. A., Dalton, R. J., Greene, S., & Huckfeldt, R., "The Social Calculus of Voting: Interpersonal, Media, and Organizational Influences on Presidential Choices," 2002, *American Political Science Review* 96, no. 1, pp. 57–73; Heatherly, K. A., &

Lu, Y., "Filtering Out the Other Side? Cross-cutting and Like Minded Discussions on Social Networking Sites," 2016, *New Media & Society*, 1–19, retrieved from doi:0.1177/1461444816634677

60 Easley, J., "Here's the Proof that Jill Stein and Gary Johnson Cost Hillary Clinton the Election," *Politics USA*, November, 9, 2016, retrieved from www.politicususa.com/2016/11/09/proof-jill-stein-gary-johnson-cost-hillary-clinton-election.html

61 The term unfriend applies here in a general sense, cutting off communication from a person with whom there was a previous online connection through any social networking platform. It is not meant to represent only the use of the "friend" feature on the popular Facebook platform.

62 Givanniello, M. A., "Echo Chambers: Voter-to-voter Communication and Political Competition Working Paper," *Semantic Scholar*, November 21, 2016, retrieved from https://pdfs.semanticscholar.org/f7ba/e6260f3b8f17d46e34d2c1b7464fafd95822.pdf

63 Heatherly, K. A., & Lu, Y., 2016.

64 Lee, B., & Bearman, P., "Important Matter in Political Context," 2017, *Sociological Science* 4, pp. 1–30, retrieved from doi:10.15195/v4.a1

65 Foos & de Rooij, 2016; Mutz, D. C., "Cross-cutting Social Networks: Testing Democratic Theory in Practice," 2002, *American Political Science Review* 96, no. 1, pp. 111–26, retrieved from www.jstor.org/stable/3117813.

66 Galeotti, A., & Mattozzi, A., "'Personal Influence': Social Context and Political Competition," 2011, *American Economic Journal: Microeconomics* 3, no. 1, pp. 307–27, retrieved from www.jstor.org/stable/41237179; Hassell & Weeks, 2016; Heatherly & Lu, 2016.

67 Hedberg et al., 2017; Reilly & Hedberg, 2022.

68 ANES Guide, November 11, 2015a, retrieved February 28, 2017, from Party Identification 7-Point Scale: www.electionstudies.org/nesguide/toptable/tab2a_1.htm

69 Keith, B. E., Magelby, D. B., Nelson, C. J., Orr, E. A., Westlye, M. C., & Wolfinger, R. E., *The Myth of the Independent Voter*, University of California Press, 1992.

70 Klar, S., *Independent Politics: How American Disdain for Parties Leads to Political Inaction*, Cambridge University Press, 2016.

71 Zschirnt, 2011.

72 Hedberg et al., 2017; Reilly & Hedberg, 2022.

73 Burt, R. S., "Network Items and the General Social Survey," 1984, *Social Networks* 6, no. 4, pp. 293–339, retrieved from http://dx.doi.org/10.1016/0378-8733(84)90007-8

74 Reilly & Hedberg, 2022.

75 Prior, M., "News vs Entertainment: How Increasing Media Choice Widens Gaps in Political Knowledge and Turnout," 2005, *American Journal of Political Science* 49, no. 3, pp. 577–92, retrieved from doi:10.1111/j.1540-5907.2005.00143.x; Rainie, L., Smith, A., Schlozman, K. L., Brady, H., & Verba, S., "Social Media and Political Engagement," *Pew Research Center*, October 19, 2012, retrieved from www.pewinternet.org/2012/10/19/social-media-and-political-engagement/

76 Reilly & Hedberg, 2022.

77 Gottfried & Shearer, 2016.

78 Hedberg et al., 2017.

79 Ibid. p. 8.

80 Ibid.

81 Ibid., p. 4.

82 Burt, 2004; Fuchs, 2009.

83 Foos & de Rooij, 2016; Meraz, 2012.

84 Burt, 2004; Fuchs, 2009; Reilly & Hedberg, 2022.

85 Settle, J. E., & Carlson, T. N., "Opting Out of Political Discussions," 2019, *Political Communication* 36, no. 3, pp. 476–96.

86 Pattie & Johnston, 2008.

87 Garret et al., 2016.
88 Ekstrom, P. D., Smith, B. A., Williams, A. L., & Kim, H., "Social Network Disagreement and Preferred Candidate Preferences," 2020, *American Politics Research* 48, no. 1, pp. 132–54.
89 Hedberg et al., 2017; Reilly & Hedberg, 2022.
90 Pattie & Johnson, 2008.
91 Reilly & Hedberg, 2022.
92 Vaccari, C., "From Echo Chamber to Persuasive Devise? Rethinking the Role of the Internet in Campaigns," 2012, *New Media & Society* 15, no. 1, pp. 109–127.
93 Reilly & Hedberg, 2022.

6

FREE THE VOTERS

The Legal Barriers and Biases Against Independents

There is a dirty little secret that sophisticates have been hiding from the masses for three or four decades. The secret is that the two-party system is dying . . . the two-party system has been kept alive with artificial respiration through state laws biased against third parties and through artificial insemination by federal subsidies and other protections sold to the public as "campaign reform." The two-party system would collapse in a moment if all the tubes and IVs were pulled out.

—Theodore Lowi, 1992[1]

When Lenora Fulani, the African-American developmental psychologist, decided to run for president as an independent in 1988, she had a simple but daunting strategy: to qualify for federal primary matching funds, get on the ballot in all 50 states, and run a national campaign calling for a sweeping program of political reform to establish a nonpartisan framework for fair elections. Fully expecting that Jesse Jackson and his Rainbow crusade would be denied the Democratic Party presidential nomination, Fulani's independent bid would give Black and progressive voters an independent option once Jackson's campaign had crested.[2]

Fulani was used to hitting ceilings erected to keep Black people and women on the bottom rungs of the ladder. But as she later told Judy Woodruff on the *PBS Newshour* when asked about the challenges of running for high office, the discrimination against being an independent was unlike anything she had previously experienced.[3] The campaign did not have to wait long for its first such roadblock, one thrown across her path by the national regulators of the election process, the FEC.

The FEC—founded in 1975 after the Watergate-era scandals in which brown paper bags filled with cash funded late-night break-ins at Democratic Party

DOI: 10.4324/9781003240808-7

headquarters—was charged with enforcing the strict standards for campaign fundraising and spending set out in the 1974 amendments to the Federal Election Campaign Act (FECA, originally passed in 1971). To incentivize and police the new rules, the FECA offered a public-funding program to match every qualified dollar raised. This included a primary-phase matching-funds program that insurgent and independent candidates who met the stiff threshold requirements could take advantage of. The major-party candidates generally qualified easily. Independents had to muster considerable strength and infrastructure to qualify. To begin soliciting campaign funds, federal regulations required that Fulani form, name, and file an authorized campaign committee with the FEC. She named her political vehicle Lenora B. Fulani's Committee for Fair Elections, a choice designed to demonstrate the mission of her presidential candidacy.

Then came an absurdist encounter where Kafkaesque applications of the rules revealed the true character of a bureaucracy. The commissioners questioned the name of the committee and threatened to disqualify her. What did the notion of "Fair Elections" have to do with a presidential campaign? In the view of the FEC, it was illegitimate—even deceptive—to link the contest for the US presidency with a call for reform and fair elections. The commissioners raised concerns that "no reference to the office she is seeking is included in the name of her principal campaign committee."[4]

The commissioners, all party nominees in accordance with the uniquely partisan design of the FEC—the only federal regulatory agency with an even number of commissioners, thereby guaranteeing equity between the two major parties—had more questions. They worried "whether the type of presidential candidacy" would be "acceptable."[5] By "type," the commissioners questioned "whether this campaign is a civic group or a presidential election effort."[6] Thusly, the commissioners were poised to conclude that there was only one kind of "acceptable" presidential campaign, potentially ruling out that a legitimate motive for running for public office is to popularize or mainstream a cause or issue. Still, they had one more bone to pick that year with the radical, Black developmental psychologist. They objected to the fact that Fulani was seeking the presidential nomination of multiple independent parties in different states. Fulani chose this route both to fortify her ballot access drive, the requirements for which were onerous in the extreme, and to lay the groundwork for a national, independent electoral coalition. The commissioners doubted the validity of this approach. The FEC's legal counsel had to bring the commissioners to heel with this conclusion:

> Two of the questions raised to Counsel were the name of this Committee (Lenora B. Fulani's Committee for Fair Elections) and the fact that the candidate is seeking the nomination of several political parties in different states. Counsel has concluded that neither of these would bar the receipt of matching funds.[7]

The biases inherent in the partisan commissioners' first impressions highlight a not-so-hidden tension in the larger political drama of American politics. That tension revolves around America's now built-in default to a two-party system, the barriers that discourage or derail independent and third-party efforts, and the ways in which the regulatory matrix can be brittle and unwelcoming to new players, especially those attempting to introduce new practices and approaches. The FEC itself, a bipartisan, not nonpartisan apparatus, embodied that bias from its inception.

As previously mentioned, the only federal regulatory body to have six rather than five members, allowing the commission's three GOP members and three Democrat members to deadlock if necessary, the FEC has had a clear function.[8] While Democrats and Republicans may be forced by the voters to trade control of Congress, the White House, and the judiciary, the electoral process itself must be in the permanent and jointly held custody of the two parties. Calls to reform and restructure the FEC have abounded for decades, to no avail. The Brennan Center for Justice published a scathing report in 2019 that documented the FEC's decline from mere partisan abuse to absolute dysfunction. "Congress needs to fix this problem," the report declared "but in a way that preserves safeguards against partisan abuse of the Commission's power and bureaucratic overreach that could stifle political expression."[9] Unfortunately, Congress in its current state is the last place to turn to for leadership on reforming the political system. What's more, even though the Brennan Center recommended reducing the number of commissioners to five while providing an automatic slot for an independent, the question of *how* to select an independent commissioner, in a manner equitable to the right to nominate reserved for the parties, is unanswered by would-be reformers. If party leaders get to vet and approve nominees, why not create a process in which leaders of the independent movement vet and approve the independent nominee?

More than a generation before Fulani's outlier presidential bid, in the landmark work *The Age of Reform*,[10] historian Richard Hofstadter examined the historical role of third parties:

> Third parties have often played an important role in our politics, but it is different in kind from the role of the governing parties. Major parties have lived more for patronage than principles; their goal has been to bind together a sufficiently large coalition of diverse interests to get into power; and once in power, to arrange sufficiently satisfactory compromises of interests to remain there. Minor parties have been attached to some special idea or interest, and they have generally expressed their positions through firm and identifiable programs and interests. Their function has not been to win or govern, but to agitate, educate, generate new ideas, and supply the dynamic element in our political life.

The Fulani candidacy was mainly intended to perform the role Hofstadter described, namely to "supply the dynamic element in our political life."[11] The commissioners, who owed their nomination (formal appointment by the president is merely a technicality) to one or the other of the major political parties, resist any kind of dynamism. It should be no surprise then that Senate Minority Leader Mitch McConnell insists on personally screening the party's nominees to the FEC.[12]

Ultimately, the Fulani campaign was certified by the FEC, and Lenora B. Fulani's Committee for Fair Elections raised one million matchable dollars. She was forced to spend the bulk of the million-dollar match on her 50-state ballot access drives. She had to navigate a maze of qualifying regulations in which a Democrat or Republican must collect 50,000 petition signatures, while an independent must garner a million. Having to go to court 11 times to compel a recalcitrant and partisan state supervisory agency to put her on that state's ballot,[13] Fulani went on to become the first African American and woman in US history to achieve access to the presidential ballot in all 50 states.

Independent and third-party presidential candidates before and after Fulani have held up a mirror to the intricate matrix of post- and pre-Watergate structural inequities imposed on candidates, voters, and parties choosing to identify as someone or something other than a Republican or Democrat. Some examples are John Anderson (1980), Dennis Serrette and Sonia Johnson (1984), Ron Paul (1988), Ross Perot (1992/1996), Ralph Nader (2000/2004), Patrick Buchanan (2000), Jill Stein and Gary Johnson (2012 and 2016).[14]

These inequities not only persist to this day, in some cases they have been bolstered. The Klobachar–Manchin compromise democracy reform bill,[15] written to win collaborative support from the GOP, eliminates the federal primary matching funds program altogether, which is now utilized only by minor-party and independent presidential candidates. Some states that have allowed open primaries for generations—including Idaho, South Carolina, Missouri, Louisiana, and Hawaii—have recently taken steps to preclude nonaligned voters from participating. During the onset of the COVID pandemic, then-New York Governor Andrew Cuomo rammed through new rules for obtaining legal ballot status for minor parties that nearly tripled the vote threshold.[16]

Currently, there is a very public and overheated battle over voting procedures, vote counting, election certification, and the conduct of elections between Democrats and Republicans in Congress and in a maze of state governments. In this environment, Lowi's "dirty little secret" is more explosive today than it was when he coined the phrase. While the Democratic Party reform agenda is built around *Protecting the Vote* by battling various forms of suppression (real or imagined), and the Republican mantra is to *Stop the Steal* by combatting fraud (imagined or real), the need to *Free the Vote and the Voter* from the heavy restraints and manipulations at the hands of institutionalized party politics remains largely ignored.

Through the Looking Glass of Partisan Bias

The legal barriers and instances of political bias against independents are lengthy and well documented. You can't run for judge in West Virginia as anything other than a Democrat or Republican.[17] If you are an independent, you may not serve as an Election Day poll worker in New York state. In Florida, changing election laws via citizen referendum requires a threshold of 60 percent of the vote—thus, a 2020 initiative for top-two nonpartisan primaries that would have allowed independent voters to cast ballots in the first round of voting was defeated in spite of winning 57 percent of the vote.[18] In Arizona, the major parties receive voter lists from the state for free; independent candidates and campaigns must pay for them. The CPD—a bipartisan club calling itself a commission—can exclude candidates from the debate stage if they don't consistently poll 15 percent in three national polls before the debates take place. Multiple legal efforts to nullify the CPD's control over the presidential debates have hit a brick wall. Taxpayers who are politically nonaligned must finance party primaries that they are barred from casting ballots in. If candidates want the endorsement of more than one party in a run for political office, they can do so only in eight states.[19] In Texas, if you are petitioning to run as an independent, you can collect signatures only from voters who did not cast a ballot in a primary. In Arkansas, you cannot hire a petitioner from out of state. Some states allow independents to vote in primaries, but only if that voter joins the party on the day of the election. The state then makes it cumbersome for voters to regain their independent status. Independent voters, candidates, and parties are consistently relegated to a second-class status.

Some attempts to remedy these inequities have been brought to Congress, only to die in committee. The late John Conyers of Detroit, a veteran champion of the civil rights agenda and among the original founders of the Congressional Black Caucus, sponsored HR 1582, the Fair Election Act, in 1987, to eradicate the shocking inequities in ballot access requirements for independent candidates seeking federal office. It never got out of committee. Congressman Tim Penny of Minnesota, a Democrat who later became an independent, sponsored HR 1753, the Democracy in Presidential Debates Act, in 1993, a bill to open access to presidential debates for independent candidates. The bill never got out of committee. Congressman John Delaney of Maryland introduced a bill in 2014, HR 5334, the Open Our Democracy Act, to require primaries in federal contests to allow independent voters to participate. The bill never got out of committee. The barriers are numerous. They are statutory, regulatory, court-ordered, cultural, and baked into the everyday practice and mindset of American politics. And yet a clear and constitutionally sound evaluation and reset of these practices has not made its way onto the national agenda, even though America is in the throes of a democracy crisis, and even though between four and five out of 10 voting-age Americans identify as independent.

Balancing Party Interest and Public Interest

Since the late 1960s, the United States Supreme Court (SCOTUS) has periodically overturned onerous ballot access requirements for independent candidates, as in *Williams v. Rhodes* (1968), *Illinois v. Socialist Workers Party* (1979), and the landmark *Anderson v. Celebrezze* (1983).[20] The Supreme Court also upheld onerous ballot access requirements that independents had hoped to overturn, as in *Jenness v. Fortson* (1971) and *American Party of Texas v. White* (1974).[21] The Supreme Court struck down repressive filing fees imposed on independents, as in *Bullock v. Carter* (1972) and *Lubin v. Panish* (1974), and loyalty oaths, as in *Communist Party of Indiana v. Whitcomb* (1974).[22] In *Storer v. Brown* (1974), the high court allowed the state of California to bar independent ballot access to a candidate who had been registered in a political party within a year of the election in question, enshrining the so-called sore loser principle that protected the major parties from an independent breakaway.[23] In the same decision, SCOTUS compelled the state of California to create a pathway for both independent candidates and independent parties, which it had previously refused to do.

Arguably, the Court has been "all over the map" with respect to the rights of independents, regardless of whether the Court had a Republican or Democrat majority. The imperative has been to balance stability and "state interest" with constitutionally protected freedoms of association, political expression, and equal protection under the law. Even with the ongoing efforts to balance those interests, the sympathies of the Court—though the Constitution doesn't mention parties at all—have tended to fall in line with protecting the party system in general and the two parties in particular.

Abner Mikva, the renowned DC circuit court judge, showed his alarm at this bias in a dissenting opinion rendered in a 1988 case, *Fulani v. Brady*, in which Fulani challenged her exclusion from the CPD-sponsored presidential debates. The circuit court held that Fulani did not have standing to pursue her claim. In a scathing dissent, Judge Mikva held the opposite. In 1991, emphasizing the profound implications of the DC circuit court's bias, Mikva wrote:

> The problems of conducting national elections through the electronic media have become nigh impossible to solve. The "simple" difficulty of reaching voters, the more complicated difficulty of substantively informing them, and the need for huge sums to fund such communications all drive an engine of chaos in the national campaign regimen. Congress and the courts have struggled with this urgent matter, often with frustration. But whatever its proper role in correcting imbalances and imperfections in the status quo, government certainly must not abandon its posture of nonpartisanship. The government of any democracy, let alone one shaped by the values of our Constitution's First Amendment, must avoid tilting the electoral playing field, lest the democracy itself become tarnished.[24]

Judge Mikva's sober admonition, rendered in the context of a seemingly minor controversy, speaks volumes in today's context. Insofar as Mikva saw the potential for "tilting the electoral playing field," he opened a window on a critical feature of the structural bias against independents. Making room for alternatives, however much the Constitution proposes a level of neutrality and fairness, has come complete with relating to those alternatives as "outsiders." Fairness is surely a bedrock principle of American democracy. But the impulse to protect and privilege the institutions in power and to marginalize the outsiders is operative everywhere. However much the courts, or lawmakers, or even many reformers, assert principles of fairness, they strive to do so while making sure to contain and restrain the growth potential of any independent alternatives.

Twin Cities Showdown

In the spring of 1994, a sitting representative in District 65A, Andy Dawkins—a white Democrat—was running for reelection in a majority Black district. In addition to running on Minnesota's Democrat Farm Labor (DFL) ticket as he had in the past, he was asked by the Twin Cities Area New Party, a minor party with a permanent line on the ballot, to run on its ticket as well. This cross-party endorsement, known as fusion, was banned by the state legislature in Minnesota, and Dawkins, an attorney himself, knew that running as a fusion candidate would test the constitutionality of the ban.

Before accepting the cross-endorsement, Dawkins decided to test the strategy with his own constituents. His argument to the voters of District 65 was that the Black community had been taken for granted by the Democrats and the move to run on the New Party line, giving voters an option as to which line they would choose to vote on would signal a willingness to go independent. This new leverage would alter the dynamics between the African-American community and the party. Dawkins's offer of a leverage strategy was welcomed by his constituents and he agreed to accept the New Party endorsement.[25] But when the nominating petitions were filed, local elections officials refused to accept them. The Dawkins cross-nomination became the subject of legal action that went all the way to the SCOTUS in *Michele L. Timmons v. Twin Cities Area New Party*. Though the Court of Appeals reversed the circuit court's ruling upholding the constitutionality of the fusion ban, the Supreme Court reversed the Court of Appeals in 1997 and declared the state's ban to be constitutional.

The Court's decision was not without considerable controversy, as it closed off the option of fusion strategies for an independent movement that was just establishing its power and potential competitiveness with the dominant two parties. Fusion, or cross-nomination, was thought to be a valuable tool for expanding the base of the emergent independent movement in some circles. It had been conceived and popularized in the West and Midwest in the late 19th century during the Populist and Progressive eras when local and state independent parties used fusion to win elections by coalescing with a major party—typically the Democrats, though in the South the fusion coalitions focused on the Republicans. At that time parties, not the states, printed ballots. Creating fluid partnerships was simple and desirable.[26] The Supreme Court's decision in 1997 was a blow to those looking to pursue and nationalize this strategy outside of the few states that permitted it.[27]

Three US Supreme Court justices dissented in the *Timmons* case: Justices John Paul Stevens, Ruth Bader Ginsburg, and David Souter.[28] Stevens wrote the dissent, and in it he provides a detailed catalogue, not only of the judicial errors of the majority but also of the inherent bias of those who view the two-party system as sacrosanct. Stevens succinctly puts his finger on the matter:

> In most States, perhaps in all, there are two and only two major parties. It is not surprising, therefore, that most States have enacted election laws that impose burdens on the development and growth of third parties. The law at issue in this case is undeniably such a law. The fact that the law was both intended to disadvantage minor parties and has had that effect is a matter that should weigh against, rather than in favor of, its constitutionality.[29]

Stevens, a lifelong Republican elevated to the Supreme Court by President Gerald Ford, did not discount the argument that society has an interest in "political stability." But he charged that the majority, in upholding the constitutionality of Minnesota's ban on fusion, went far beyond such a mandate, writing: "Indeed, the activity banned by Minnesota's law is the formation of coalitions, not the division and dissension of 'splintered parties and unrestrained factionalism.'"[30]

Stevens—who later dissented in *Citizens United* on the grounds that the majority decision was "a rejection of the common sense of the American people, who have recognized a need to prevent corporations from undermining self-government"[31]—recognized in the New Party case that the majority on the Court were undermining the right of new and non-establishment political forces to grow and develop:

> A fusion ban burdens the right of a minor party to broaden its base of support because of the political reality that the dominance of the major parties frequently makes a vote for a minor party or an independent candidate a "wasted" vote.[32]

The Presidential Debates

Since 1984, when the US Court of Appeals District of Columbia circuit ruled that there was no constitutional basis to allow Citizens' Party presidential candidate Sonia Johnson into the televised general election presidential debates, there has been at least one lawsuit challenging the exclusion of independent or minor-party candidates from the debates in all but one presidential election cycle. Plaintiffs and amicus supporters in such suits have included candidates Ross Perot, Ralph Nader, Pat Buchanan, Lenora Fulani, Jill Stein, and Gary Johnson; the Libertarian, Green, Reform, and New Alliance parties; and pro-democracy organizations Level the Playing Field, Our America Initiative, Committee for a Unified Independent Party, and Independent Voter Project; among others. Their efforts have been supported by commentary in such publications as *the New York Times* and *the Atlantic*.

In an editorial printed on September 18, 1996, *the New York Times* proposed that a genuinely nonpartisan organization take over hosting the debates:

> by deciding yesterday to exclude Ross Perot from this year's debates, the commission proved itself to be a tool of the two dominant parties rather than a guardian of the public interest. This commission has no legal standing to monopolize debates, and it is time for some more fair-minded group to get into the business of sponsoring these important events.[33]

Almost 20 years later, Larry Diamond, a senior fellow at the Hoover Institution and Freeman Spogli Institute at Stanford University, penned an article in the May 8, 2015 issue of *the Atlantic*, calling out the CPD and calling for more open presidential debates:

> Even more formidable is the obstacle imposed by a crucial but little known and unaccountable gatekeeper, the Commission on Presidential Debates (CPD). Members of this unelected and unaccountable commission have established a rule that makes it impossible for an independent, nonpartisan, or third-party ticket to gain access to the general-election debates.[34]

He went on to report on the results of direct engagement with the CPD and closed with a historical perspective:

> When a Petition for Rulemaking was filed with the FEC and posted for public comment in December, all but one of the 1,252 public comments endorsed the request for a new rule. Only the CPD claimed there was no need for a change. Despite this overwhelming backing, the CPD has stonewalled. In fact, the 17-member board has refused even to meet with the four-dozen signers of the Change the Rule letter.
>
> For more than two centuries, the United States has been a beacon of hope for democracy worldwide. For the last century, the United States has been the world's most successful and powerful democracy. But both of these elements of global leadership are now rapidly eroding. Making the election for America's highest office more open and competitive might renew the vigor and promise of its democracy.[35]

The US Supreme Court has never taken a case that opposed the partisan selection process used in the presidential debates. This despite creative and compelling legal argumentation that has included challenges to the tax-exempt status of debate sponsors. The FECA stipulates that debate sponsors must be tax-exempt organizations, and the Internal Revenue Code states that all tax-exempt organizations be nonpartisan. (Other suits have raised that the exclusion of independent and minor-party candidates from the debates violates everything from the candidates' First Amendment rights to the Sherman Antitrust Act of 1890.)

When the League of Women Voters (the League) allowed independent John Anderson into the 1980 presidential debates, incumbent Democrat Jimmy Carter refused to take the podium alongside him. (Anderson ended up in a one-on-one debate with Republican Ronald Reagan.) The only other independent to grace the debate stage was Ross Perot in 1992, largely because both major-party nominees believed his presence would help them. When Perot requested entrance into the debates in 1996, after a 19 percent showing in the '92 election, the CPD refused him on the grounds that he wasn't polling high enough that year.

The CPD has been the gatekeeper of the presidential debates since 1988, when it wrested sponsorship rights from the League of Women Voters. The CPD was then led by the sitting chairs of the Republican and Democratic party national committees, Frank Fahrenkopf and Paul Kirk. Despite this, they have consistently claimed that they are a nonpartisan organization.

According to *the New York Times* account of the CPD's founding press conference:

> In response to questions, Mr. Fahrenkopf indicated that the new Commission on Presidential Debates . . . was not likely to look with favor on including third-party candidates in the debates. Mr. Kirk was less equivocal, saying he personally believed the panel should exclude third-party candidates from the debates.[36]

The League fought tooth and nail to maintain its sponsorship of the debates. Initially, a compromise was worked out where the CPD would sponsor the first debate and the League would sponsor the second. But when major-party candidates George Bush and Michael Dukakis issued a joint demand to control the selection of questioners, the composition of the audience, hall access for the press, and other issues, the League pulled out. In a press release announcing that they were withdrawing their sponsorship of the second debate, League president Nancy Neuman said,

> It has become clear to us that the candidates' organizations aim to add debates to their list of campaign-trail charades devoid of substance, spontaneity and honest answers to tough questions. The League has no intention of becoming an accessory to the hoodwinking of the American public.[37]

The CPD took the reins of the second debate. After 1992, the CPD adopted the current standard: ballot access in enough states to be mathematically capable of winning a majority of the electoral college votes and a 15 percent or greater showing in the average of five national opinion polls.

However, the poll question for which the 15 percent threshold is based is: "Which presidential candidate would you *vote for* if the election were held today?" not "Which presidential candidates would you *like to see in the debates?*"

In 2000, the Committee for a Unified Independent Party (CUIP)[38] launched a grassroots and media effort called a Campaign to Change the Question. A CUIP press release issued on January 12 stated:

> Not only is the poll question it proposes a manipulation, but the fact that the polling partnerships will be asking voters their candidate preference without informing them that the results of the poll they are taking will determine who is admitted to the debates is a fraud on the public. The American people have a right to know the implications of answering questions in a particular way. Informed voting is the essence of democracy.[39]

The longest-running challenge to the two-party monopoly control of the presidential debate process was initiated by Level the Playing Field (LPF), an organization led by Peter Ackerman, a former investment banker turned pro-democracy leader in non-violent conflict resolution.[40] In September 2014, LPF filed the first of two administrative complaints with the FEC, charging that the CPD's 15 percent polling threshold violated the law and requesting that the FEC (which has oversight authority over the CPD) address the situation. LPF also filed a Petition for Rulemaking asking the FEC to revise its debate regulations to prohibit the use of the 15 percent threshold.

The FEC dismissed both complaints, claiming that LPF lacked standing in the matter since it was not a presidential campaign or political party and also finding no reason to believe that CPD violated the debate regulations. It also declined to initiate new rulemaking.

In early 2015, LPF organized a Change the Rule campaign that promoted a new standard for accessing general election debates:

> On April 30 any candidate, party, or nominating process with ballot access in states that collectively have at least 270 Electoral College votes [i.e., a majority of the electoral college votes] would notify the CPD of that access. If there is more than one, then whoever has gathered the most signatures as part of the ballot access process will participate in the debates with the Democratic and Republican nominees.[41]

A letter in support for this rule change was made public on March 17, 2015 in *The Hill*, a newspaper popular with political insiders that covers the goings-on in Washington, DC. Among the signers of the letter were John Anderson (independent presidential candidate in 1980), former Director of National Intelligence Dennis Blair, former Secretary of Defense William S. Cohen, Senator Angus King, General Stanley A. McChrystal, Kansas independent Greg Orman, Rep. Tim Penny, former Chair of the FEC Bradley A. Smith, Admiral James G. Stavridis, and former Director of the New York Stock Exchange John C. Whitehead.[42]

In August 2015, LPF and Peter Ackerman joined forces with the Libertarian and Green parties and filed a lawsuit against the FEC in the US District Court of the District of Columbia. In February 2017, the District Court remanded the case to the FEC, with Judge Tanya Chutkan writing that the FEC had "acted arbitrarily and capriciously and contrary to law."[43]

By February 2020, the case was before the US Court of Appeals of the District of Columbia Circuit, the second highest court in the land. The assumption that partisan behavior could only mean one major party acting against the other was so strong that, during oral argument, Judge Cornelia T. L. Pillard, one of three judges on the panel, had to clarify for her brethren that the plaintiffs were contending that the bias in question was *both* parties (in concert) against non-major-party presidential candidates.

An appeal to the US Supreme Court was denied. The case was returned to the district court, which ruled in favor of the FEC on November 13, 2021, stating, "There is no legal requirement that the commission make it easier for independent candidates to run for president of the United States."[44]

Farewell to Factionalism, Say the Factions

In his oft-quoted farewell address in 1796, George Washington cautioned the new nation against the "baneful effects of the spirit of party generally"[45] as he warned against "the alternate domination of one faction over another, sharpened by the spirit of revenge, natural to party dissension, which in different ages and countries has perpetrated the most horrid enormities, is itself a frightful despotism."[46] Ironically, perhaps, one form of that modern-day despotism is the extent to which the parties—now fully in jointly held power—use that power to delay and defeat independent competition by invoking the idea that allowing them to flourish will promote factionalism. The factions that usurped power in the form of the two-party system now lean into the need to prevent factionalism.

A problem, though, is that the United States now has as its largest segment of the electorate some 80 million Americans who object to that usurpation and define themselves as other than the present-day factions. Washington observed,

> If, in the opinion of the people, the distribution or modification of the constitutional powers be in any particular wrong, let it be corrected by an amendment in the way which the Constitution designates. But let there be no change by usurpation; for though this, in one instance, may be the instrument of good, it is the customary weapon by which free governments are destroyed.[47]

Notes

1 Lowi, Theodore, "The Party Crasher," *New York Times Magazine*, August 23, 1992, retrieved from www.nytimes.com/1992/08/23/magazine/the-party-crasher. html?searchResultPosition=4

2 This campaign was called "Two Roads are Better than One." Jackson's Democratic Party bid was the first road; Fulani's independent run was the second. After Jackson was sidelined by the Democratic Party, Fulani staged a 5,000-person rally in Atlanta outside of the Democratic Convention and urged his supporters to back her effort and create a long-term independent road.

3 Interview with Judy Woodruff, *PBS NewsHour*, 1992, retrieved from www.youtube. com/watch?v=YpeYCvPQPn4

4 Memo from Lawrence M. Noble, General Counsel, FEC, to Robert J. Costa, Assistant Staff Director, Audit Division, FEC, and Kim L. Bright-Coleman, Special Assistant to General Counsel, FEC. Subject: Threshold Submission and Letter of Candidate Certifications and Agreements Received from Lenora B. Fulani/Lenora B. Fulani's Committee for Fair Elections, January 13, 1987 and December 28, 1987, p. 1.

5 Memo from Robert J. Costa, Assistant Staff Director, Audit Division, FEC, to The Commissioners. Subject: Eligibility of Lenora B. Fulani to Receive Primary Matching Funds, January 15, 1988, p. 2.

6 Ibid.

7 Ibid; FEC counsel also concluded the Commissioners' concerns about the "type" of campaign Fulani would run would not disqualify her from the matching funds program, Ibid.

8 The composition of the FEC is set in 2 U.S.C., §437c: Federal Election Commission:

> (a) Establishment; membership; term of office; vacancies; qualifications; compensation; chairman and vice chairman. (1) There is established a commission to be known as the Federal Election Commission. The Commission is composed of the Secretary of the Senate and the Clerk of the House of Representatives or their designees, ex officio and without the right to vote, and 6 members appointed by the President, by and with the advice and consent of the Senate. *No more than 3 members of the Commission appointed under this paragraph may be affiliated with the same political party.* [Emphasis added]

9 Weiner, Daniel I., "Fixing the FEC: An Agenda for Reform," *Brennan Center for Justice*, 2019, pp. 11–12.

10 Hofstadter, Richard, *The Age of Reform*, Vintage, 1955, p. 97.

11 Ibid.

12 Weiner, Daniel I., 2019, p. 2.

13 *Ballot Access News*, the following issues: 11/87 New York, p. 4, retrieved from www.ballot-access.org/1987/BAN.1987.11-19-87.pdf; 1/88 West Virginia, p. 5, retrieved from www.ballot-access.org/1988/BAN.1988.01-20-88.pdf; 4/88 California (new lawsuits filed), p. 4, and North Carolina, p. 1, retrieved from www.ballot-access.org/1988/BAN.1988.04-19-88.pdf; 5/88 Florida, p. 1, and Texas, p. 3, retrieved from www.ballot-access.org/1988/BAN.1988.05-23-88.pdf; 7/88 Michigan, p. 1, retrieved from www.ballot-access.org/1988/BAN.1988.07-08-88.pdf; 8/1/88 Nebraska, p. 1, retrieved from www.ballot-access.org/1988/BAN.1988.08-01-88.pdf; 8/27/88, North Carolina, p. 1, retrieved from www.ballot-access.org/1988/BAN.1988.08-27-88. pdf; 9/88 California, (Peace and Freedom Party), p. 2, retrieved from www.ballot-access. org/1988/BAN.1988.09-16-88.pdf; 10/88 Arizona, p. 2, retrieved from www.ballot-access.org/1988/BAN.1988.10-12-88.pdf; http://ballot-access.org/print-issues.

14 For campaigns of John Anderson, Ron Paul, Ross Perot, Ralph Nader and Patrick Buchannan, see Wikipedia, "List of United States Presidential Candidates," retrieved

from https://en.wikipedia.org/wiki/List_of_United_States_presidential_candidates; for candidates in 1984, Dennis Serrette and Sonia Johnson, see Wikipedia, "1984 United States Presidential Election," retrieved from https://en.wikipedia.org/wiki/1984_United_States_presidential_election

15 Muller, Tiffany, "Manchin Offers a Path Forward on Voting Rights With Compromise Bill," *Democracy Docket*, September 17, 2021, retrieved from www.democracydocket.com/news/manchin-offers-a-path-forward-on-voting-rights-with-compromise-bill

16 "The Sinister Attack on Ballot Access in New York," *lp.org*, August 26, 2021, retrieved from www.lp.org/the-sinister-attack-on-ballot-access-in-new-york/

17 See process of running for judge in West Virginia, retrieved from https://ballotpedia.org/Partisan_election_of_judges

18 "Top-Two Open Primaries for State Offices Initiative, 2020" *Ballotpedia*, 2020, retrieved from https://ballotpedia.org/Florida_Amendment_3,_Top-Two_Open_Primaries_for_State_Offices_Initiative_(2020)

19 According to Ballotpedia, Connecticut, Delaware, Idaho, Mississippi, New York, Oregon, South Carolina and Vermont are the only states with fusion voting, retrieved from https://ballotpedia.org/Fusion_voting

20 *Williams v. Rhodes*, 1968, retrieved from Justia, https://supreme.justia.com/cases/federal/us/393/23/; *Illinois v. Socialist Workers Party*, 1979, retrieved from https://supreme.justia.com/cases/federal/us/440/173/; *Anderson v. Celebrezze*, 1983, retrieved from Justia, https://supreme.justia.com/cases/federal/us/460/780/.

21 *Jenness v. Fortson*, 1971, retrieved from Justia, https://supreme.justia.com/cases/federal/us/403/431/; *American Party of Texas v. White*, 1974, retrieved from Justia, https://supreme.justia.com/cases/federal/us/415/767/

22 *Bullock v. Carter*, 1972, retrieved from Justia, https://supreme.justia.com/cases/federal/us/405/134/; *Lubin v. Panish*, 1974, retrieved from Justia, https://supreme.justia.com/cases/federal/us/415/709/, *Communist Party of Indiana v. Whitcomb*, 1974, retrieved from Justia, https://supreme.justia.com/cases/federal/us/414/441/

23 *Storer v. Brown*, 1974, Retrieved from Justia, https://supreme.justia.com/cases/federal/us/415/724/

24 Mikva, Judge Abner, *Fulani v Brady*, decided June 14, 1991, Judge Abner Mika, dissenting, Section IV, retrieved from https://casetext.com/case/fulani-v-brady

25 Private conversation between Dawkins and Jacqueline S. Salit, November 29, 2021.

26 Legal Information Institute, retrieved from www.law.cornell.edu/supct/html/95-1608.ZS.html

27 Michael Bloomberg won the mayoral race in New York City in 2001 as a fusion candidate, running both on the Republican Party line and the Independence Party line. He received 59,091 votes on the IP line, almost double his margin of victory. New York state is a significant example of how fusion can determine outcomes and allow third parties greater leverage.

28 Justice Souter signed onto the first two sections of the dissent, not the third.

29 Legal Information Institute, *Michele L. TIMMONS, v. TWIN CITIES AREA NEW PARTY,* Part III, #46, retrieved from www.law.cornell.edu/supremecourt/text/520/351

30 Ibid., 1997, Part II, #43.

31 Legal Information Institute, *Citizens United v. Federal Election Commission*, Justice Stevens' dissent, Part V, second paragraph, retrieved from www.law.cornell.edu/supct/html/08-205.ZX.html

32 *Michele L. TIMMONS, v. TWIN CITIES AREA NEW PARTY*, 1997, Notes, #1.

33 Gailey, Phil, "Democrats and Republicans Form Panel to Hold Presidential Debates," *New York Times,* February 19, 1987, retrieved from www.nytimes.com/1987/02/19/us/democrats-and-republicans-form-panel-to-hold-presidential-debates.html?pagewanted=1

34 Diamond, Larry, "Ending the Presidential-Debate Duopoly," *The Atlantic*, May 8, 2015, retrieved from www.theatlantic.com/politics/archive/2015/05/ending-the-presidential-debate-duopoly/392480/

35 Ibid.

36 Gailey, Phil, 1987.

37 "League Refuses to 'Help Perpetuate a Fraud,'" *League of Women Voters Press Release*, October 3, 1988, retrieved from www.lwv.org/newsroom/press-releases/league-refuses-help-perpetrate-fraud

38 CUIP is now best known as Independent Voting, with IndependentVoting.org a DBA of CUIP's.

39 Quote from Dr. Lenora Fulani, CUIP Press Release, "Campaign Launched to Change the Commission on Presidential Debates Polling Question," January 12, 2000.

40 Ackerman founded the International Center on Nonviolent Conflict in 2002 and sat on the Atlantic Council and the Council on Foreign Relations. Source: Wikipedia.

41 Change the Rule, 2015, retrieved from www.changetherule.org

42 Easley, Jonathan, "Adding Independent Voices to the Debate," *The Hill*, March 17, 2015, retrieved from https://thehill.com/homenews/campaign/236046-adding-independent-voices-to-the-debate. Based on Letter of Support posted by Americans Elect, February 26, 2015, retrieved from www.americanselect.org/news/2018/8/21/change-the-rule

43 Ackerman, Peter, & Shapiro, Alexandra, "A Victory in the Battle to Open Presidential Elections," February 12, 2017, retrieved from www.realclearpolitics.com/articles/2017/02/12/a_victory_in_the_battle_to_open_presidential_elections_133060.html

44 Ryan, Tim, "Court Rejects Push to Have Debates Welcome 3rd Party Candidates," *Courthouse News.com*, June 12, 2020, retrieved from www.courthousenews.com/court-rejects-push-to-have-debates-welcome-3rd-party-candidates/

45 "Transcript of President George Washington's Farewell Address," *ourdocuments.gov*, retrieved from www.ourdocuments.gov/doc.php?flash=false&doc=15&page=transcript

46 Ibid.

47 Ibid.

7

INDEPENDENTS SPEAK

"We're Not a Party. We're a Mindset"[1]

In a series of excerpts from nearly two dozen interviews with independent voters from a range of backgrounds and from around the country, we learn about the ways in which they see themselves and are misconceived in the media. In the excerpts, taken from transcriptions of a video montage that was produced for the annual Anti-Corruption Awards by IndependentVoting.org held on October 25, 2021, independents speak for themselves as independents and what they see as misconceptions about them in the media. In one after another excerpt, we see how independents assert themselves as neither ideologically driven nor unsure of their convictions around the need to reform the ways in which politics is done—the culture of politics—and stifling bipartisan control of the electoral process. Perhaps, most critically, one hears repeatedly their call for being treated with respect and recognized as independents—neither closet Democrats nor Republicans—and deeply concerned about moving the country forward in inclusive and democratic ways.

DOI: 10.4324/9781003240808-8

Greg Orman (Olathe, Kansas) is an entrepreneur, businessman, and leading voice in the US political independent movement. In 2014, he ran as an independent for US Senate in Kansas and won 43 percent of the vote.

Source: Photo courtesy of Mark Shaiken, used with permission.

Jeanette Schultz (Dayton, Ohio) is retired from a career in computer management, a member of the Dayton League of Women Voters, and a recent independent activist.

Source: Photo courtesy of Susan Miller, used with permission.

The biggest thing the media gets wrong about independents is, frankly, a misconception they have about all politics. They think it's all about ideology. Therefore, they're critical of independents because they say they don't share a common ideology. I like to push back on that by pointing out that neither do Republicans or Democrats. If you look at the deep divisions in both of the major parties, you realize that politics just isn't about ideology. Why people are independent, however, tends to be very similar. We're independent because we think this two-party system is irreparably broken, and we need to introduce a third force in our politics if we're going to get our country back to the business of solving problems for the American people. And the American people are hurting. They feel like they're being left behind, and as a result of that, not only are they becoming independents in bigger numbers, but they're also more and more alienated and dissatisfied with their own parties. In fact, I think that in most instances, roughly half of Republicans and half of Democrats aren't Democrats or Republicans because they like their party. Rather, they're Democrats and Republicans because they hate the other party. That's not the foundation upon which we can build a nation and that's why we need independents.

The biggest misconception that the media has is that we independents are leaners—leaners for one party or the other. We're not leaners. In fact, if anything, I'm running away from both parties. I don't want to be put in either a red box or a blue box. And I'm tired of being categorized as such. So when they talk about us in the polls, for instance, they always say, "Well, they're leaning this way now, they're leaning that way." No, we're either voting against something, and usually not even for something, because we haven't been given much of a choice as independents. So when you ask me if I lean, I definitely do not lean! Both parties are for themselves and for their own power, not for us, the people, and I'm tired of it.

One of the things that's important to me for people to know about independents is that it's critical in terms of the overall health of the democracy for people to be able to maintain the capacity for original thought. They don't have to be told what a platform is, they don't have to be told what their positions are on a particular situation. They stop and they think about the issues themselves and they follow their own research and thinking. One of the things that's critical about that is, for me, I don't see how it's possible for any thinking person to be a member of a party, because there's always going to be a party platform, there's always going to be the primary voice of the party, there's always going to be the leaning—left or right—and no issue, or no group of issues, is ever going to fit neatly into one party or the other. So, instead of just maintaining this rigid mindset of "it's my party's way or no way," which is killing us, then the thinking person must be an independent. There's just no way around it. Another reason why I feel so adamant that people need to be independents and need to understand the independent mindset is what we stand for because even now, at least for the last 30 years in Washington, it literally does not matter the validity of any legislation. If it's presented by one party, it's fought by the other—period. And that's killing us. One of the worst things that could have happened to the environmental movement was for Al Gore to host the documentary An Inconvenient Truth because the minute he did that, it became a political issue, it became something that the Democrats were behind, ergo the Republicans—to them it's a joke. To them it's fake science. Once people get into that deep of a party mindset, then the thinking process is gone. And with that goes democracy, without original thought there cannot be a democracy. Without people researching and thinking and looking into issues themselves, regardless of what the issue may be, and forming their own opinion, and acting on that opinion, there is no democracy. There's a few puppet masters, and a bunch of sheep. And sheep, by definition, are not independent.

Aaron James (Memphis, Tennessee) is a retired architect and the founder and leader of Tennessee Independents.

Source: Photo courtesy of Jamie Harmon, used with permission.

Rev. Gregory Seal Livingston (Brooklyn, New York) is an ordained minister and a civil rights and community leader. He is also the founder and president of the newly formed civil rights organization EquanomicsGlobal.

Source: Photo courtesy of Rev Gregory Seal Livingston, used with permission.

What do independents need to know about America? America's unchecked partyism has metastasized into the political/industrial complex, printing dollars and taking the American electorate for granted. However, independents need not be daunted by partisan power and propaganda. Why? Because entrenched partyism is fundamentally flawed, and any system that is fundamentally flawed will eventually implode upon itself. This "ism" is not the womb of democracy. The matrix of our enfranchisement, our vote, is of the people, for the people, by the people. This civic choice must never be segregated by race, gender, pedigree, or socioeconomic status. Enfranchisement is the sacred right of every citizen, labels notwithstanding. And just as we, the people, have declared our independence from monarchies, aristocracies, and confederacies, we, the independents, must untiringly work, fight, strive, and labor to make and keep our tax-funded republic open, accessible, and politically unfettered for all the people all the time.

Eric Bronner (Webster Groves, Michigan) is an attorney and the founder of Veterans for Political Innovation, a nonprofit that organizes the military-connected community to support targeted electoral reforms.

Source: Photo courtesy of Holly Kunze Photography, used with permission.

I'm a navy veteran, and supposedly about 49 percent of veterans identify as independent or unaffiliated voters, and I think there's a reason for that. When we commit to serving our country, we all swear an oath to support and defend the Constitution. We don't swear an oath to a political party or a political leader. Our duty and our obligation is to the Constitution, and that is what we want to continue serving. And, unfortunately, in our current system, as an independent voter, our options are all too often far too limited.

"Independents" is an ironic label, given that we believe that Americans are actually highly independent. Our COVID-19 experience has just been an illustration of that. The political parties act as if we're on separate planets. "Independent" means we're not being controlled by the parties. We prefer voting for the best choice regardless of party position. We respect America's rich diversity. Sadly, many qualified voters choose not to vote. However, a great many independents are denied their voting rights by election rules imposed by parties trying to maintain their control. Independents work hard to improve voter choice, not restrict it. In fact, most of the current ideas for improving election systems originated with independents. We want our nation's problems solved, not used as weapons against us.

Al Bell (Peoria, Arizona) is an active member of Independents for Arizona and served on Eyes on 2020, Independent Voting's national cabinet.

Source: Photo courtesy of Al Bell, used with permission.

As independents, we are not undecided; we're unimpressed. Unimpressed with having to settle for the lesser of two evils, the scarce choice in the marketplace of ideas, unimpressed with a system that promotes us versus them, and rewards the demonization of anyone who has a different point of view. Unimpressed with leaders who spew hatred into our discourse and kneel at the altar of partisanship at the expense of those whom they pledge to serve. Unimpressed with a lack of transparency, a lack of accountability, and a lack of solutions year after year after year. We want politicians who are elected for their problem-solving abilities, not their party alliances. We want leaders who are open-minded enough to listen to all sides of an issue. We want those who can bridge the divide between points of view and find real, lasting solutions. We are independents, and we are here to stay.

Damien Hughes (Gate City, Virginia) is a software developer and is active in the Virginia Independent Voters Association.

Source: Photo courtesy of Damien Hughes, used with permission.

Elaine Stephen (Wichita, Kansas) is the co-leader of Kansans Demand Better and Rank the Vote Kansas and was a full-time volunteer on Greg Orman's 2018 independent campaign for Kansas governor. Orman, a businessman who had been previously registered as a Republican and then as a Democrat, ran as an independent for U.S. Senate in Kansas in 2014 and then for Governor in 2018, but suspended his gubernatorial campaign operations when polling showed that he would not be able to defeat the two major party candidates.

Source: Photo courtesy of Terri Whitley Photography, used with permission.

Katie Fahey (Grand Rapids, Michigan) is executive director of The People. In 2018, she founded and led a successful grassroots campaign to end gerrymandering in Michigan.

Source: Photo courtesy of The People, used with permission.

Independents are a diverse group of people who, largely, have chosen not to belong to a party. We obviously have the option to join either of the two major parties or the minor parties, but we want to be independent. We don't want to be affiliated with a red team or a blue team and be part of a whole tribalism problem that is dividing this country into two parts. The founders warned about America being divided into factions, and that's what we see happening today. In the middle are independents, caught in between these two warring factions. Yet, independents are not necessarily "in the middle." We are a diverse group of people who have a diverse set of perspectives that bounces all over the place across the spectrum, depending on the issue. Yet, instead of talking to us about those issues, the media and elected officials or candidates just try to use us or take us for granted that we're going to flip to their side or the other side, instead of actually engaging us. Independents are a huge bloc—over 40 percent of the electorate—and yet we basically get ignored and/or used instead of being respected. And our point about tribalism isn't being taken as valid.

It's not that we don't have strong political beliefs, or that we don't vote for candidate A or B. It's that right now, we care more about the collective American people and getting a government that's actually accountable to all of us than we do about certain polarizing political candidates or talking points. We care about a political system that isn't going to discriminate against any American based on who they voted for. And what the United States really needs to know about us independents right now is that we believe until we get a government that's going to be accountable to all of us, we can't rest. This is about a country that will derive its power from us, not the red or the blue, but deriving its power from us, its people.

Independent voters are the single greatest untapped resource in our nation today. We're the majority—no political party has as many registered voters. That gives us a tremendous amount of power. We can determine elections. Smart candidates know that and speak to independents. Use that power.

Lisa Schnebly Heidinger (Arizona) is an author, independent activist, and board member at Arizona Humanities and Arizona Historical Advisory Commission.

Source: Photo courtesy of Larry Schnebly, used with permission.

I think that Americans need to know that independents believe in bold yet practical solutions. We independents want to be more included in the election systems and want to be getting more involved in the political process in a more fair and accessible way.

Darius Holt (Indian Head, Maryland) is a librarian technician in Washington, DC and was a political science major at the College of Southern Maryland.

Source: Photo courtesy of Darius Holt, used with permission.

Mike Pierson (Leggett, California) is a custodian at the Leggett Valley Unified School District whose interest in independent politics was first ignited by Ross Perot's independent presidential campaign in 1992.

Source: Photo courtesy of Mike Pierson, used with permission.

Jackie Fuller (Alexandria, Virginia) is an entrepreneur and a longtime advocate for electoral reform. She has a blog called the Black Independent Voter Network.

Source: Photo courtesy of Jackie Fuller, used with permission.

What does America need to know about independent voters? First of all, you need to know you're not alone. Almost half of us are independents at this point in time. It can seem—if you listen to mainstream media—like we're the weird ones, the outcasts, the outsiders, like everybody who's serious is either a Republican or a Democrat, and if you're not, then you're not on board. The reality is that both Republicans and Democrats are shrinking. More and more of us are not willing to be beholden to those parties or their platforms. What does the mainstream media get wrong about independents? They get all kinds of things wrong about us. They get it wrong about how many of us are there, how many of us are actually serious about politics, they're wrong about our intentions and what we want to see. They try to call us shadow partisans, they say we're just Republicans and Democrats who won't admit it. But the reality is there's a lot more of us who want alternatives to these parties who can win elections. We don't want to be beholden to Republicans and Democrats. We want alternatives, we want our voting systems to allow those alternatives, and that's one of the things that I hope to see happen.

I would definitely have to say that independents are definitely not a monolith. That's a big thing for sure. And when you speak to a lot of independents, more than likely they are not seeing themselves as attached to a political party, or maybe even, in some cases, to ideology. They want to make sure they're voting for the person and not the party. Though some can be leaning toward the left, right, or center, they're looking at issues. And if you feel that a political party or a politician isn't effectively addressing the issues, then of course you don't want to be affiliated with people who are not doing things that are of interest, the things that are important to you. Independents don't care about a candidate's political affiliation or personal life. I want to make sure that you're able to do the job, that you're not being influenced by special interests, by a particular PAC committee. They want to make sure that they are getting the candidate that best represents them.

Above all else, we strongly believe in country over party. We believe in voting for the best person for the job. We believe in principles, the laws, morals, and doing the right thing for the country. We don't identify with any party who votes party over country, we don't appreciate national parties running primary elections with our money, keeping us independents from voting by having to choose one side or another. Our members run from ultraconservative to ultraliberal, and there is no single way to define us.

Jose Torres (Jacksonville, Florida) is a business systems analyst who played a key role in the Florida Fair and Open Primaries' ballot initiative campaign for top-two open primaries in 2020.

Source: Photo courtesy of Jose Torres, used with permission.

The United States needs to know that independents like me are not undecided voters. We have definitive values, and we vote. Independents are dedicated to the idea of a rational decision process for public policy issues and the restructuring of the electoral process. A rational decision process is dedicated to achieving sustainable solutions to our problems. This means a representative is not constrained by partisan requirements, often to the detriment of their constituents. We do this by changing the structure of elections. Elections should have open primaries to allow all voters to vote. Gerrymandering, the flagrant restructuring of voting districts, should be drawn by a nonpartisan committee. Public funding of elections should be available to third-party candidates. These changes do not abolish the political party. To the contrary, elections will be more representative of the people—all the people. Voter turnout is currently so low we risk losing a pluralistic society that provides for our own economic and cultural strength. These extreme wings of the Democratic and Republican party are creating opposing, totalitarian regimes that are always in constant conflict. They have gone tribal in their political zeal. I don't want to be part of this destruction. I want the work to get done. As the late Senator John McCain said, "We are getting nothing done." I am a registered independent because I want us to be exceptional, to honor the idea of selfless service that is worth the sacrifice of all those who gave their lives for our country.

Mark Ritter (Frankfort, Kentucky) is a retired lieutenant colonel from a 34-year career with the Army Reserve and previously worked with the Kentucky Department for Environmental Protection. He is a leader at Independent Kentucky.

Source: Photo courtesy of Mark Ritter, used with permission.

Mickey Edwards (Princeton, New Jersey) is a former Republican Congressman from Oklahoma, taught at Harvard, and is now a visiting lecturer in public and international affairs at Princeton University's Woodrow Wilson School.

Source: Photo courtesy of Beth Babs and Babs Photography, used with permission.

Independents are not one monolithic group in the center. They are a range. They're people of various opinions, some more to the left, some more to the right. But they are not bound to a political party. They will look at the candidates, they will look at the issues on their merits, and they're not locked in. There's actually a large number of them, over 40 percent of Americans now consider themselves independents, and they don't want to be handed a menu of options by a party. They want to just say, "I like this person. He may not be the party I usually vote with, but his ideas are right, his personality is right, his knowledge is right, and that's who I want."

Chad Peace (San Diego, California) is the founder and president of IVC Media LLC, a nationally recognized leader in election law and voter rights, legal strategist for the Independent Voter Project, and a partner at the law firm of Peace & Shea LLP.

Source: Photo courtesy of IVC Media LLC, used with permission.

I think the biggest misconception about independents is that you can fit them into a box. Independents, by definition, span the political spectrum. They're often left of the Democratic Party, right of the Republican Party, and a bunch of them in between. Even within the parties, independents can't exist within the parties. I know that, coming from an organization that calls itself the Independent Voter Project, we mistakenly get attacked as being anti-party because we're the Independent Voter Project. I think there's extreme irony in a lot of that because a lot of independents like ourselves actually believe that by reforming the process we'll actually end up with stronger parties, not weaker parties. So, I think that misconception is that somehow because you're an independent you want to blow up the system and everybody in it is terrible is one that's a negative connotation about independents. And it's actually not just misdirected; it's opposite of where a lot of independents are coming from who want to see a better system. When we say we're independent it means we're independent of the system that is not representative of Republicans, Democrats, and everybody else that we believe representatives should be paying attention to.

I think what the United States needs to know about independent voters is that first and foremost it's the fastest growing segment of the electorate. That's not a recent phenomenon but it seems to be accelerating. And my take on that is that people are very frustrated with the choices that we seem to have, which often can consist of you can wear the blue shirt or you can wear the red shirt—or you can wear the red shirt or you can wear the blue shirt. And I think it also reflects the increased availability of information about issues and candidates, thanks to the Internet, and the fundamental independent spirit of American voters. We cherish that sense that each and every person makes up his or her own mind and doesn't need somebody to tell them how to do that. This is a strong and growing force in electoral politics that I don't think gets the credit or the visibility that it's often due.

David Thornburgh (Philadelphia, Pennsylvania) is the president and CEO of the Committee of Seventy, a Philadelphia-based civic leadership organization.

Source: Photo, Rebecca Thornburgh, used with permission.

There's a couple of media narratives that I think are just a little off. One of them is that independent voters are essentially mushy-headed on the one hand; on the other hand, "can't make up my mind" types. And I think that's wrong. My experience of independent voters—and I am one—what we know about them is that they're literally independent. You'll find independent voters who you would think of as almost libertarians, you'll find some who are uber-progressives, and everything in between. It's hard to characterize, but none of that adds up to this sense of mushy-headed, can't make up my mind.

The second narrative that I think is a little off is that independent voters are really partisan wolves in sheep's clothing. That they're somehow closet partisans. And this is all part of some elaborate game that's being played by the two parties. And that's just plain wrong. One thing that we do know about independent voters is that they are less partisan, meaning that they are less wearing their team colors each and every day. And how do we know that? Because if they were more partisan, they would be members of the two parties. And we should embrace that as a positive. In these hyper-partisan, acidic times, we should embrace people who are less partisan, who are bringing their own independent thinking to elections. We've got to work hard to change the narrative that's often out there. A lot of our politics and a lot of our academic research that feeds our politics are conditioned by you have only two choices. You can be Republican or Democrat. And once you look at everything through that lens, it literally colors your judgment about people who are not choosing to be part of that process. And again, this is the fastest growing segment of the electorate, so it seems to me, it demands a lot more attention and a lot more research and a broader view of what the American electorate is all about.

Julia Hemsworth (Brooklyn, New York) is an administrative assistant at Independent Voting and an illustrator whose design skills are used to help promote Independent Voting's mission.

Source: Photo courtesy of Julia Hemsworth, used with permission.

The biggest misconception in the media about independent voters is why independent voters are important. The media loves to frame independents in relation to the two major parties. Independents are extremists who don't think the parties go far enough. Independents are closet partisans who don't want to admit to being loyal to a party. Independents are undecided voters who are to be taken advantage of in elections. But all of that kind of misses the bigger picture, which is that independents are important because they're independent—because they exist. Being independent isn't just this political title that people take on; it's a statement of noncompliance. And it's not just a whisper of dissent. Independents should be the majority voice. Gallup consistently reports that about 40–50 percent of the American population identifies as independents. But not only does our legislature not reflect this majority, there's virtually no representation for anything but Democrat and Republican. So what's important about independents is that this system isn't working for us. It's hurting us. And people are starting to do something about it.

One of the greatest misconceptions is that we are people who are lost. When, in actuality, we are people who found ourselves and found our voice, not because of the push or pull of a party but by the convictions of our hearts, our minds, our souls, about what Americans can be, what the United States should be. So we express ourselves independently so we can really speak our truth and effectuate power in our communities.

Rev. Carl McCluster (Bridgeport, Connecticut) is senior pastor of Shiloh Baptist Church in Bridgeport and the founder of Faith Community Development Corporation.

Source: Photo courtesy of Rev. Carl McCluster, used with permission.

To me, the biggest misconception about independent voters is that we are secretly partisan and that we have some loyalty to a political party. In reality, my vision as an independent voter is for the political future of the country to depend on the perspectives of the voters on the right path forward. I believe that politics is a conduit for the will of the people, not the will of the political parties. That's why I registered as an independent.

Ron Dumas (Asheville, North Carolina) is a student at the University of North Carolina, Asheville and a student leader of a policy initiative program focused on providing food security to college students.

Source: Photo courtesy of Carri Flanagan, used with permission.

Steve Hough (Southport, Florida) is a retired accountant and the founder and director of Florida Fair and Open Primaries, which ran a ballot initiative in 2020 for top-two open primaries that garnered 57 percent of the vote, just short of the 60 percent needed to pass.

Source: Photo courtesy of Steve Hough, used with permission.

Jane Kleeb (Hastings, Nebraska) is the chair of the Nebraska Democratic Party.

Source: Photo courtesy of Mary Anne Andrei, used with permission.

The major misconception is that we don't really exist, at least not in the numbers being consistently reported by Gallup. As you may now, Gallup has been polling on party affiliation for 30 years. And, as of last month, 40 percent responded as being independent. That's after hitting an all-time high of 50 percent in January of this year. So why aren't we being taken more seriously? The problem with this poll is that since 1991, a follow-up question has been asked: whether an independent leans Democrat or Republican. The responses to that question are normally pretty evenly split, so pundits conclude that independents are merely closet Democrats and Republicans. As an independent, I can't vote in Florida's primaries, but I always vote in the general election. In almost every case, there are only two choices. This is true for every independent voter and sets up the opportunity to ask the leaner question. In my view, the media would better serve us by highlighting how election rules are written to impede outside competition and reinforce the duopoly rather than questioning whether we are truly independent.

***

The rising tide of independent voters has been changing the ways in which even partisan officials are willing to acknowledge their importance—principally, in order to win elections but also as "bridge builders." Jane Kleeb, who serves as chair of the Nebraska Democratic Party and is a founder and president of Bold Alliance and a board member of Our Revolution, offered her perspective in the plainest of terms for the video montage produced for Independent-Voting.org's 2021 Anti-Corruption Awards:

You are the game changers of 2020. You are the bridge builders across our country. You are the swing voters who can decide any election. As you all know in the room, 46 percent of America's electorate consider themselves independent. In the great state of Nebraska, where I am the proud Democratic Party chair, independents are the fastest growing voting bloc. As we head into the 2020 election, it is simply not acceptable that close to 26 million independent voters do not have access to vote for a presidential candidate during the primary. As chair of the Nebraska Democratic Party, I was proud to lead the charge to change that rule here in our state. In 2020, independent voters will be able to help decide who the next nominee is for the Democratic Party. And why would we do anything different? Independents get an opportunity to vote for our candidates in the general election, and we need them standing with us, shoulder to shoulder, in order to win elections. So you should also be able to vote in our primary elections. I join you . . . and you can count on me as an ally to make sure that more states are allowing independents to vote in their primaries.

Note

1   Opening quote from transcription of a focus group participant appearing in McFadden, E., Daugherty, D., Hedberg, E., & Garcia, J. (2015). "Who is Arizona's Independent Voter?" retrieved from https://morrisoninstitute.asu.edu/node/179, p. 10 (retrieved on November 5, 2021). All other excerpts in this chapter come from a transcript made by Caroline Donnola of videos used for a montage produced for the 20th Annual Anti-Corruption Awards by IndependentVoting.org on October 25, 2021. See www.2021aca.com/watch (retrieved November 5, 2021).

8

WHAT BINDS INDEPENDENTS TOGETHER?

Historically, pandemics have forced humans to break with the past and imagine their world anew. This one is no different. It is a portal, a gateway between one world and the next.

We can choose to walk through it, dragging the carcasses of our prejudice and hatred, our avarice, our data banks and dead ideas, our dead rivers and smoky skies behind us. Or we can walk through lightly, with little luggage, ready to imagine another world. And ready to fight for it.

—Arundhati Roy, "The Pandemic Is a Portal," April 2020[1]

In all the controversy about independent voters, about whether they are "really" independent, about whether they are intrinsically or definitionally moderates, about whether they are a force that can be organized, there is little attention paid to the underlying values that this wide-ranging community of Americans embraces. Values are difficult to discern for any group of voters, since the vast majority of polling and reporting focuses on issues, candidates, and policy. While that data can imply a set of values, the data itself can be tinged with a certain bias. Arundhati Roy poignantly links "our data banks and dead ideas," which is to say that many of the conceptual and technological tools we use to understand the world are not only outmoded, they are holding back the development of the global community. Acting in response to changes in the US electorate is likewise hampered by outmoded frameworks and tools.

Independent voters—who, according to exit polls, make up between 25 percent and 31 percent of the voting electorate in any given general election cycle[2]— periodically lift up an outsider candidate and bring him or her from the borders to the center of political action, as with both Barack Obama and Donald Trump. At other times they can act as a kind of barrier to stem the floodwaters of partisan

DOI: 10.4324/9781003240808-9

domination, as they did in 2020, when they backed the Democratic presidential candidate by 13 points, a 17-point swing from 2016.

One could liken them to sandbags, a low-tech but highly effective barrier to floodwaters that threaten to engulf a terrain, like those used by the Army Corps of Engineers or local fire departments. The sand contains a mix of minerals with different properties. For example, many types of sand contain particles of quartz, which have a hardness rating of seven on the Mohs scale.[3] The quartz, mixed with other particles in sand, contributes to its porosity; in other words, the level of coarseness. The coarser the sand, the less porous it is. While it might seem counterintuitive, this is true because when floodwaters hit a wall of sandbags, the silt and clay in the rushing water fill the gaps in the sand, making it harder for the water to pass through. The sand becomes a better barrier as the mixture becomes muddier, heavier, and almost cement-like.

Independent voters, who as a force are made up of multiple particles spanning the ideological spectrum, crossing socioeconomic categories, and deriving from many different racial and geographic identities, bind together at certain moments and under certain conditions to prevent one or the other of the major political parties from washing over the country. Concretely (no pun intended), independents decided the fortunes of the last three presidents, switching from a Democrat to a Republican to a Democrat. Though pollsters, analysts, and politicians have tried to ascribe a certain set of traditional political categories to these Americans or to negate their influence altogether, neither approach captures the evolving mindset of the independent voter. Some traditional political scientists have viewed the idea that independent voters could be a force for positive culture change as being as likely as a soup sandwich.

Yourdictionary.com defines a soup sandwich as "something that is not as it should be; something disorganized or unfinished."[4] That is, perhaps, an apt description of independent voters at this stage of history. Surely as a force they are unfinished. But in spite of that, or perhaps because of it, independents have been the swing factor in deciding key election outcomes over the last 25 years.

But even as they swing, even if they are disorganized or unfinished, can their values be discerned? If the conceptual and technological tools we use to understand the state of the US electorate are indeed outmoded, there is no better example than the peculiarity of the Obama-to-Trump voter, estimated at between nine million and ten million people.[5] If our understanding of politics is based on left/right ideology, there is no possibility of understanding such a phenomenon. Other factors must be at work.

In a 2019 CNN segment titled "Pulse of the People," anchor Alisyn Camerota hosted a panel discussion focused on the Rust Belt states of Wisconsin, Pennsylvania, Michigan, and Indiana with a diverse group of six people who voted for Obama in 2012 and then voted for Trump in 2016.

Of these six panelists, in this instance all self-described "lifelong Democrats," two African-American men made statements that appeared to stun the CNN anchor. When she asked how these voters could "like both these people," meaning Obama and Trump, one said, "Just because I'm born Black I'm supposed to have this allegiance to the Democratic Party." Another saw Trump's campaign as a "big middle finger to the establishment and all of politics." Even those who had voted for Trump in 2016, but subsequently regretted it, hoped that a Trump presidency could shake up the establishment and move the country forward, similar to how they had felt about Obama.

Not surprisingly, even Obama had left many voters disappointed with his embrace of the partisan system. Former Senator Bill Bradley told PBS journalist Charlie Rose in May 2012 that the loss of faith was not a mystery. Bradley said that Obama "took this soaring idealism and tried to fit it into a culture in Washington that was antithetical to it."[6]

In January 2021, inspired by a sense that many Trump voters were miscast and misunderstood by the mass media, independent activist Cathy Stewart launched a program to reach out to Trump voters. Stewart, vice president of National Development at Independent Voting, was perfectly situated for such a task, having spent decades creating cross-partisan, cross-ideological coalitions from the days of the Patriot and Reform parties of the 1990s to the Michael Bloomberg mayoral campaigns of the 2000s.

The calls to Trump voters, which reached mostly rural and suburban areas, were designed to investigate some of the values that Stewart suspected were shared by many Americans, regardless of how they may have voted in the 2020 presidential election. This listening tour took place against the backdrop of nonstop trashing by many on the left of the 74 million Americans who voted to reelect Trump. Regardless of how one feels about the former president, the question that progressive independents like Stewart felt needed addressing was, "What about those 74 million voters?" Stewart's volunteer calling team—all independents who considered themselves progressives—sought to have a genuine, open-ended dialogue. Was it possible to "bring us all together" when the parties had done their damnedest to tear the American people apart? And could independents play a key role in challenging this state of affairs? Stewart thought the phone calls might be a helpful barometer.

The outreach went to 51 voters in 18 states. Of those, 83 percent voted for Trump, 2 percent for Biden, 2 percent didn't vote (but would have voted for Trump), and 14 percent declined to answer. The party affiliation breakdown was 47 percent Republicans, 22 percent independents, 4 percent Democrats, and 24 percent declined to answer.

When asked whether they thought the American people are divided, or whether we are being divided, 63 percent thought we are being divided. Many spoke about the role that the parties and the media play in how Americans are being torn apart. They were asked how they rated a series of values, which Stewart suspected might be shared by a broad range of Americans. Fairness was rated very important by 58 percent, important by 40 percent, and not important by 2 percent. When asked how they view the importance of justice, they responded very important (70 percent), important (28 percent), and not important (2 percent).

Other questions were more open-ended, such as, "How are you feeling about this moment? What worries you?" One typical response was, "I am concerned about the direction of the country. . . . Politicians are serving themselves, not the country, not us." Another said, "We need to get along although we have differences. We need to find better ways than we have."

Most of these conversations lasted for 30–50 minutes. The design of the dialogue was to give the interviewees plenty of room to express their thoughts and feelings about the state of politics in the United States. One of the callers, Arizona independent Al Bell, noted,

> Listening is learning. I am not aware of a more transformative tool for escaping the painful abyss of our current political environment. Without it, we have nowhere to go. . . . Listening loudly involves turning up the earpiece and muting the microphone physically and mentally. It was a struggle—and eminently worthwhile.[7]

Not surprisingly, the conversations impacted the interviewers as well as the interviewees. The callers described these dialogues as a cultural experience as much as a political one. Some of the takeaways from Stewart? The conversations were "therapeutic, on both sides, establishing that it is possible to have conversations that open doors, and that shine a light on American values that resonate deeply."[8]

Perhaps, the most striking aspect of these exchanges was the extent to which Trump voters expressed their appreciation for getting this call. "No one ever asked me these questions," said one. Many had the experience of having been vilified for their support of Trump. Several stated that they had lost friends in the process. And they were grateful to be able to have a civil conversation about their perspective and concerns.

The Independent Mindset

While independent voting patterns have been heavily scrutinized, the idea of an independent "mindset," as one independent described the phenomenon, offers a window into the values that drive these voters.[9] In addition to being ardently pro-reform (90 percent think the presidential primaries should be open to all voters, regardless of affiliation or non-affiliation)[10] and ardently disappointed in the two-party system (66 percent say the reason they decided to become independent is that the two-party system has failed the country and puts its own interests ahead of the people),[11] independents increasingly exhibit a politic that might be described as "humanist libertarian."

A survey released by the Pew Research Center illuminates these values.[12] It found that 66 percent of independents feel that the economic system in this country "unfairly favors powerful interests," three points higher than the combined number for all voters. A majority of independents (57 percent) say "the U.S. needs to continue to make changes to give blacks equal rights with whites." And 66 percent of independents believe that immigrants strengthen the country rather than burden it (23 percent). Sixty-two percent oppose "substantially expanding the wall along the U.S. border with Mexico." The theme of fairness resonates with independent voters, as 70 percent favored the right to same-sex marriage.

With respect to attitudes about environmental problems and policy, a January 2019 Hill-HarrisX survey found that 64 percent of independents feel current environmental patterns are "extremely" or "somewhat" troubling.[13] While independents hold certain progressive values, they are much more libertarian than traditional progressives when it comes to the role and scale of government. By a small margin, 48 percent to 43 percent say they believe that "government regulation is necessary to protect the public interest," rather than "government regulation of business does more harm than good." By another small margin, 47 percent of independents prefer "smaller government providing fewer services" while 44 percent prefer "bigger government providing more services."

This distinction sets up an interesting contrast with progressives in the Democratic Party. The younger generation of the Democratic Party elected to Congress, for example, consists largely of Big Government advocates. Many Democratic Party leaders are conflicted about whether nonpartisan reforms should be supported to empower independent voters. This conflict pits party loyalty against demands for across-the-board fairness in the democratic process. Whereas Democratic Party activists tend to see the corporate sector as the pinnacle of corruption, many independents believe that while Wall Street is guilty of many sins, the political system itself produces the most pernicious and actionable corruption. On the other side of the aisle, Republicans often preach that Big Government represents the fundamental evil in US society. Independents have a strong libertarian streak. But they also see a particular and necessary role for government in redressing the overreach of capitalism. Economist Pat Choate, Ross Perot's vice-presidential running mate in 1996, put the matter succinctly in his 2009 book *Saving Capitalism*. "We are at an in-between time—a tumultuous moment when free-market absolutism is dying, but a widely acceptable form of sustainable twenty-first-century capitalism has not yet been born."[14] Independent voters experience that impasse keenly.

Defining Independence

Seeking out the message or the meaning of political choices that voters make, beyond who gets elected or which party is put into power, is rarely examined by the commentariat. With respect to independent voters, that work is even less fully formed.

Political scientists Samara Klar and Yanna Krupnikov are one exception. In their book, *Independent Politics*,[15] they attempt to look below the surface at the motivations for identifying as an independent in this highly partisan, highly politicized environment.

> Independents tend not to look all that different from partisans. But they do tend to be more averse to identifying themselves as a partisan when there is a negative stigma associated with partisanship. So, it's really the arguments, the hostility, the negativity that seems to be driving this behavior.[16]

Put another way, Klar and Krupnikov are identifying independents as reacting to the form of political life more than the content per se. Many political scientists have taken Klar's findings to support their contention that there is no such thing as a real independent, but they miss the point. Independents are making an urgent statement, a rejection of the culture of American political life itself. What could be more defining of values than that? Klar goes on: "They're not actually changing their views on politics. . . . [Independents] are simply recusing themselves from publicly identifying as a partisan."[17]

This "recusal" by 40–50 percent of the country should be considered a statement of values. A pretty shattering one at that. Instead, it is swept under the rug by the "experts." Commenting on Klar's work and the observations of other political scientists that parties are weak but partisanship is strong, the political newsletter *FiveThirtyEight* concluded: "That sounds counterintuitive given how many more Americans are identifying as independent, but remember that most aren't actually independent."[18]

What does it mean to be "actually independent" and who gets to define that? When an estimated 60,000 independent voters cast ballots in Maine in 2018, to veto the legislature's overturning of a citizens' initiative to install ranked choice voting, they did so even though independents would still be banned from voting in Maine primaries, a problem that ranked choice voting did not cure. This was a values statement, a process statement, a statement about an egregious overreach by the state legislature, a statement about the form of political life. Independents hold those values dear even when they are not the direct beneficiaries of them, as was the case in Maine.[19] And those values are as real and impactful as any vote cast in an election or any position on any issue framed by the parties and politicians. Arguably, given the state of politics today, they are even more real.

Notes

1 Roy, Arundhati, "The Pandemic is a Portal," *Financial Times*, April 3, 2020, retrieved from www.ft.com/content/10d8f5e8-74eb-11ea-95fe-fcd274e920ca
2 For example, in the 2020 presidential election, 26 percent of those who voted in the general election identified as independent: retrieved from www.cnn.com/election/2020/exit-polls/president/national-results

3 The Mohs scale is used to measure the hardness or softness of minerals, with diamonds set at 10.

4 Yourdictionary.com, retrieved from www.yourdictionary.com/soup-sandwich

5 Skelley, Geoffrey, "Just How Many Obama 2012-Trump 2016 Voters Were There?," *CenterforPolitics.org*, June 1, 2017, retrieved from https://centerforpolitics.org/crystalball/articles/just-how-many-obama-2012-trump-2016-voters-were-there/

6 Bradley, Bill, "Charlie Rose," May 8, 2012, retrieved from https://charlierose.com/videos/23653

7 Interview with Cathy Stewart, November 22, 2021.

8 Ibid.

9 Hedberg, Eric, Reilly, Thom, Daugherty, David, & Garcia, Joseph, "Voters, Media and Social Networks," *Morrison Institute for Public Policy*, April 2017, p. 2.

10 "Confronting a New Reality," *Independent Voting Survey*, Fall 2020, retrieved from https://independentvoting.org/survey-report/

11 Ibid.

12 "Political Independents: Who They Are, What They Think," *Pew Research Center*, March 14, 2019.

13 Sheffield, Matthew, "Most Favor Policies to Improve Environment, But Are Divided Over Paying for it," *The Hill*, from Hill-HarrisX survey, January 25, 2019.

14 Choate, Pat, *Saving Capitalism: Keeping America Strong*, Vintage Books, division of Random House, September 8, 2009, p. xiv.

15 Klar, Samara, & Krupnikov, Yanna, *Independent Politics*, Cambridge University Press, January 2016.

16 Skelley, Geoffrey, "Few Americans who Identify as Independent are Actually Independent. That's Really Bad for Politics," *FiveThirtyEight*, April 15, 2021, retrieved from https://fivethirtyeight.com/features/few-americans-who-identify-as-independent-are-actually-independent-thats-really-bad-for-politics/

17 Ibid.

18 Ibid.

19 In June 2021, both chambers of Maine's legislature voted in favor of opening the primaries to independent voters. The approved bill has to go through appropriations before it can be sent to the governor for signing. If approved, it would go into effect in 2024.

9

DEMOCRACY'S DILEMMA

Partisan primaries are the biggest form of voter suppression that there is in this country because people are not allowed to vote for whom they want. People are forced to vote for who the parties want them to vote for and it is time we change that.

—Danny Ortega[1]

Today, it may seem impossible to imagine the US government without its two major political parties. We operate as a two-party system currently dominated by the Democrats and Republicans, one of which has won every presidential election in the United States since 1852 and they have controlled the US Congress.[2] Over the course of the history of the republic, voices varied and powerful, from George Washington to W. E. B. Du Bois, have spoken long and loudly against the perils of a party system.

In 1787, when the Framers to the Constitutional Convention gathered in Philadelphia to design a new democratic republic, they entirely and purposely omitted political parties from the new nation's founding document.

This was no accident. The founders viewed parties as "factions" that had no legitimate place in the republic, harboring a deep distrust that was shaped by their experience under British government and their study of ancient history.[3]

On September 19, 1796, when Washington gave his farewell address, he warned against the deep threats and dangers of a bipartisan government when he said:

The alternate domination of one faction over another, sharpened by the spirit of revenge, natural to party dissension, which in different ages and countries has perpetrated the most horrid enormities, is itself a frightful despotism.[4]

DOI: 10.4324/9781003240808-10

In a further display of his prescience, he warned about political disinformation and propaganda.[5] A feature of party factions, he said, is "to misrepresent the opinions and aims of" other parties and regions, distorting reality and spreading falsehoods. Washington warned that the nation could not do enough to protect itself from this.[6]

The United States' second president, John Adams, also worried that "a division of the republic into two great parties . . . is to be dreaded as the great political evil."[7] Likewise, Alexander Hamilton feared parties as "the most fatal disease" of government and had hoped the United States could dispense of such groups,[8] while Benjamin Franklin warned of the "infinite mutual abuse of parties, tearing to pieces the best of characters."[9]

In the 1830s, Frenchman Alexis de Tocqueville in his famous observations of the US political life chronicled in *Democracy in America* characterized parties as dangerous and often a destructive force, "an evil inherent in free government."[10]

Further, he characterized American parties on his journey to America:

> I can't conceive of a sorrier spectacle in the world than that of different coteries (they don't deserve the name of parties) which to-day divide the Union. You see operating in broad daylight in their bosoms all the small and shameful passions which are usually hidden with great care at the bottom of the human heart.
>
> As for the interest of the country, no one thinks of it; and if they talk about it, it's only for the form. . . . It's pitiful to see what coarse insults, what small vilifications and what impudent calumnies fill the journals which serve them as party organs, and with what shameless scorn for all social decencies they daily arraign before the bar of public opinion the honour of families and the secrets of domestic hearth.[11]

Two Partyism Breeds Corruption

In 1881, President James Garfield was assassinated by Charles Guiteau, a disgruntled office seeker who was rejected by Garfield. Congress responded by enacting The Pendleton Act in 1883 to curb patronage practices at all levels of government, setting up a nonpartisan civil service system for such appointments. This move from patronage to civil service reform was an effort to weaken the control of political parties that had previously controlled job appointments and government contracts in federal, state, and local government.[12]

Political patronage, corruption, and the spoils system were at their peak in the late 1800s and early 1900s. New York's Tammany Hall and the notorious Boss Tweed best exemplified these practices. Tammany Hall was an organization based in New York City that became famous for the extent of its political corruption. Between 1854 and 1934, Tammany Hall essentially controlled Democratic Party politics, and thereby the local governments in New York City.

Three progressive figures—US Presidents Theodore Roosevelt and Woodrow Wilson and editor and a co-founder of the magazine *The New Republic* Herbert Croly—emerged during this time as a result of this widespread corruption and took specific aim at party politics, hoping to weaken the two-party control of US political life.[13]

Croly viewed the two-party system as undermining the ability of the people to control their own destiny because it:

> proposes to accomplish for the people a fundamental political task which they ought to accomplish for themselves. It seeks to interpose two authoritative partisan organizations between the people and their government. It demands of them that they act and think in politics not under the influence of their natural class or personal convictions, but according to the necessities of an artificial partisan classification.[14]

Warnings about the evils of bipartisan parties in the United States were not delivered only from the founders, observers, presidents, and reformers of the US democracy but echoed by US sociologists, civil rights leaders, and one of the founders of the National Association for the Advancement of Colored People (NAACP) W. E. B. Du Bois in his famous essay, "Why I Won't Vote," appearing in *The Nation*:

> In 1956, I shall not go to the polls. I have not registered. I believe that democracy has so far disappeared in the United States that no 'two evils' exist. There is but one evil party with two names, and it will be elected despite all I can do or say.[15]

Today, myriad political figures routinely criticize the grip the two-party system has on American life. "The party business is an evil business," asserted former California Governor Arnold Schwarzenegger:

> because they really don't care about the people at all. They say "OK, my ideology is right wing, and this is what we want to force on them." And the other side, "mine is left wing and that's what we want to promote." So they make the rules and they go and identify those things and they're not really interested in getting things done. They're more interested in what gets them elected.[16]

Even highly partisan former Senate Majority Leader Harry Reid recently lamented, that while he had tremendous affection for the two parties, he felt "our system has become so filled with tribalism, it's hard for me to comprehend. I know there is tremendous dissatisfaction, which is causing many people, many young people, to not be party-affiliated."[17]

The consequence is that today, America has an impenetrable two-party system, the situation that the Framers and reformers feared most. And it shows no signs of resolving. The two parties thrive on divisions by geography and cultural values in a zero-sum, winner-take-all electoral system. Political parties have effectively short-circuited the design intentions of our constitutional democracy.

Limitations of a Two-Party Partisan Political System

Growing dissatisfaction with the party system and voter frustration with a polarized and paralyzed government have fueled a breakdown in self-government and public trust. As previously noted, between 40 percent and 50 percent of US citizens now identify as independents, one important indicator of the disintegration of traditional political institutions.

The distrust of traditional two-party power and the proliferation of self-identifying independents are among the most volatile phenomena in US politics today. How are we to understand these dynamics and how can we remedy a situation where government and governing are captive to party power? What structural reforms, cultural changes, and institutional redesigns are necessary to establish an independent democracy, to free the electoral arena from partisan control, and to create a functional and free 21st-century political process? What is the unique role of independent voters—those who have made a statement of noncompliance with the party system—in this historical moment? As previously addressed, independents are barred or restricted from primary voting or coerced into joining a party in half of the 50 states. In many states and local jurisdictions, the primary is the decision-making round of voting, thus a hidden form of voter suppression has been allowed to flourish just below the surface.

The limitations imposed by the nation's two-party partisan political system and the hyperpolarization occurring as a result are profound, as the consequences play out on a daily basis. Alarmingly, a recent study by Yale political scientists Matthew Graham and Milan Svolik[18] found that only a small fraction of US voters are willing to sacrifice their partisan interests to defend democratic principles. The pair found that only 3.5 percent of US voters would vote against their preferred candidates as punishment for undemocratic behavior, such as press restrictions, disenfranchising voters, or supporting gerrymandering.[19] A growing number of Americans on each side see the members of the other party not as political opponents but as existential threats.

Clearly, former President Trump exacerbated the decline in civil discourse and the rise in party division. This fueled his and his allies' efforts to overturn the results of the November 2020 election, fed by repeated lies about widespread voter fraud. But Trump's corrosive crusade cunningly built on the growing pockets of distrust in the overall neutrality of the electoral system. The truth is US democracy was in deep trouble long before Trump was elected president. Business leaders Katherine Gehl and Michael Porter, in their book *The*

Politics Industry: How Political Innovation Can Break Partisan Gridlock and Save Our Democracy (2020), argue that the "rules that shape day-to-day behavior and outcomes"[20] of the US political system have been perverted and they were created by and for the benefit of the Democratic and Republican parties. The authors are among many contending that there must be a reengineering of the election processes that address a few key areas: party primaries and plurality or winner-take-all voting.[21]

Scholars and citizens alike have pursued implementing a series of alternatives and modifications to party-driven democracy. The previously mentioned reformer Croly[22] provides a useful lens to look at the impact of this distortion: The two-party system undermines "the ability of the people to control their own destiny by interposing two authoritative partisan organizations between the people and their government. The question is, what institutional and structural design changes can impact on this?"

There are constitutional changes that take the form of proposed amendments to the US Constitution. Over the recent years, a wide range of ideas, such as a requirement for a balanced federal budget; shrinking federal authority; limiting the Supreme Court to a term of 18 years; abolishing the electoral college; banning gerrymandering; and getting "dark money" out of politics has been discussed and even pursued.[23]

Addressing some of the shortcomings of American democracy by amending the US Constitution or calling on Congress to form a constitutional convention to propose amendments present some serious challenges. The former is exceedingly difficult and the latter dangerous. The country's foundational laws are hard to change. Under the present circumstances, a convention would certainly be extremely contentious and highly politicized and its results impossible to predict. Congress and the states have never called one. An amendment to the Constitution proposed by Congress requires a two-thirds majority in both the House and Senate. After the amendment is approved by Congress, it must be ratified by the legislatures of three-fourths of the states before it is added, a hurdle that is difficult to overcome. Perhaps, more to the point is the question of whether and how to effect cultural and political developments in the body politic such that a constitutional amendment process could take place in a more wholesome and unifying environment.

Structural reforms and designs have been implemented to varying degrees in the United States with a goal of making our democracy more responsive, fair, transparent, and representative. These include local and state forms of proportional representation/multiparty system, nonpartisan redistricting, open primaries, and nonpartisan primaries and general elections. Opposition to these reforms by the Democratic and Republican parties has, in many cases, been fierce, as these initiatives have threatened their entrenched duopoly. Often, voters have had to bypass their elected representatives and enact these measures directly by popular vote. These reforms have demonstrated some notable achievements as discussed later.

Still, we must ask how do we evaluate and discuss the potential impact of these reforms given that the entire system has been controlled by partisanship?

Proportional Representation/Multiparty System

Proportional representation is a governing system in which divisions in an electorate are reflected proportionately in the elected body.[24] Despite the United States being the oldest continuous democracy in the world,[25] many of the world's industrialized nations have surpassed the United States in how to fairly elect their representatives. Practically every democracy in the world has embraced some variation of proportional representation through multi-member districts for electing their national legislatures.[26]

There are several reasons two major parties dominate the political system in the United States. Forty-eight states have a standard winner-takes-all electoral system for counting presidential votes. This winner-takes-all principle applies in presidential elections. When a presidential candidate garners the most votes in any particular state, all of the electoral votes from that state are awarded to the candidate. In all states but Maine and Nebraska, the presidential candidate must win a plurality of votes to win all of the electoral votes. This is termed "unit rule," under which a delegation to a national political convention casts its entire vote as a unit as determined by a majority vote.[27] Under winner-take-all, 51 percent of the vote controls 100 percent of the power, and a consistent minority of approximately 40 percent gets nothing.[28] Under proportional representation, 51 percent of the vote would control (roughly) 51 percent of the power, and that 49 percent minority would get (roughly) 49 percent of the legislative seats. A proportional representational electoral system ensures that the majority preference is respected while also ensuring that significant minorities are not left completely unrepresented.[29]

Research has found time and again that governance works better in multiparty proportional systems. These systems produce higher voter turnout,[30] including better representation for minority and underrepresented populations.[31] Citizens consistently report being more satisfied with governance systems that have proportional representation,[32] and partisan debates are less negative.[33]

According to Lee Drutman, a senior fellow at New America and the author of *Breaking the Two-Party Doom Loop: The Case for Multiparty Democracy in America* (2020):[34]

> Multiparty democracy is not perfect. But it is far superior in supporting the diversity, bargaining, and compromise that the Framers, and especially Madison, designed America's institutions around, and which they saw as essential to the fragile experiment of self-government. The country must break the binary hyper-partisanship so at odds with its governing institutions, and so dangerous for self-governance. It must become a multiparty democracy.[35]

However, proportional multiparty democracies are still party-based. A sizable number of independent voters indicate a popular yearning for a system that does not privilege parties at all.

And using Croly's lens, how does this system lessen the role the parties play between the people and their government and help citizens develop their civic capabilities? Would moving to a multiparty democracy reduce the control of the parties? Would having more parties, ironically, lessen the control of the parties? And what about citizens who don't want to be in a party?

Nonpartisan Redistricting

Gerrymandering is a deeply undemocratic practice that inherently disenfranchises voters by manipulating electoral district boundaries in favor of a political party or incumbent. Every ten years after the decennial census data has been collected and processed, all 435 congressional districts are redrawn. Electoral maps must follow the principle of "one person, one vote," in which each district has a substantially similar number of people.[36] However, in the majority of states, the state legislature ultimately determines how these districts are constructed. Typically, the party in power tends to draw them to maximize its advantage. States where one party controls both chambers of the legislature and the office of governor can pass redistricting maps that favor their party without much opposition. Since most congressional districts are already gerrymandered, protecting incumbents is a priority. Not only are members of the US House of Representatives consistently reelected 97 percent of the time,[37] but the United States is the only industrialized democracy in the world that still allows incumbent legislators to draw their own districts—one of a litany of ways the major parties institute mechanisms for their self-preservation.[38]

Law Professor McKay Cunningham of Concordia University explains it this way:

> Partisan gerrymandering benefits the legislators and parties drawing the direct lines, but it carries a host of negative consequences for the electorate. Academic research into Congressional behavior yields at least one fixed finding: more than anything else, winning elections motivates politicians. But if opposition is effectively neutralized, the negative consequences include less responsiveness, less accountability, less ideological diversity, less compromise and less institutional legitimacy. . . . If the general election is assured through partisan gerrymandering, the primary becomes a contest of radicals. The most extreme candidate often secures the party nomination, promoting incumbents to eschew any semblance of compromise or moderation while in office.[39]

While the practice is more often associated with federal congressional districts, it is widespread and impacts state legislative districts, county commissions, city councils, and even school board members. States must follow federal law requirements, such as having voting districts contain equal populations, each congressional district needing to be represented by a single member, and they must be in compliance with the Voting Rights Act. Beyond federal mandates, states often utilize several other factors when drawing district lines, such as contiguity (single, unbroken shape), racial fairness, the preservation of communities of interest, and compactness. However, elected individuals and their two-party accomplices employ a host of techniques to reduce racial and political party power and create districts that favor incumbent politicians over challengers.[40] If districts are drawn fairly, the public can elect representatives who reflect the views of the population as a whole. But if the district lines are manipulated through partisan gerrymandering, fair representation of citizens is thwarted and voter apathy and disillusionment increase.

Gerrymandering has occurred in the United States since its founding. The term "gerrymander" originated in 1812, when Massachusetts Governor Elbridge Gerry, "a Founding Father, signer of the Declaration of Independence, reluctant framer of the Constitution, congressman, diplomat, and the fifth vice-president,"[41] approved an oddly shaped partisan map that was reported to resemble a salamander. Combined with his last name, this produced the term "gerrymander."[42]

The 2019 US Supreme Court, in *Rucho v. Common Cause*,[43] basically closed the door on using the federal courts as an option to combat redistricting abuses by ruling 5–4 that there was no objective standard for adjudication when determining whether a map went too far in locking in partisan advantage. Additionally, the two major parties have been reluctant to give up the ability to draw and gerrymander districts and have blocked reform efforts that include creating independent redistricting bodies. This leaves citizens with few alternatives to get around their elected representatives. Besides being an often arduous and difficult process, only half the states (26) currently have some form of initiative or referendum allowing citizens to directly engage in policy making.[44] Most states that equip their citizens with direct democracy tools are in the West with 60 percent of all initiative activity occurring in six states: Arizona, California, Colorado, North Dakota, Oregon, and Washington. Initially, Eastern and Southern states left out these direct democracy tools from their state constitutions primarily out of fear that direct democracy would empower Blacks and immigrants.[45]

While state legislatures maintain a tight grip over redistricting, alternative models do exist in a few states. A state's redistricting authority can be classified as legislature-dominant, where the legislature maintains final authority to draw district maps; a commission, which is legislatively empowered to draft and enact district boundaries; or a hybrid, where the legislature shares redistricting authority with a commission. For congressional redistricting, state legislatures in 33 states play the dominant role. In eight states (Arizona, California, Colorado, Hawaii, Idaho, Michigan, New Jersey, and Washington), commissions draw congressional district lines. In two states (New York and Virginia), hybrid systems are used, in which the legislatures share redistricting authority with commissions. The remaining states comprise one congressional district each, rendering redistricting unnecessary.[46] California was one of the first to create a citizen commission. But there is no uniform standard for such commissions, and some have become paralyzed by partisanship.[47]

Good government groups have been advocating for states to turn over their redistricting process to nonpartisan commissions. These are bodies that are theoretically not motivated by partisan concerns and instead draft and enact maps with other goals in mind, like fostering competition, preserving communities of interest, and drawing more compact districts.[48] California went so far as to establish independent voting commissions made up of citizens who volunteer to serve. However, even these independent commissions are not immune to partisan meddling.[49]

US citizens overwhelmingly are opposed to partisan gerrymandering and support independent redistricting commissions;[50] however, the partisan practices persist. Moreover, extreme gerrymandering has gotten substantially worse over the last decade, as technology has made it easier to draw gerrymandered districts with intense precision.[51]

What is the proper way to evaluate redistricting reform? Is it by virtue of the end product—how "fair" are the lines? And what is fair—balance between the parties or complete neutrality? Or should the value of independent commissions be evaluated by virtue of what they accomplish before they even draw their first map, which removes the parties from one way they stand in between the people and their government?

Open Primaries

In the United States, in most elections, candidates compete in two contests to win their seat: a primary election and a general election. While the general is open to all voters in a jurisdiction, in many states the primary is divided by party and limited to registered party members.

If you are an independent voter who is not affiliated with a party, you are likely blocked from voting in a primary. Since general elections are overwhelmingly noncompetitive, getting excluded from a primary can mean getting excluded from the election altogether. In 2020, 26 million independent voters were barred from voting in presidential primaries.[52]

Primary elections were created during the progressive era to give voters more direct say in the nominations process. Today, primaries are used in three distinct ways: first, in most states, to determine which candidates for state and federal office will receive the nomination of the Democratic or Republican parties (and to a lesser extent minor parties like the Green and Libertarian); second, in four states (California, Washington, Nebraska, and Alaska) to determine, in a nonpartisan way, which candidates will advance from the first round (primary) to the second round (general); and finally, to elect delegates to attend the national conventions of the Democrats and Republicans to decide a presidential nominee. The rules for primary participation vary from state to state and oftentimes within the same state. Arizona, for example, allows independent voters to participate in primary elections for state and federal office but not to participate in presidential primaries. Add to this confusion the fact that 30 states register voters by party and 20 states do not, so the meaning/experience of an "open" primary in a partisan registration state and nonpartisan registration state are different.

Some reformers suggest eliminating primaries outright. The argument is that primaries are low turnout elections, and they are dominated by the most ideologically extreme members from the Democratic and Republican parties. Furthermore, primaries significantly underrepresent poor and working-class citizens and minorities of color. Focusing voters' attention on one high-stakes general election, it is argued, would help maximize turnout.[53]

Christian Grose (2020) of the University of Southern California's Schwarzenegger Institute found that open primaries and top-two primaries are associated with reduced legislator extremity and result in more moderate legislators.[54] This study was the first to find this by analyzing the voting behavior of members of Congress.[55] They also result in elected officials reaching out beyond their party to all the voters in order to get elected and stay in office.[56] Additionally, they are associated with higher voter turnout from women of color who are independents.[57] In contrast, closed primaries have been found to have a disparaging effect on people of color, specifically independents of color. A recent study by Grose, Raquel Centeno, Nancy Hernandez, and Kayla Wolf of the University of Southern California found that "Independent and third-party voters across four of the racial groups [studied] are more likely to vote in an open or top-two primary rather than a closed primary."[58] The study found that Latinx and Asian Americans were more likely to be registered as independent and had the lowest predicted primary turnouts when compared to Black and white independents. Similarly, Asian-American independents had the lowest predicted turnout in a closed primary state. The researchers found that closed primaries had large demobilizing impacts on voters of color.

While US citizens consistently support having open primaries,[59] there is a good deal of opposition toward it from the Democratic and Republican parties. A key question is whether the only goal with open primaries should be to moderate the outcome. Might there be other ways to look at this? Might another goal be to create a level and fair playing field for all voters?

Nonpartisan Primaries and General Elections

Top-candidate primaries and ranked-choice voting are two examples of nonpartisan election reforms. Top-candidate primaries are an election process in which all candidates running for an office, regardless of party affiliation, are listed on the same primary ballot. While top-two primaries are the most common version of a top-candidate primary, top-four and final-five primaries also let voters choose candidates from any party. With the top-four and final-five primary models, however, the top vote-getters move on to a general election. In all these primaries, the top candidates who receive the highest number of votes, regardless of party affiliation, advance to the general election, making it possible for two members of the same party to run against one another in a general election.[60]

As of 2020, the top-two primary elects slightly less than one-fifth of the members of the House each year.[61] Washington became the first state to adopt a top-two primary system for congressional and state-level elections in 2004, with California doing the same in 2010. In 2020, a ballot initiative was approved in Alaska creating a top-four primary system for state and congressional elections. This initiative also included provisions establishing ranked-choice voting for state executive, state legislative, congressional, and presidential elections. Nebraska employs a top-two primary system in state legislative elections; however, because its legislature is nonpartisan, no party affiliation is listed in association with any candidate.

Louisiana does not use a two-party system but allows all candidates to run in the general election and, in the event that no candidate receives a majority of the votes (50 percent + 1 vote), the top two vote-getters run against one another in a runoff. While not a true top-two primary, the two-round electoral system is based on the same founding principles.

Supporters of the top-two primary system believe that it allows for a more accurate reflection of the will of the electorate and encourages candidates to take more moderate stances. According to Jesse Crosson of the Center for the Study of Democratic Politics at Princeton University, "According to proponents of the top-two primary, the partisan neutral, two-stage nature of the system leverages the participation of minority party voters in safe districts in order to elect more moderate winners."[62] This belief comes from the idea that in a top-two system, in order to get on the ballot, candidates must appeal to voters of all political affiliations, moving their stances closer to the center.[63] Researchers have found top-two and open primaries are associated with more moderate legislators[64] while other studies have found more of a modest or inconsistent approach.[65]

Ranked-choice voting (RCV) is a system within which constituents vote for multiple candidates, in order of preference.[66] In an RCV system, the candidate who receives more than half of the first-choice votes in races that only elect one winner will win. However, if there is no majority winner within the first-choice votes, then votes are subject to a new counting system, often an "instant runoff." In this instance, the candidate with the fewest total votes is eliminated from the race, and votes are re-tallied for the remaining candidates. Voters whose first-choice votes went toward the eliminated candidate will have their second-choice votes counted, and tabulation will continue until there is a candidate who has won the majority of votes.[67]

In jurisdictions with multi-winner positions (such as city council or school board) or who elect multiple winners for a legislative body, a variant of RCV is more likely to be used: proportional RCV. In proportional RCV, winning candidates must reach only the voting threshold—the minimum percentage of votes to guarantee winning the seat—in order to win one of the seats up for grabs. For example, a single-seat election needs 50 percent + 1 vote, a two-seat election needs 33.3 percent + 1 vote, a three-seat election needs 25 percent + 1 vote, and so on.[68]

Proponents assert that the expected benefits of RCV include greater openness of the electoral arena to new parties and independents, greater ideological moderation, and greater voter satisfaction.[69] Ranked-choice voting was designed to encourage centrism and, in many cases, independent candidates. According to Evan Falchuk, a former independent gubernatorial candidate for governor in Massachusetts, "Ranked-choice voting helps you not have to feel as if you're voting for the lesser of two evils."[70]

Opponents have argued that RCV is unnecessarily complex and confuses voters. It introduces many more steps, and more complexity than would be expected otherwise in a traditional tabulation of results.[71] Others have argued that absent substantial voter education, the system will effectively disenfranchise voters, especially older individuals and voters of color.[72]

Ranked-choice voting is currently seeing relatively limited use here in the United States. However, its popularity is increasing. Lawmakers in 29 states are considering measures that would adopt RCV in some form, in local, statewide, or presidential primary elections.[73] Currently, a total of only 43 jurisdictions utilize RCV, including two states, one county, 29 cities outside of Utah, and 23 cities in Utah. Particularly noteworthy out of the jurisdictions that use RCV are the states of Alaska and Maine, who use it in all statewide and presidential elections. Outside of the United States, RCV is used nationally by six countries: Australia, Ireland, New Zealand, Malta, Northern Ireland, and Scotland. Additionally, India, Nepal, and Pakistan use proportional RCV for their national offices, including Senate and, in Pakistan, the presidency.[74]

Ensuring Voting Access

The most recent iteration of restoring and fortifying two portions of the Voting Rights Act of 1965 removed by the US Supreme Court in 2013 and 2021 has taken the form of the John Lewis Voting Rights Act, named in honor of the Alabama native son, voting rights advocate, and longtime Democratic congressman. The bill, H.R. 4, sponsored by Alabama Representative Traci A. Sewall, with 223 cosponsors, was introduced on August 17, 2021, in the House, followed in the US Senate by Vermont Senator Patrick Leahy with 48 cosponsors. However, less than three months after being introduced it was voted down in the US Senate. If passed and implemented, the bill would have helped to ensure voting rights for Black and minority voters by making it more difficult to discriminate against such voters through a litany of proactive measures and mechanisms. These would have included broadening the scope of the courts, restoring federal pre-clearance, and oversight regarding redistricting and voter I.D., as well as offering multilingual election materials, expanding voting locations and hours, and maintaining voter rolls.[75]

Such measures would undoubtedly be of value to ensure voting rights, but they could go only so far. That is, such measures would tend to favor Democratic electoral victories over Republican candidates, doing little to address the plurality of voters in the nation—the independent voter—without the inclusion of proportional voting, inclusive and open primaries, top-candidate primaries, and RCV. In other words, if passed, the proposed Lewis legislation to ensure voting rights along the lines of the original (and fortified) Voting Rights Act would maintain the status quo and fail to develop our democracy by encouraging new kinds of coalitions that are cross-ideological and perhaps even post-ideologically driven.

Adding to the more developmental and democratic measures are two additional state-based mechanisms to help ensure electoral participation and voting access to all: ballot-access reform and same-day voter registration.

The nation would benefit from having more non-major-party candidates on the ballot and making voter registration and casting one's ballot easier. Having more candidates and greater access is not simply a moral proposition—the notion that anyone should run for office and that anyone 18 and above (some argue lowering the voting age to 16) should be able to cast a vote for public office because that is what an inclusive democracy is all about. To the authors of this book, the issue is also a developmental one: Greater electoral participation (as candidates and voters) might lead to innovation in policy through a richer and varied political culture.

First, there is the issue of having a candidate who is neither the Democratic or Republican nominee get on the ballot. As election reform attorneys Jeremy Gruber, Michael A. Hardy, and Harry Kresky note in "Let All Voters Vote: Independents and the Expansion of Voting Rights in the United States," appearing in the *Touro Law Review*,

> Across the country, an increasing number of congressional and state elections are largely pro forma because of partisan gerrymandering and a patchwork of restrictive ballot access laws. Indeed, election competitiveness across the country is at a 40-year low, with only five percent of Americans living in districts with elections won by five percent or less.[76]

Quite simply, if one is not able to have one's name appear on the ballot for public office, then his or her likelihood of being competitive is effectively zero (write-in candidates notwithstanding). Richard Winger, editor of *Ballot Access*

News, has tracked the inequities across the nation over the past 35 years, with digital archives available since 2004.[77] Examples of highly restricted ballot access include North Carolina's election rules, which require more than 100,000 signatures to have one's name appear on the ballot for statewide office if one runs as an independent, versus no signatures required if one is either the Democratic or Republican nominee.

Second, there is the issue of voting access to supplement the proposed Lewis legislation. Currently, 20 states and Washington, DC have same-day voter registration. The measure allows qualified residents to both register *and* vote at the same time during early voting periods; all, except for two of these states (Montana and North Carolina), offer election-day registration. (Alaska allows same-day voter registration but for only president and vice president.)

Together, these measures would increase the voices of people through increased electoral participation and voting access.

How to Assess Reforms in a World Controlled by Partisanship?

These institutional reforms and designs appear to have a good deal of promise in advancing laudable goals, such as electing moderates and/or moderating the behavior of elected officials, reducing negative campaigning, assuring minority (political and racial) representation, and increasing voter participation. However, assessing their impact is challenging because their implementation takes place in the context of complete partisan control. And none of them seem to engage the question Croly asserted, namely addressing the extent to which the parties have inserted themselves "between the people and their government." Perhaps the question is, To what extent might these various reforms taken together lessen the obstructionist and corrosive role the parties play in between the people and their government? Toward what end? In order to create new electoral possibilities and coalitions as part of a new political culture that is more democratic, inclusive, and responsive to the challenges facing the nation and the world.

Notes

1 Gruber, J., & Opdycke, J., "The Next Great Migration: The Rise of Independent Voters," p. 3, retrieved from https://d3n8a8pro7vhmx.cloudfront.net/openprimaries/pages/4575/attachments/original/1637687269/ROI_Report_R1-1-compressed.pdf?1637687269

2 Anthony, G., & Carl, A., "Two-Party System: A Case Study of United States of America." 2019, *IDOSR Journal of Communication and English*, 4, no. 1, pp. 18–26. Retrieved from www.idosr.org/wp-content/uploads/2019/10/IDOSR-JCE-41-18–26–2019.pdf; Eldersveld, S. J., "The American Party System: Origins and Development." In H. Walton Jr. (Ed), *Political Parties in American Society*, Palgrave Macmillan, 2020, pp. 43–65. retrieved from https://doi.org/10.1007/978-1–137–11290-3_3

3 Chernow, R., *Alexander Hamilton*, Penguin Books, 2004.

4 S. Doc No. 106–21, 2000, retrieved from www.govinfo.gov/content/pkg/GPO-CDOC-106sdoc21/pdf/GPO-CDOC-106sdoc21.pdf

5 Chervinsky, L., *The History of Fake News from George Washington to Donald Trump*, *Governing*, December 8, 2021, retrieved from www.governing.com/context/the-history-of-fake-news-from-george-washington-to-donald-trump\

6 Ibid.

7 University of Virginia Press, *Founders Online: From John Adams to Jonathan Jackson, 2 October 1780*, *Founders.Archives.Gov*, October 1780, retrieved from https://founders.archives.gov/documents/Adams/06-10-02–0113

8 Chernow, 2004, p. 390.

9 Hofstadter, R., *The Idea of a Party System*, first edition, University of California Press, 1968.

10 de Tocqueville, A., *Democracy in America* (Vintage Books ed., Vol. 1), Vintage Books, 1948.

11 Pierson, G. W., *Tocqueville and Beaumont in America*, first edition, Oxford University Press, 1938, p. 657.

12 Reilly, T., *Rethinking Public Sector Compensation*, Taylor & Francis, 2014.

13 Ibid; Postell, J., "The Rise and Fall of Political Parties in America," *The Heritage Foundation*, 2018, retrieved from www.heritage.org/political-process/report/the-rise-and-fall-political-parties-america

14 Croly, H. D., *Progressive Democracy*, Macmillan Co., 1914, p. 341.

15 *"Why I Won't Vote" by W.E.B Du Bois [Published in The Nation Magazine, 1956]*, July 31, 2016, PISB Publications, retrieved from https://pisbpublications.wordpress.com/2016/07/31/why-i-wont-vote-by-w-e-b-dubois-published-in-the-nation-magazine-1956/.

16 J. Salit, Personal Communication, 2021.

17 T. Reilly & J. Salit, Personal Communication, 2019.

18 Graham, M. H., & Svolik, M. W., "Democracy in America? Partisanship, Polarization, and the Robustness of Support for Democracy in the United States," 2020, *American Political Science Review*, 114, no. 2, pp. 392–409, retrieved from https://doi.org/10.1017/s0003055420000052

19 Ibid.

20 Gehl, K. M., & Porter, M. E., *The Politics Industry: How Political Innovation Can Break Partisan Gridlock and Save Our Democracy*, Harvard Business Review Press, 2020.

21 Ibid.

22 Croly, 1914.

23 *About ALEC*. American Legislative Exchange Council, n.d., retrieved from www.alec.org/about/; Hasan, M., Eight Simple Steps to Fix American Democracy. *New Statesman*, September 3, 2021, retrieved from www.newstatesman.com/world/americas/north-america/2018/11/eight-simple-steps-fix-american-democracy; "The Democracy Amendments," *Free Speech For People*, April 29, 2021, retrieved from https://freespeechforpeople.org/democracy-amendments/; "5 Radical Solutions to Fix Our Busted Government," *Time*, December 2, 2016, retrieved from https://time.com/4585012/technocracy-how-to-fix-government/

24 Wikipedia Contributors, "Proportional Representation," *Wikipedia*, November 24, 2021, retrieved from: https://en.wikipedia.org/wiki/Proportional_representation

25 Boix, C., Miller, M., & Rosato, S., "A Complete Data Set of Political Regimes, 1800–2007," 2013, *Comparative Political Studies*, 46, no. 12, pp. 1523–54, retrieved from https://doi.org/10.1177/0010414012463905

26 *Comparative Data—AceProject.Org*. (n.d.), retrieved from https://aceproject.org/epic-en

27 *The Two-Party System | Boundless Political Science*. Lumen Learning. (n.d.), retrieved from https://courses.lumenlearning.com/boundless-politicalscience/chapter/the-two-party-system/

28 Among political scientists, "Duvenger's law" holds that plurality rule, as with "first past the post" systems, tends to favor the two major parties.

29 Mulroy, S., *Rethinking US Election Law: Unskewing the System (Rethinking Law)* (Reprint ed.), Edward Elgar Pub., 2020.

30 Selb, P., "A Deeper Look at the Proportionality—Turnout Nexus," 2008, *Comparative Political Studies*, 42, no. 4, pp. 527–548, retrieved from https://doi.org/10.1177/0010414008327427; Blais, A., & Dobrzynska, A., "Turnout in Electoral Democracies," 1998, *European Journal of Political Research*, 33, no. 2, pp. 239–61, retrieved from https://doi.org/10.1111/1475-6765.00382

31 Lijphart, A., *Thinking about Democracy*, Taylor & Francis, 2007; Negri, M., "Minority Representation in Proportional Representation Systems," Unpublished manuscript, University of St. Andrews, 2014.

32 Altman, D., Flavin, P., & Radcliff, B., "Democratic Institutions and Subjective Well-Being," 2017, *Political Studies* 65, no. 3, pp. 685–704, retrieved from https://doi.org/10.1177/0032321716683203; Radcliff, B., *The Political Economy of Human Happiness: How Voters' Choices Determine the Quality of Life*, Cambridge University Press, 2013.

33 Elmelund-Præstekær, C., "Negative Campaigning in a Multiparty System," 2008, *Representation* 44, no. 1, pp. 27–39, retrieved from https://doi.org/10.1080/00344890701869082

34 Drutman, L., *Breaking the Two-Party Doom Loop: The Case for Multiparty Democracy in America*, Oxford University Press, 2020.

35 Drutman, L., "The Two-Party System Broke the Constitution," *The Atlantic*, January 2, 2020b, retrieved from www.theatlantic.com/ideas/archive/2020/01/two-party-system-broke-constitution/604213/

36 Legal Information Institute, retrieved from www.law.cornell.edu/wex/one-person_one-vote_rule

37 "Reelection Rates Over the Years," OpenSecrets., n.d., retrieved from www.opensecrets.org/elections-overview/reelection-rates

38 Mulroy, 2020.

39 Cunningham, M., "Gerrymandering and Conceit: The Supreme Court's Conflict With Itself," 2017, *SSRN Electronic Journal*, retrieved from. https://doi.org/10.2139/ssrn.2989985

40 "Fighting Gerrymandering in the States," *Indivisible*, July 16, 2021, retrieved from https://indivisible.org/resource/fighting-gerrymandering-states

41 Magazine, S., "Where Did the Term "Gerrymander" Come From?" *Smithsonian Magazine*, July 20, 2017, retrieved from www.smithsonianmag.com/history/where-did-term-gerrymander-come-180964118/

42 Kruzel, J., "Supreme Court Decision Could Set off Gerrymandering 'Arms Race.'" *The Hill*, August 8, 2021, retrieved from https://thehill.com/regulation/court-battles/566631-supreme-court-decision-could-set-off-gerrymandering-arms-race

43 *RUCHO v. COMMON CAUSE*. LII/Legal Information Institute, June 27, 2019, retrieved from www.law.cornell.edu/supremecourt/text/18-422#writing-18-422_SYLLABUS

44 "Forms of Direct Democracy in the American States," *Ballotpedia*, (n.d.), retrieved from https://ballotpedia.org/Forms_of_direct_democracy_in_the_American_states; "Initiative and Referendum Processes," *NCSL.Org*, 2021, retrieved from www.ncsl.org/research/elections-and-campaigns/initiative-and-referendum-processes.aspx#/

45 Altic, J., & Pallay, G., "Opinion | Ballot Measures: American Direct Democracy at Work" *The New York Times*, August 31, 2016, retrieved from www.nytimes.com/2016/08/31/opinion/campaign-stops/ballot-measures-american-direct-democracy-at-work.html.

46 "State-by-state Redistricting Procedures," *Ballotpedia*. (n.d.), retrieved from https://ballotpedia.org/State-by-state_redistricting_procedures

47 Pildes, R. H., "Why the Center Does Not Hold: The Causes of Hyperpolarized Democracy in America," 2011, *California Law Review* 99, no. 2, pp. 273–333, retrieved from www.jstor.org/stable/23018603

48 Williamson, R. D., "Examining the Effects of Partisan Redistricting on Candidate Entry Decisions," 2019, *Election Law Journal: Rules, Politics, and Policy* 18, no. 3, pp. 214–226, retrieved from https://doi.org/10.1089/elj.2018.0505

49 Oxford University Press. "Is Gerrymandering 'Poisoning the Well' of Democracy?" *OUPblog*, October 28, 2020, retrieved from https://blog.oup.com/2020/10/is-gerry-mandering-poisoning-the-well-of-democracy/; Greenblott, A., Redistricting Reform is Easier Said Than Done, *Governing*, December 3, 2021, retrieved from www.govern-ing.com/now/redistricting-reform-is-easier-said-than-done

50 Kruzel, J., "American Voters Largely United Against Partisan Gerrymandering, Polling Shows," *The Hill*, August 4, 2021a, retrieved from https://thehill.com/homenews/state-watch/566327-american-voters-largely-united-against-partisan-gerryman-dering-polling; "Bipartisan Poll Shows Strong Support for Redistricting Reform," *Campaign Legal Center*, 2019, retrieved from https://campaignlegal.org/update/bipartisan-poll-shows-strong-support-redistricting-reform; Tyson, R., "National Electoral Reforms Survey," *R Street Institute*, 2021, retrieved from www.rstreet.org/wp-content/uploads/2021/02/National-Survey-Memo_2-8-21.pdf; "New National Bipartisan Redistricting Poll," *Campaign Legal Center*, January 28, 2019, retrieved from https://campaignlegal.org/document/new-national-bipartisan-redistricting-poll

51 Greenblott, 2021.

52 *Ballot Access News*, Volume 25, Number 10 (March 1, 2020).

53 Pierce, R. O. C., "Eliminate Primary Elections to restore Our Strong Democracy," *The Hill*, July 12, 2019, retrieved from https://thehill.com/opinion/campaign/452844-eliminate-primary-elections-to-restore-our-strong-democracy; Gehl, K. B. O. M., "Opinion: It's Time to Get Rid of Party Primaries," *CNN*, March 12, 2021, retrieved from https://edition.cnn.com/2021/03/12/opinions/reform-american-political-primaries-gehl/index.html; Troiano, N., "Party Primaries Must Go," *The Atlantic*, March 30, 2021, retrieved from www.theatlantic.com/ideas/archive/2021/03/party-primaries-must-go/618428/

54 Grose, 2020.

55 Miller, J., "Top-two and Open Primaries Lead to Less Extreme Lawmak-ers," *USC News*, May 21, 2020, retrieved from https://news.usc.edu/170366/top-two-open-primary-elections-less-extreme-lawmakers-usc-study/

56 Grose, 2020.

57 Centeno, R., Grose, C. R., Hernandez, N., & Wolf, K., *The Demobilizing Effect of Primary Electoral Institutions on Voters of Color*. Presented at 2021 Midwest Political Science Association, 2021.

58 Ibid.

59 "AP-NORC Poll: Americans Want Nomination System Changed," *AP NEWS*, May 31, 2016, retrieved from https://apnews.com/article/f5821f2774c14c39ad00c-1777f9ec6ea; Florida Poll, *Open Primaries*, (n.d.), retrieved from www.openprimaries.org/florida_poll

60 Ballotpedia., "Top-two Primary," *Ballotpedia*, (n.d.), retrieved from https://ballotpedia.org/Top-two_primary

61 Miller, J., "Top-two and Open Primary Elections Produce Less Extreme Law-makers," *USC News*, May 21, 2020, retrieved from https://news.usc.edu/170366/top-two-open-primary-elections-less-extreme-lawmakers-usc-study/

62 Crosson, J., "Extreme Districts, Moderate Winners: Same Party Challenges, and Deter-rence in Top-two Primaries." 2018, *Political Science Research and Methods*, pp. 1–17.

63 "Myths and Facts," *Open Primaries*, (n.d.), retrieved from www.openprimaries.org/myths_and_facts

64 Grose, 2020; Crosson, 2018.

65 McGhee, E., & Shor, B., "Has the Top Two Primary Elected More Moderates?" 2017, *Perspectives on Politics* 15, no. 4, pp. 1053–1066, retrieved from doi:10.1017/S1537592717002158

66 Kambhampaty, A. P., "New York City Voters Just Adopted Ranked-Choice Voting in Elections. Here's How It Works," *Time*, November 6, 2019, retrieved from https://time.com/5718941/ranked-choice-voting/

67 DeLeon, R. E., *San Francisco and Instant Runoff Voting: An Analysis of the SFSU/PRI Exit Poll Data Assessing voter Opinions About Ranked Choice Voting in the November 2004 Board of Supervisors Elections*," 2005, retrieved from http://archive.fairvote.org/media/irv/deleon2004_sanfran.pdf

68 "Proportional Ranked Choice Voting," *FairVote*, (n.d.), retrieved from www.fairvote.org/prcv#how_prcv_works

69 "Supporting Ranked Choice Voting," *Election Reformers Network*, (n.d.), retrieved from https://electionreformers.org/supporting-ranked-choice-voting/; Cerrone, J., & McClintock, C., "*Ranked-Choice Voting, Runoff, and Democracy Insights from Maine and Other U.S. States,*" 2021, retrieved from https://papers.ssrn.com/sol3/papers.cfm?abstract_id=3769409

70 Brooks, A., "A Greater Choice" Or "Confusing": Arguments For And Against Ranked Choice Voting In WBUR Debate | WBUR News," *WBUR.Org*, October 14, 2020, retrieved from www.wbur.org/news/2020/10/14/wbur-debate-question-2-ranked-choice-voting

71 Gagnon, M. O. C., "Ranked-choice Voting Makes Elections Unnecessarily Complex and Confusing," *Bangor Daily News*, August 5, 2020, retrieved from https://bangordailynews.com/2020/08/05/opinion/ranked-choice-voting-makes-elections-unnecessarily-complex-and-confusing-2/

72 Rubinstein, D., Mays, J. C., & Fitzsimmons, E. G., "Why Some N.Y.C. Lawmakers Want to Rethink Ranked-Choice Voting," *The New York Times*, June 30, 2021, retrieved from www.nytimes.com/2020/12/09/nyregion/ranked-choice-lawsuit-voting.html

73 Vasilogambros, M., "Ranked-Choice Voting Gains Momentum Nationwide." *The Pew Charitable Trusts*, March 12, 2021, retrieved from www.pewtrusts.org/en/research-and-analysis/blogs/stateline/2021/03/12/ranked-choice-voting-gains-momentum-nationwide

74 FairVote.org, "Ranked Choice Voting/Instant Runoff," *FairVote*, 2021, retrieved from www.fairvote.org/rcv#where_is_ranked_choice_voting_used

75 See U.S. Congress website on sponsored bills and status www.congress.gov/bill/117th-congress/house-bill/4

76 Gruber, Jeremy, Hardy, Michael A., & Kresky, Harry, "Let All Voters Vote: Independents and the Expansion of Voting Rights in the United States," 2019, *Touro Law Review* 35, no. 2, Art. 4: 652.

77 Winger, Richard, editor, *Ballot Access News*, 2022, retrieved from https://ballot-access.org/

10

DEVELOPING DEMOCRACY

> When a man as uncouth and reckless as Trump becomes president by running against the nation's elites, it's a strong signal that the elites are the problem. We're talking here about the elites of both parties.
>
> —Robert W. Merry, 2017[1]

For 160 years there has been an enduring debate over the Emancipation Proclamation. The war powers pronouncement by President Abraham Lincoln was issued on January 1, 1863, formally abolishing slavery in the states and territories that remained in revolt against the Union two years into the Civil War. A dry and legalistic document, which some contended had no legal force, drew mixed reviews.

For some, like Ohio's Republican US Representative Albert Gallatin Riddle, it was "the greatest human utterance" that was "speaking a new world into being by Omnipotence."[2] The so-called radicals in Congress applauded the action.[3] According to William Stoddard, Lincoln's private secretary who copied the Proclamation, Lincoln's critics in the newspaper world "rose in anger to remind Lincoln that this is a war for the Union only, and they never gave him any authority to run it as an Abolition war."[4] Frederick Douglass, the great abolitionist and orator, an ally of Lincoln, gave a poignant and pitiless critique of the Proclamation:

> Had there been one expression of sound moral feeling against Slavery, one word of regret and shame that this accursed system had remained so long the disgrace and scandal of the Republic, one word of satisfaction in the hope of burying slavery and the rebellion in one common grave, a thrill of joy would have run round the world, but no such word was said, and no such joy was kindled.[5]

DOI: 10.4324/9781003240808-11

For his part, Lincoln had labored and vacillated over the document for at least two years, waiting to build his case as Congress passed a series of confiscatory acts that freed certain slaves in certain areas under certain conditions, and several of his military leaders issued their own emancipations in the field, in large measure to recruit newly freed slaves to fight for the Union army. Navigating the distance between his call to save the Union and his—some say reluctant—call to end the practice of human bondage, Lincoln seemingly believed that the timing of the Proclamation and the technical and passionless nature of the document would allow him to fuse the two: "Now we have got the harpoon fairly into the monster slavery, we must take care that in his extremity, he does not shipwreck the Country."[6]

Lincoln did not live to see the passage of the 13th Amendment, the act that did finally and legally abolish slavery in the United States of America. Nor did he live to see the era of Reconstruction, wherein the United States attempted, but largely failed, at a social, economic, and cultural reorganization to stamp out the legacy of slavery and integrate the Black population into the mainstream of the country's life.[7] Perhaps at its best, though, the Emancipation Proclamation was less a document than a moment when it was publicly acknowledged by a president that there could be no Union without abolition. That nothing could be transformed without everything being transformed.

It would be foolish and ahistorical to equate today's political divisions and the shortcomings of the present system with the horrors of slavery or the brutality of the United States's bloodiest and most violent war, even if it has become popular in some liberal and right-wing circles to do so. Barbara F. Walter—an expert on international security, with an emphasis on civil wars, and professor at the University of California at San Diego—in her new book, *How Civil War Starts*,[8] suggests the United States is closer to civil war than many think. Similarly, *the New York Times* columnist Thomas Friedman, in an article titled "The American Civil War, Part II," wrote:

"In a tribal world it's rule or die, compromise is a sin, enemies must be crushed, and power must be held at all costs."[9] But the hysteria and the commentary on the hysteria mask a fundamental failure in the US political system that has hit a critical point of no return. As political scientist Morris Fiorina at the Hoover Institute at Stanford University observed after the 2016 election,

> [T]he socioeconomic transformations occurring in the United States and around the world have created problems that call into question old solutions and cut across political coalitions. One might naively think that, in response, a healthy party system would show more creativity, but the parties have not become more creative.[10]

Far from it. Fiorina adds, "small wonder that 40% of the American citizenry declines to pledge allegiance to either party."[11]

If, as Fiorina and 40 percent of the country suggest, the US party system has proven to be unhealthy, how do we fix it? And if we are faced with a situation where the mechanisms for fixing the system are controlled by the parties themselves, how do the American people free ourselves from the bondage of partisanship? When, where, and how will we arrive at the moment, with leadership that is sufficiently independent and emboldened to declare it, that we can emancipate ourselves from an old and decaying party system and re-create a democracy for the 21st century?

None of the reforms outlined in Chapter 9 can ultimately "right the ship" in an environment where the entire system is under complete partisan control. Arguably, some could have the effect of intensifying that control if they are not part of a total reorganization. Through the lens of Herbert Croly,[12] the road to transformative reform will have to embrace more daring changes that weaken partisan control, lessen the role the parties play as mediators between the people and their government, and help citizens develop their civic capabilities. Perhaps, the United States needs a postmodern Emancipation Proclamation that inaugurates a multilevel campaign to abolish partisanship.

Expand the Nonpartisan Ballot

Nonpartisan elections are the norm at the local level for most county, municipal, and school board elections. This is a direct result of reforms that were ushered in at the turn of the last century during the Progressive Era to combat corruption and weaken the reign of party bosses and machine politics. The Progressives believed that by removing partisan politics, the entrenched machines dominating local governments would crack, making room for municipal governments to be more responsive to their citizens. In addition to the nonpartisan ballot, other reforms during this period included measures allowing direct democracy tools for citizens, such as citizen initiatives and options to recall elected officials (primarily in the West), the secret ballot and direct primaries, and the introduction of the council-manager form of government, which allowed councils to appoint nonpartisan professionally trained city mangers to oversee operations.[13]

Today, all these reforms have been broadly adopted, with the nonpartisan ballot for local elections almost universally embraced. Over three-quarters of local governments currently elect their representatives through nonpartisan ballots.[14] Nonpartisan elections for judges are also common, as less than 20 percent of states elect their judges at the Supreme Court, intermediate, appellate, or general jurisdiction level in a partisan matter.[15] Likewise, most school board elections are nonpartisan.[16] Nebraska has the only state legislature that is entirely nonpartisan.

Despite the widespread adoption of many of the Progressive Era reforms that sought to weaken control of the two political parties, many scholars have asserted that parties are essential to ensuring a strong democracy. American political scientist and educator E. E. Schattschneider, in his book *Party Government* (1942), famously proclaimed:

> The political parties created democracy and . . . modern democracy is unthinkable save in terms of the parties. . . . The parties are not therefore merely appendages of modern government; they are in the center of it and play a determinative and creative role in it.[17]

Party identification has long been a chief component of voter decision-making;[18] therefore, it is not surprising that much of the research on nonpartisan elections has focused on how voters would make decisions without referring to the cues and political playbook of the parties. Would voters be less informed and less likely to vote if they are required to learn (or at least be generally familiar with) the platforms of every candidate? And in the absence of a party ballot, what cues would they use?

Early research suggested that nonpartisan ballots provide an advantage to Republican candidates due to a combination of voter behavior and resource differences.[19] However, studies that found the Republican-advantage premise were done earlier in an era of urban politics. More recent reexamination has either found this effect to be minimal or nonexistent; and more recent studies have found that taking away party labels has been shown to increase chances of minority party candidates.[20] Absent party labels, voters tend to rely on a broad range of cues available to them, such as gender, race, ethnicity, religion, prestige, occupational background, and incumbency.[21] This is especially true for down-ballot candidates. Voter information devoid of partisan ideology is critical for these nonpartisan elections.

Nonpartisan elections have dominated the landscape of local governments for the past century and have been an effective tool in reducing the gamesmanship that goes on in party politics. In nonpartisan primaries, candidates can more easily express their actual beliefs, rather than pander to their party and craft their positions on issues to appeal to the more ideological voters who tend to turn out more often for partisan primaries. It also eliminates blind, straight-party voting where uninformed voters follow their party regardless of the merits of the individual candidates.

A critical step toward reversing the decline in our democracy and freeing us from the two-party death grip suffocating us would be to expand nonpartisan elections and nonpartisan appointments dramatically and significantly. This includes not only making further inroads at the local government level and judicial offices but expanding the nonpartisan ballot upward to include governorships, state constitutional offices, state legislators (similar to Nebraska's unicameral system), and even Congressional and Senate offices.

Everything associated with elections—including election boards, Secretary of State offices and other senior officials overseeing elections, as well as the composition of the FEC—should be nonpartisan. In 33 of the 50 states, the position of secretary of state is elected in a partisan manner.[22] With the growing distrust that currently exists over the neutrality of our elections, how in the world does it make sense to have election officials run as partisans and thus be accountable to a party when their job is to be neutral referees of elections? In races for 2022, state and county offices with direct oversight of elections, a number of outspoken Trump loyalists supporting his discredited claims about the 2020 election are front-runners in Republican primaries for secretary of state across the United States.[23] Regardless of the outcome of those contests, the fact that electoral process matters are so permeated with partisan political agendas is a measure of the deterioration of American democracy.

The United States is the only democracy in the world that permits partisan contests for election officials. In other democracies, elections are run by independent commissions or governmental agencies shielded from political influence.[24] Senior elections officials who oversee federal, state, and local elections must either be appointed by neutral bodies or via a neutral nonpartisan selection process or, if elected, run as a nonpartisan. Furthermore, these officials should be required to swear an oath of impartiality or face recall or removal.

As previously mentioned, the FEC, created in 1974, whose purpose is to enforce campaign-finance laws in US federal elections,[25] is the only federal regulatory agency with an even number of commissioners to guarantee equity between the two major parties. There are no members who are nonaligned, nonpartisan, and/or independent. The Commission has been designed to deadlock with six members as a way to ensure the two-party system remains dominant in the United States. This Commission should at a minimum have nonpartisan representation and an odd number of members; however, ideally, its entire membership should comprise nonaligned and nonpartisan individuals. Its job is to protect the integrity of the electoral process, not the relative or combined interests of the parties.

Nebraska's Democracy Reforms

Expanding the nonpartisan ballot upwards from local government to state and federal offices would eliminate a significant part of the divisiveness, gridlock, and the "two authoritative partisan organizations between the people and their government."[26] The state that has done this (at least at the state level) and has gone the furthest in dealing with the problem of the entrenched two-party system holistically is Nebraska. In 1934, Nebraskans enacted a broad set of democracy reforms, voting to eliminate half their state legislature and enact a nonpartisan election system. Nebraska's legislature is unique among all state legislatures in the nation because it has a single-house system, a unicameral legislature. Unicameralism is the practice of having only one legislative chamber.[27] Unlike other states, Nebraska's legislative leadership is not based on party affiliation, and it is the only state legislature that is entirely nonpartisan.

As part of the democracy reforms, Nebraska also enacted top-two nonpartisan primaries for the legislature, abolished party identification in the legislature, and abolished the partisan committee structure and minority/majority caucus structure. The Legislature's nonpartisan structure has allowed the formation of alliances and inter-party strategizing as the norm, not the exception. Coalitions have developed issue by issue, including tackling messy topics and passing legislation abolishing the death penalty, implementing immigration reform, raising the gasoline tax, and increasing the minimum wage.[28]

The cumulative impact of these reforms is significant but far from comprehensive. Nebraska still has gerrymandering, and the nonpartisan system is used only for the state legislature, not statewide or for federal offices. And even within the nonpartisan legislature, partisan politics surfaces in a million ways. But it's a state that took a shot at removing the role of the parties in several ways at once, and it seems to have impacted the culture and legislative behavior.[29]

Conclusion

How can we expand on the Nebraska experiment and develop more "holistic combinations" of democracy reform? How can we free American voters from the corrosive control of political parties?

This would require a clear and inviolable *separation between the institutions of government and the functions of political parties.* Any and all offices that govern, adjudicate, or administer any aspects of the electoral process must be elected without party affiliation. For those positions that are made by appointment, appointees must be independent of party designation. Bipartisan does not equal nonpartisan. Any and all elections for public office should include all voters, regardless of their stated affiliations. No American should be required to join a political party or organization as a condition of voting. No taxpayer dollars should be used for party business, including primaries, if the parties decide to hold them as a means of endorsing a candidate. No constraints on voter or candidate mobility should be permitted. Sore-loser laws, which are in effect in 47 states,[30] and currently bar candidates from running as an independent if they lose a primary, should be abolished. Anti-fusion laws in place in 42 states that prevent political coalitions from forming should be abolished. Maximum fluidity and flexibility should be the watchwords. Any and all laws and regulations enacted by the parties to protect their incumbency, control, or advantage should be declared unconstitutional. Ballot access laws should be fair, equitable, and nondiscriminatory against independents. Section 5 of the Voting Rights Act should be restored. Voter registration should be automatic and nonpartisan. It is not the job of the states or taxpayers to maintain voter rolls for the parties.

In sum, these reforms and others that seal off the destructive and distortive influence of partisanship are not sufficient to save our democracy. Only the American people—mobilized, empowered, educated, and creative—can accomplish that. Independent voters—in their search for the politics of otherness, statement of noncompliance, and volatile antiestablishment leanings—have begun to show the way.

Notes

1 Robert, W. Merry, "Removing Trump Won't Solve America's Crisis," *America Conservative*, May 18, 2017, retrieved December 26, 2021, from www.theamericanconservative.com/articles/removing-trump-wont-solve-americas-crisis/

2 Guelzo, Allen, *Lincoln's Emancipation Proclamation: The End of Slavery in America*, Simon & Schuster, 2006, p. 178.

3 Ibid.

4 Ibid, p. 179.

5 Douglass, Frederick, *Douglass' Monthly*, January 1863, retrieved from https://transcription.si.edu/view/13223/ACM-2007.19.27_02

6 Guelzo, Ibid, p. 160.

7 Reconstruction began in 1863 with Union control of the Upper South but mostly went into effect after the conclusion of the Civil War in 1865. See Foner, Eric, *Reconstruction: America's Unfinished Revolution, 1863–1877*, Harper Perennial Modern Classics, 2014.

8 Walter, Barbara, *How Civil War Starts: And How to Stop Them*, Crown Publishing, 2022.

9 Friedman, T., "The American Civil War, Part II," *The New York Times*, October 2, 2018, retrieved from www.nytimes.com/2018/10/02/opinion/the-american-civil-war-part-ii.html

10 Fiorina, Morris P., *Unstable Majorities, Polarization, Party Sorting & Political Stalemate*, Hoover Institution Press, 2017, pp. 218–219.

11 Ibid.

12 Croly, H. D., *Progressive democracy*. Macmillan Co., 1914.

13 Partisanship in United States municipal elections, 2017. *Ballotpedia*. (2017), retrieved 2021, from https://ballotpedia.org/Partisanship_in_United_States_municipal_elections,_2017#History_of_local_nonpartisanship; Reilly, T., *The Failure of Governance in Bell, California*, Lexington Books, 2016; Wright, G., "Charles Adrian and the Study of Nonpartisan Elections," *Political Research Quarterly* 61, no. 1, pp. 13–16, 2008; Schaffner, B. F., Streb, M., & Wright, G., "Teams Without Uniforms: The Nonpartisan Ballot in State and Local Elections," 2001, *Political Research Quarterly* 54, no. 1, pp. 7–30.

14 Cities 101—Partisan and Non-partisan Elections, *National League of Cities*, October 23, 2020, retrieved 2021, from www.nlc.org/resource/cities-101-partisan-and-non-partisan-elections/

15 "Nonpartisan Election of Judges," *Ballotpedia*, (n.d.), retrieved 2021, from https://ballotpedia.org/Nonpartisan_election_of_judges

16 "*Nonpartisan*" *Ballotpedia*, n.d., retrieved from https://ballotpedia.org/Nonpartisan

17 Schattschneider, E., *Party Government*, Farrar & Rinehart, 1942, p. 1.

18 Campbell, A., *The American Voter*, J. Wiley & Sons, 1960.

19 Hawley, W. D., *Nonpartisan Elections and the Case for Party Politics*, John Wiley, 1973; Lascher, E., "The Case of the Missing Democrats: Reexamining the Republican Advantage in Nonpartisan Elections," 1991, *Western Political Quarterly*, 44, pp. 656–75; Lee, E. C., *The Politics of Nonpartisanship: A Study of California City Elections*, University of California Press, 1960.

20 Schaffner, B. F., Streb, M., & Wright, G., "A New Look at the Republican Advantage in Nonpartisan Elections," 2007, *Political Science Quarterly*, 54, pp. 7–30.

21 Adams, B., Lascher, E., & Martin, D., "Ballot Cues, Business Candidates, and Voter Choices in Local Elections," 2020, *American Political Research*, July 16, 2020; Bonneau, C. W., & Cann, D. M., "Party Identification and Vote Choice in Partisan and Nonpartisan Elections," 2015, *Political Behavior* 37, no. 1, pp. 43–66; Kirkland, P. A., & Coppock, A., "Candidate Choice Without Party Labels," 2018, *Political Behavior* 40, pp. 571–91; Wright, 2008; Schaffner, Streb, & Wright, 2001; Matson, M., & Fine, T., "Gender, Ethnicity, and Ballot information: Ballot Cues in Low-information

Elections," 2006, *State Politics and Policy Quarterly*, 6, pp. 49–72; Smith, R., & Squire, P., "The Effects of Prestige Names in Question Wording." 1990, *Public Opinion Quarterly*, 54, pp. 97–116; Squire, P., & Smith, R., "The Effect of Partisan Information on Voters in Nonpartisan Elections," 1988, *Journal of Politics*, 50, pp. 169–79; Jacobson, G. C., *The Politics of Congressional Elections*, fourth edition, Longman, 1997; Jewell, M. E., & Breaux, D., "The Effect of Incumbency on State Legislative Elections," 1988, *Legislative Studies Quarterly*, 13, pp. 495–514.

22 Wikimedia Foundation, "United States Secretary of State," *Wikipedia*, December 5, 2021, retrieved 2021, from https://en.wikipedia.org/wiki/United_States_Secretary_of_State

23 Homans, C., "Trump Loyalists Speed Into Jobs Overseeing Votes," *The New York Times*, 2021.

24 United States: Freedom in the World 2021, *Country Report, Freedom House*. (n.d.), retrieved 2021, from https://freedomhouse.org/country/united-states/freedom-world/2021; Diamond, L., Johnson, K., & Rapoport, M., "The Time Has Come for Nonpartisan State Election Leadership," *The Hill*, April 4, 2021, retrieved from https://thehill.com/opinion/campaign/546307-the-time-has-come-for-nonpartisan-state-election-leadership

25 Wikimedia Foundation, "Federal Election Commission," *Wikipedia*, November 15, 2021, retrieved from https://en.wikipedia.org/wiki/Federal_Election_Commission

26 Croly, H., *Progressive Democracy*, The Macmillan Company, 1914.

27 "Unicameralism," Ballotpedia. (2020), retrieved December 14, 2021, from https://ballotpedia.org/Unicameralism

28 "Nebraska Legislature—History of the Unicameral." *Nebraska Legislature* (n.d.), retrieved 2021, from https://nebraskalegislature.gov/about/history_unicameral.php; Gruber, J., "The Myth of the Red State," *Open Primaries*, 2015, retrieved from www.openprimaries.org/research_nebraska

29 *Nebraska Legislature.*

30 According to Ballotpedia, all states have sore loser laws, with the exception of Connecticut, Iowa, and New York. See: https://ballotpedia.org/When_states_adopted_sore_loser_laws.

AFTERWORD

Difference Without Separability

—Denise Ferreira da Silva[1]

Reilly, Salit, and Ali have produced a thoroughly well-documented harbinger of a transformative movement of voters outside of the moribund but still dominant US two-party system. Their analysis reflects the multidimensional diversity of those American voters who choose to affiliate other than with the two major political parties. Independents whose emergence defies ideological categorization are outside the political establishment but at the core of creating cutting-edge unorthodox processes for ordinary people to drive a broad expansion and revitalization of American democracy.

Independents have been catalysts for change throughout American history, and two major parties have consolidated their control of politics and elections such that today partisanship is constitutive of government. About 40–50 percent of the electorate, 70 million people, are independent voters. Independents are shut out by party control. The inclusion of independent voters requires more democracy, it requires opening the primaries, it requires a redistricting process not based on a balance between the two major parties but based on a nonpartisan process led by ordinary citizens. Independents are calling for nothing less than a total rebirth and renewal of American democracy.

At the nation's founding African Americans were constitutionally excluded from citizenship in the country which was largely built on their enslaved bodies. But there were those enslaved and free, of color and white, who spoke out and petitioned to combine opposition to slavery with the cause of American independence.[2] It took a Civil War to end slavery and then a Civil Rights Movement to begin to dismantle structural racism and fully integrate African Americans within the American nation—a purpose and promise still unfulfilled. A fundamental question remains as to whether independents can lead reform of our democracy for the full participation of all. Independent movements and leaders, as the authors detail, are trying to answer that question in the affirmative.

The methodology of independents *Bridging the Political Divide* is explored. The two parties divide the American people but quickly join together in direct opposition to any threat to their mutual vested interest in controlling the political mainstream. The phone conversations by Independent Voting volunteer callers, who consider themselves progressives, to independents who had voted for Donald Trump in the 2020 election were examples of the kind of bridge building needed to cross ideological divides. One of the callers pointed out that *"Listening is learning. I am not aware of a more transformative tool for escaping the painful abyss of our current political environment. Without it, we have nowhere to go."* Indeed, such qualitative listening and dialogue creates the possibility of moving beyond ideology and coming together to build an inclusive American community.

In the United States, the sacred fact of the vote as a nonviolent tool has meaning beyond preference for a particular candidate or party, as Taylor Branch writes in *At Canaan's Edge America in the King Years 1965–68,* "the most basic element of free government—the vote . . . Every ballot is a piece of nonviolence, signifying hard-won consent to raise politics above firepower and bloody conquest." The African-American community's long fight for full voting rights continues in the face of voter suppression today, independent voters join in demanding full and equal voting rights in all rounds of elections including the primaries. No person should be required to join a political party to exercise the right to vote.

The crisis in American democracy of governmental dysfunction, political polarization, voter suppression, closed primaries, restricted ballot access, closed debates, and gerrymandered districts extend into matters of life and death for the American people. We have experienced the ongoing crisis from the pandemic, which is occurring in the midst of a crisis in access to decent housing, quality education, employment, and the so-called *diseases of despair*—alcoholism, depression, and drug use. Millions have died due to the lack of quality health for all. A massive infusion of nonpartisanship into all aspects of government to prioritize the health and well-being of the American people over partisan self-interest is needed. Independents are an important force to bring about such better possibilities for our country meant for all.

American Dream

All to make impossibly possible
Political emancipation abstract able to fly
Standing on the cold concrete city streets
Near high rise projects and elite stores

And muddy back roads and farms of small towns
Petitioning with people from all over and back then
At Lexington and Concord at Philadelphia at Gettysburg
At Selma still. Are they free yet? Can we be?
All the declarations and intentions gone awry
Like the plants unable to breathe die
Like the last best hope she could only whisper dissent
Like the wind take her up listen ensemble sing.
Day begins again let us all begin again with none left behind
Where are all the dead except everywhere.
Can we end violence? Dr. King believed and was killed
What are we to do now? War everywhere and within.
Fragments fear, hard as the broken pieces breaking broken promises
Somehow we can write the country together anew
Even after all we have been through together make it all for all.

—Jessie Fields

Notes

1   Ferreira da Silva, D., *On Difference Without Separability*, Fundaca Bienal de Sao Paulo, 2016, pp. 57–65.
2   Ali, O., *In the Balance of Power Independent Black Politics and Third Party Movements in the United States*, Ohio University Press, 2020, pp. 14–17; Ortiz, P., *An African American and Latinx History of the United States*, Beacon Press, 2018, pp. 14–18.

TIMELINE

1776—Thomas Jefferson pens the Declaration of Independence, with the notion of inalienable rights, including "Life, Liberty, and the Pursuit of Happiness."

1789—The US Constitution is ratified with two clauses significantly entrenching slavery—Article One providing that three-fifths of the slave population is to be counted for purposes of taxation and representation in the House of Representatives and Article Four affirming the right of slave masters to recover runaway slaves.

1796—George Washington's farewell address warns against partisanship and its corrosive nature in governance.

1804–2—Tertium quids, which were various factions within the Democratic-Republican Party, are more opposed to the Federalist Party's policies than moderates within their own party. Such formations express the limitations of an emerging bipartisan system to capture the range of voices and interests outside the dominant parties.

1828—The Democratic Party is founded with Andrew Jackson as its standard-bearer; the party promotes an expansion of voting rights among white men.

1840—The Liberty Party, whose leaders call for the immediate abolition of slavery, is created in the face of bipartisan opposition by the Democratic and Whig parties.

1848—The women's rights movement is launched at the Seneca Falls Convention. The movement grows out of abolitionist circles and leaders.

1854—The Republican Party wins a plurality of seats in Congress, shifting the balance of power and beginning to displace the Whigs as the other major party.

1860—Abraham Lincoln is elected US president as the Republican candidate; the Whigs are fully displaced, ushering in the two parties that will dominate the United States through the present.

1861—Beginning of the Civil War with secession of Confederate states in the South from the Union; more than 720,000 people are killed in the four-year-long war.

1863—Reconstruction begins in the federally controlled northern part of the South; Reconstruction is the federal government's effort to rebuild the infrastructure of the South, where the war was largely fought, and the political institutions of the region.

1865–70—Ratification of the 13th, 14th, and 15th Amendments to the US Constitution abolishing slavery, extending citizenship to all African Americans, and giving Black men, 21 and older, the right to vote.

1877—End of Reconstruction with a compromise between the Democratic and Republican parties over Electoral College votes, allowing Republicans to take presidency with a promise to end federal efforts to reconstruct the South.

1890—Formation of the People's Party as part of the Black and white Populist movements.

1892—James B. Weaver runs on the People's Party ticket for president and wins approximately 9 percent of the vote.

1895—Fusion between Populists and Republicans in North Carolina win the majority of the state legislature; South Carolina begins to enact Jim Crow, the legal segregation, and disfranchisement of African Americans.

1898—Wilmington Riot in North Carolina, where Democrats overthrow the Populist-Republican-led local government through violence, killing hundreds of African Americans and effectively ending Populism in the state.

1900—Jim Crow takes hold across most of the South, leading to new challenges for independent political organizing.

1912—The "Bull Moose" Party of Theodore Roosevelt receives the largest percentage of the vote for a minor party in the 20th century; W. E. B. Du Bois initially builds a black base in the Progressive Party in 1912, but in subsequent elections supports the Socialist Party.

1920—19th Amendment passed for women's right to vote; Socialist presidential candidate Eugene V. Debs runs for office from jail.

1929—Stock market crash leads to widespread economic uncertainty and will ultimately prompt the labor movement to apply sufficient pressure on the government of Democrat Franklin D. Roosevelt to enact New Deal legislation.

1935—Key concessions made to labor movement by the Democratic Party, which will come to include the direct relief of the unemployed, minimum-wage legislation, a public works program, unemployment and old age insurance, and the abolition of child labor.

1939–43—The Communist Party and American Labor Party are active in New York City and, with the latter, in areas of the South, including Alabama, Georgia, North Carolina, Texas, and Virginia.

1948—Former Vice President Henry Wallace runs for US president with the Progressive Party, breaking with the Democratic Party; "Dixiecrat" Strom Thurmond runs for president on the States' Rights Democratic Party.

1960—Woolworth's lunch counter sit-in movement is launched in Greensboro, North Carolina; as part of the burgeoning Civil Rights Movement, African Americans form the Afro-American Party in Alabama to protest the Democratic Party's disfranchisement of Black voters in the state.

1964—Malcolm X gives his "Ballot or the Bullet" speech. Fannie Lou Hammer speaks at the Democratic National Convention in Atlantic City representing the Mississippi Freedom Democratic Party.

1965—The Voting Rights Act is passed, along with the Civil Rights Act the year prior, helping legally dismantle Jim Crow.

1966—The Black Panther Party is formed in Oakland, California, and will partner with the Peace and Freedom Party in the presidential campaign.

1968—Dr. Martin Luther King Jr. organizes the Poor People's Campaign in Washington, DC, to demand economic justice for the poor. There are efforts to recruit him to run for US president as an independent; Black Panther leader Eldridge Cleaver is nominated to run for US president on the Peace and Freedom Party line. In *Williams v. Rhodes*, the Supreme Court declared Ohio's 15 percent petition unconstitutional and placed the American Independent Party and its presidential candidate, George Wallace, on the ballot. The Court said the Ohio law violated the Equal Protection Clause of the 14th Amendment.

1971—The 26th Amendment to US Constitution is ratified, lowering the voting age from 21 to 18; the Libertarian Party is formed; in *Jenness v. Fortson* the Supreme Court affirmed a Georgia law requiring minor-party candidates to obtain the signatures of 5 percent of eligible voters on their nominating petitions. The 5 percent figure would become the benchmark for the number of signatures required of independent and minor-party candidates.

1972—The National Black Political Convention meets in Gary, Indiana, to discuss which political path is best for the Black community. Gary's mayor, Richard Hatcher, strongly advocates for a multiracial independent political alternative; in *Bullock v. Carter*, the Supreme Court declared the Texas primary filing fee system, which required the payment of fees as high as $8,900, unconstitutional on the grounds that it violated the Equal Protection Clause of the 14th Amendment.

1974—In *American Party of Texas v. White*, the Supreme Court upheld the Texas ballot access requirements for minor parties and independent candidates, including a 55-day petitioning period, starting the day after the primary election, and the barring of all primary voters from signing such petitions.

1975—The FEC is founded as a strictly bipartisan body after the Watergate-era scandals and charged with enforcing strict standards for campaign fundraising and spending set out in the 1974 amendments to the FECA, originally passed in 1971.

1976—In *Buckley v. Valeo* the Supreme Court decision found that statutory limits on campaign contributions were not violations of the 1st Amendment freedom of expression but that statutory limits on campaign spending were unconstitutional.

1979—The New Alliance Party is formed; the following year, Black nationalists and socialists convene in New Orleans to form the National Black Independent Political Party but it soon dissolves, urging a "Black revolt within the Democratic Party." Also, in *Illinois v. Socialist Workers Party*, the Supreme Court rendered unconstitutional an Illinois law that new political parties and independent candidates for elections in political subdivisions (specifically Chicago) gather more than the number of signatures required for elections for statewide office.

1983—In *Anderson v. Celebrezze*, the Supreme Court held that Ohio's March deadline for independent presidential candidates violated the 1st and 14th Amendments of the US Constitution, placing an unconstitutional burden on the voting and associational rights of supporters of independent presidential candidates, a decision cited as a precedent in all succeeding challenges to early filling deadlines.

1984—After garnering three and a half million votes, Rev. Jesse Jackson is denied the Democratic Party presidential nomination.

1987—The Harold Washington Party, named after the first African-American mayor of Chicago, gains popular support; the pseudo-governmental and bipartisan CPD is formed.

1988—Dr. Lenora Fulani, a developmental psychologist and educator, becomes the first woman and the first African American to have her name appear on the ballot of all 50 states and Washington, DC, running as an independent and third-party candidate for US president. She is excluded from the debates by the CPD and sues the IRS, asking that it withdraw tax-exempt status from the CPD because, in failing to provide objective criteria through which candidates could qualify for the debates, the CPD acted in a partisan manner. Fulani loses, but in a dissenting opinion, Judge Abner Mikva contends that the failure of the courts to grant Fulani standing and allow her case to be heard on its merits "insulates from review federal complicity in keeping minor political parties off the national stage."

1992—Ross Perot runs for US president as an independent and receives nearly 20 million votes or 19 percent; Fulani runs again for US president as an independent. Her Committee for Fair Elections challenges bipartisan control of the political process.

1995—The Reform Party is formed, building on the networks of the Patriot Party in order to support structural electoral reforms. The FEC adopts new rules, whereby debate sponsors must select the participants based on preexisting nonpartisan objective criteria. The CUIP succeeds in causing a change in the FEC regulations.

1998—The Working Families Party is formed.

2000—The Joint Center for Political and Economic Studies notes a discernible shift among African Americans away from the Democratic Party; meanwhile, a suit is filed by the CUIP in US District Court of the Southern District, which includes representatives from the Libertarian, Green, and Reform parties, aimed to overturn FEC regulations that allow the CPD to shut out third-party candidates by requiring that candidates garner the support of 15 percent of voters in national polls before they may participate. The suit is dismissed on the grounds that plaintiffs lacked standing.

2001—Michael Bloomberg is elected mayor of New York City, running as a fusion candidate on the Independence Party and Republican Party lines and supports nonpartisan electoral reforms; the national Green Party is formed.

2004—CUIP activists launched the "Let Nader Debate" campaign, a grassroots petitioning effort that called for independent presidential candidate Ralph Nader's inclusion into the debates. Thousands of signatures are gathered and sent to President George W. Bush in an open letter urging him to use his authority as president to intervene in the matter.

2007—At the May 2007 presidential debate, Democratic candidates John Edwards and Hillary Clinton were caught off camera saying they wanted to limit participation in the debates. Independents wrote letters to DNC chair Howard Dean protesting exclusion of candidates from the debates.

2008—Georgia Congresswoman Cynthia McKinney runs as the Green Party's presidential candidate; meanwhile the "Who decided Hillary was best for the Black Community?" campaign challenges the Democratic Party's support of US Senator Hillary Clinton over insurgent Barack Obama.

2012—Despite Black and white independents serving as the margin of victory for President Obama, the Democratic Party rejects an alliance with independents. President Obama believes, but it has become apparent, that it is not possible to reform the Democratic Party from within.

2013—In *Shelby County v. Holder*, the Supreme Court declares Section 5 of the Voting Rights Act to be unconstitutional, nullifying a critical component of the 1965 Voting Rights Act.

2016—Two million voters do not vote for the Democratic Party nominee, Hillary Clinton, in the general election, despite strong appeals by President Barack Obama and First Lady Michelle Obama; Black voter turnout for the Democratic Party drops 5 percentage points from the previous national election; Donald Trump running as the Republican candidate wins the presidency.

2018—Independent voters back Democratic congressional candidates by a margin of 12 points two years after the election of Trump to the US presidency.

2019—In *Rucho v. Common*, the Supreme Court effectively closed the door on using the federal courts as an option to combat redistricting abuses by ruling 5–4 that there was no objective standard for adjudication when determining whether a map went too far in locking in partisan advantage.

2020—The COVID-19 pandemic creates profound political and economic uncertainty across the nation, with disproportionate numbers of African Americans affected in urban centers, such as New York and Atlanta.

2021—Gallup records a high of 50 percent independent self-identification in its January 21–February 2 national poll.

BIBLIOGRAPHY

Preface

Croly, H. D. (1914). *Progressive Democracy*. New York: Macmillan Co.

Gallup, Inc., (2021, January 29). Party Affiliation | Gallup Historical Trends. *Gallup.Com*. Retrieved from: https://news.gallup.com/poll/15370/party-affiliation.aspx

Introduction

Abrams, S., and Fiorina, M. (2011). *Are Leaning Independents Deluded or Dishonest Weak Partisans?* CISE-ITANES Conference, Roma, Italy.

Ali, Omar H. (2020). *In the Balance of Power, Independent Black Politics and Third-Party Movements in the United States*. Athens, OH: Ohio University Press.

CNN. (2020). "National Results 2020 President Exit Polls." *CNN*. Retrieved from: www.cnn.com/election/2020/exit-polls/president/national-results

CNN. (2021). "Georgia 2020 U.S. Senate Runoff Exit Polls." *CNN*. Retrieved from: www.cnn.com/election/2020/exit-polls/president/georgia

Croly, H. (1914). *Progressive Democracy*. New York, NY: The Macmillan Company.

De Pinto, J., and Backus, F. (2020, November 7). "How Biden Won the 2020 Election: Exit Poll Analysis." *CBS News*. Retrieved from: www.cbsnews.com/news/election-2020-exit-poll-analysis-how-biden-became-the-projected-winner/

Gallup, Inc. (2021, January 29). "Party Affiliation." *Gallup*. Retrieved from: https://news.gallup.com/poll/15370/party-affiliation.aspx

Gruber, J., and Opdyke, J. (2020). "The Next Great Migration: The Rise of Independent Voters." *Open Primaries*. openprimaries.org, New York. Retrieved from: https://openprimarieseducationfund.org/wp-content/uploads/2020/11/ROI_Report_R1.pdf.

Jones, J. M. (2022, January 17). "U.S. Political Party Preferences Shifted Greatly During 2021." *Gallup*. Retrieved from: https://news.gallup.com/poll/388781/political-party-preferences-shifted-greatly-during-2021.aspx.

Keith, B. E., Magleby, D. B., Nelson, C. J., Orr, E., Westlye, M. C., and Wolfinger, R. E. (1992). *The Myth of the Independent Voter.* Los Angeles, CA: University of California Press.

Pew Research Center. (2014, March 7). "Millennials in Adulthood." *Pew Research Center.* Retrieved from: www.pewresearch.org/social-trends/2014/03/07/millennials-in-adulthood/

Pew Research Center. (2019, December 31). "Trends in Party Affiliation Among Demographic Groups." *Pew Research Center.* Retrieved from: www.pewresearch.org/politics/2018/03/20/1-trends-in-party-affiliation-among-demographic-groups/

Salit, J. (2017, June). "Finding Otherness: A Blueprint for an Independent Conversation About 2020." *Independent Voting.* Retrieved from: www.dropbox.com/s/4xdwahq4afm1sjb/Finding%20Otherness%20by%20J%20Salit.pdf?dl=0

Salit, J., and Reilly, T. (2020). "Can Independent Voters Save American Democracy?" In Orr, D. et al. (Eds), *Democracy Unchained: How to Rebuild Government for the People.* New York, NY: The New Press. pp. 323–336.

Statista. (2020, March 12). "Share of U.S. Iraq and Afghanistan Veterans by Political Party 2020." *Statista.* Retrieved from: www.statista.com/statistics/976355/share-us-iraq-afghanistan-veterans-political-party/

Walter, A. (2021, November 30). "Biden Has Slipped With Independents, Can He Win Them Back?." *Cook Political Report.* Retrieved from: www.cookpolitical.com/analysis/national/national-politics/biden-has-slipped-independents-can-he-win-them-back

Chapter 1

Baldwin, J. (1998). "*The Discovery of What It Means to Be An American,*" *James Baldwin: Collected Essays,* The Library of America, p. 137.

Balz, D., and Clement, S. (2017, April 23). "Nearing 100 Days, Trump's Approval at Record Lows but His Base is Holding." *The Washington Post.* Retrieved from: www.washingtonpost.com/politics/nearing-100-days-trumps-approval-at-record-lows-but-his-base-is-holding/2017/04/22/a513a466–26b4–11e7-b503–9d616bd5a305_story.html

Broder, D. S. (1993, July 7). "Perot: A Midsummer Night's Dream—or Nightmare." *The Washington Post.* Retrieved from: www.washingtonpost.com/archive/opinions/1993/07/11/perot-a-midsummer-nights-dream-or-nightmare/08c73b41-b85b-43f6-be8d-d3e62e070779/

Campbell, A., Converse, P. E., Miller, W. E., and Stokes, D. E. (1960). *The American Voter* (unabridged edition). Chicago, IL: University of Chicago Press. pp. 137, 537–538, 553.

CNN. (2008). "Election Center 2008 Exit Poll Data." *CNN.* Retrieved from: www.cnn.com/ELECTION/2008/results/polls.main/

CNN. (2016). "2016 U.S. Presidential Election Exit Polls." *CNN.* Retrieved from: www.cnn.com/election/2016/results/exit-polls

CNN. (2020a). "Arizona Election Results 2020 Presidential Election." *CNN.* Retrieved from: www.cnn.com/election/2020/exit-polls/president/arizona

CNN. (2020b). "Georgia Election Results 2020 Presidential Election." *CNN.* Retrieved from: www.cnn.com/election/2020/exit-polls/president/georgia

CNN. (2020c). "National Election Results 2020 Presidential Election." *CNN.* Retrieved from: www.cnn.com/election/2020/exit-polls/president/national-results

CNN. (2020d). "Pennsylvania Election Results 2020 Presidential Election." *CNN.* Retrieved from: www.cnn.com/election/2020/exit-polls/president/pennsylvania

CNN. (2020e). "Wisconsin Election Results 2020 Presidential Election." *CNN*. Retrieved from: www.cnn.com/election/2020/exit-polls/president/wisconsin.

Cook, C. (2020, June 26). "As Is Their Habit, Independents Seem to Be Breaking Against the Incumbent." *The Cook Political Report*. Retrieved from: www.cookpolitical.com/analysis/national/national-politics/their-habit-independents-seem-be-breaking-against-incumbent

Craighill, P. (2014, April 1). "Iraq and Afghan Vets are Conservative. But They're Not all Republicans." *The Washington Post*. Retrieved from: www.washingtonpost.com/news/the-fix/wp/2014/04/01/iraq-and-afghan-vets-are-conservative-but-theyre-not-all-republicans

CSPAN. (1993, July 7). "Ross Perot Voter Survey." *CSPAN*. Retrieved from: www.c-span.org/video/?44509-1/ross-perot-voter-survey

Drutman, L. (2019, September 24). "The Moderate Middle Is a Myth." *FiveThirtyEight*. Retrieved from: https://fivethirtyeight.com/features/the-moderate-middle-is-a-myth/

Fukuyama, F. (1992). *The End of History and the Last Man*. New York, NY: Free Press.

Fukuyama, F. (2011). *The Origins of Political Order: From Prehuman Times to the French Revolution*. New York, NY: Farrar, Straus & Giroux. pp. 7.

Geoffrey, S. (2017, June 1). "Just How Many Obama 2012-Trump 2016 Voters Were There?" *UVA Center for Politics*. Retrieved from: https://centerforpolitics.org/crystalball/articles/just-how-many-obama-2012-trump-2016-voters-were-there/

Heilemann, J. (2009, January 19). "The New Politics: Barack Obama: Party of One." *New York Magazine*. Retrieved from: https://nymag.com/news/features/all-new/53380/.

Hickey, P. (2021, July 22). "Declaration of Independents—Nevada's New Voters." *Reno Gazette Journal*. Retrieved from: https://eu.rgj.com/story/opinion/columnists/2021/07/22/declaration-independents-nevadas-new-voters-pat-hickey/8053360002/

Holzman, L., and Morss, J. (2000). *Postmodern Psychologies, Societal Practice, and Political Life*. Abingdon: Routledge. pp. 169–170.

Karp, W. (1993). *Indispensable Enemies: The Politics of Misrule in America*. New York, NY: Franklin Square Press. pp. 22.

Gallup. (2021). "Party Affiliation." *Gallup*. Retrieved from: https://news.gallup.com/poll/15370/party-affiliation.aspx

Independent Voting. (2020). "Confronting a New Reality: Independents Speak Out." *Independent Voting*. Retrieved from https://independentvoting.org/survey-report

Infoplease. (n.d.). "Presidents Elected without a Majority." *Infoplease*. Retrieved from: www.infoplease.com/us/government/elections/presidents-elected-without-a-majority

OpenPrimaries. (2020). "The Next Great Migration: The Rise of Independent Voters." *OpenPrimaries*. pp. 13, 27–56.

Pew Research Center. (2011, May 4). "Beyond Red vs. Blue: The Political Typology." *Pew Research Center*. Retrieved from: www.pewresearch.org/politics/2011/05/04/beyond-red-vs-blue-the-political-typology/

Pew Research Center. (2015, April 7). "Trends in Party Identification, 1939–2014." *Pew Research Center*. Retrieved from: www.pewresearch.org/politics/interactives/party-id-trend/

Pew Research Center. (2018, March 20). "Trends in Party Affiliation Among Demographic Groups." *Pew Research Center*. Retrieved from: www.pewresearch.org/politics/2018/03/20/1-trends-in-party-affiliation-among-demographic-groups

Quinnipiac University. (2021, August 4). "Biden Loses Ground on His Handling of COVID-19 Response, Quinnipiac University National Poll Finds; Infrastructure Bill Gets a Thumbs Up by a 2 to 1 Margin." *Quinnipiac University*. Retrieved from: https://poll.qu.edu/poll-release?releaseid=3814

Roper Center. (1992). "How Groups Voted in 1992." *Roper Center*. Retrieved from: www.ropercenter.uconn.edu/elections/how_groups_voted/voted_92.html#. Ttbc8GP0vZJ

Salit, J. (2012). *Independents Rising: Outsider Movements, Third Parties, and the Struggle for a Post-Partisan America*. London: Palgrave Macmillan. pp. 35.

Stiglitz, J. (2015). *The Great Divide: Unequal Societies and What We Can Do About Them*. New York, NY: Norton. pp. 421.

The Washington Post. (2010). "2010 U.S. House Election Exit Polls." *The Washington Post*. Retrieved from: www.washingtonpost.com/wp-srv/special/politics/election-results-2010/exit-poll/

Winston, D. (2021, July 14). "Election Day 2022 will be Independents' Day." Retrieved from: www.rollcall.com/2021/07/14/election-day-2022-will-be-independents-day/

Chapter 2

Ali, O. H. (2010). *In the Lion's Mouth: Black Populism in the New South*. Jackson, MS: University Press of Mississippi.

Anderson, B. (2006). *Imagined Communities: Reflections on the Origin and Spread of Nationalism* (Second Ed.). London, UK: Verso.

Cecelski, D. S., and Tyson, T. B. (1998). *Democracy Betrayed: The Wilmington Riot of 1898 and its Legacy*. Chapel Hill, NC: The University of North Carolina Press.

Dahl, R. A. (2000). *On Democracy*. London: Yale University Press.

Douglass, F. (1857, August 4). "West Indian Emancipation Address." In *The Frederick Douglass Papers*. 1(1). New Haven, CT: Yale University Press.

DuBois, W. E. B. (1903). *The Souls of Black Folk*. Chicago, IL: A.C. McClurg & Co.

Foner, E. (2014). *Reconstruction: America's Unfinished Revolution, 1863–1877*. New York, NY: Harper-Collins.

Gillespie, J. D. (2012). *Challengers to Duopoly: Why Third Parties Matter in American Two-Party Politics*. Columbia, SC: The University of South Carolina Press.

Goldberg, P. (1992). "The Independent Tradition Gives Birth to America's Premier Black Independent, Lenora B. Fulani." In *When Democracy Is on the Job, America Works*. New York, NY: Fulani for President.

Green, D. J. (2010). *Third Party Matters: Politics, Presidents, and Third Parties in American History*. Santa Barbara, CA: Praeger.

Hahn, S. (2005). *A Nation Under Our Feet: Black Political Struggles in the Rural South from Slavery to the Great Migration*. Cambridge, MA: Harvard University Press.

Hammer, F. L. (1964). "Fannie Lou Hammer: Testimony at the Democratic National Convention." *The American Yawp Reader*. Stanford University Press. Retrieved from: www.americanyawp.com/reader/27-the-sixties/fannie-lou-hamer-testimony-at-the-democratic-national-convention-1964/.

Moore, L. N. (2018). *The Defeat of Black Power: Civil Rights and the National Black Political Convention of 1972*. Baton Rouge, LA: Louisiana State University Press.

Rosenstone, S. J., Behr, R. L., and Lazarus, E. H. (1996). *Third Parties in America: Citizen Response to Major Party Failure* (Second Ed.). Princeton, NJ: Princeton University Press.

Royster, J., and Jacqueline. (2016). *Southern Horrors and Other Writings: The Anti-Lynching Campaign of Ida B. Wells, 1892–1900* (Second Ed.). Boston, MA: Bedford St. Martin's Press.

Scott, J. C. (1992). *Domination and the Arts of Resistance: Hidden Transcripts*. New Haven, CT: Yale University Press.

Washington, G. (1769). "George Washington's Farewell Address." *Independent Chronicle.* Retrieved from: https://avalon.law.yale.edu/18th_century/washing.asp

Chapter 3

Abrams, S., & Fiorina, M. (2011). *Are Leaning Independents Deluded or Dishonest Weak Partisans?* CISE-ITANES Conference, Roma, Italy.

Barber, M., & McCarty, N. (2013). "Causes and Consequences of Polarization." In *Task Force on Negotiating Agreement.* Washington, DC: American Political Science Association. pp. 19–53.

Bitzer, J., Cooper, C., Manzo, W., & Roberts, S. (2021, November 4–5). *The Rise of the Unaffiliated Voter in North Carolina.* Prepared for Presentation at the State of the Parties 2020 and Beyond Virtual Conference. Ray C. Bliss Institute of Applied Politics, University of Akron.

Broder, D. S. (1972). *The Party's Over: The Failure of Politics in America* (First Ed.). Manhattan, NY: Harper & Row.

Brody, R. (1991). "Stability and Change in Party Identification: Presidential to Off-Years." *Reasoning and Choice,* pp. 179–205. Retrieved from: https://doi.org/10.1017/cbo9780511720468.011

Brody, R. A. (1978). *Change and Stability in the Components of Partisan Identification.* NES Conference on Party Identification, Tallahassee, Florida.

Brody, R. A., & Rothenberg, L. S. (1988). "The Instability of Partisanship: An Analysis of the 1980 Presidential Election." *British Journal of Political Science,* 18(4), pp. 445–465. Retrieved from: https://doi.org/10.1017/s0007123400005214

Bump, P. (2016, January 11). "The Growing Myth of the 'Independent' Voter." *The Washington Post.* Retrieved from: www.washingtonpost.com/news/the-fix/wp/2016/01/11/independents-outnumber-democrats-and-republicans-but-theyre-not-very-independent/

Campbell, A., Converse, P. E., Miller, W. E., Stokes, D. E. (1960). *The American Voter.* Hoboken, NJ: Wiley.

CNN. (2008). "Local Exit Polls—Election Center 2008—Elections & Politics from CNN. com." *CNN.* Retrieved from: https://edition.cnn.com/ELECTION/2008/results/polls/#USP00p1

CNN. (2016). "2016 Election Results: Exit Polls." *CNN.* Retrieved from: https://edition.cnn.com/election/2016/results/exit-polls

CNN. (2020a). "Georgia 2020 U.S. Senate Runoff Exit Polls." *CNN.* Retrieved from: https://edition.cnn.com/election/2020/exit-polls/senate-runoff/georgia

CNN. (2020b). "National Results 2020 President Exit Polls." *CNN.* Retrieved from: https://edition.cnn.com/election/2020/exit-polls/president/national-results

Data Center. (2021, July 28). "ANES | American National Election Studies." Retrieved from: https://electionstudies.org/data-center/

de Neufville, R. (2018, October 6). "Do Independent Voters Matter?" *Big Think.* Retrieved from: http://bigthink.com/politeia/do-independent-voters-matter

Drum, K. (2014, April 23). "Most Independent Voters Aren't, Really." *Mother Jones.* Retrieved from: www.motherjones.com/kevin-drum/2014/04/most-independent-voters-arent-really/

Enten, H. (2016, March 8). "Americans Aren't Becoming More Politically Independent, They Just Like Saying They Are." *FiveThirtyEight.* Retrieved from: https://fivethirtyeight.com/features/americans-arent-becoming-more-politically-independent-they-just-like-saying-they-are/

Eris, D. (2011, November 15). "Debunking the Myth of the Myth of the Independent Voter." *IVN.Us.* Retrieved from: https://ivn.us/2010/11/24/debunking-myth-myth-independent-voter/

Fiorina, M. (2016, October 12). "Independents: The Marginal Members of an Electoral Coalition." *Hoover Institution.* Retrieved from: www.hoover.org/research/independents-marginal-members-electoral-coalition

Fiorina, M. P. (2017). *Unstable Majorities: Polarization, Party Sorting, and Political Stalemate.* Stanford, CA: Hoover Institution Press.

Franklin, C. H. (1984). "Issue Preferences, Socialization, and the Evolution of Party Identification." *American Journal of Political Science*, 28(3), pp. 459. Retrieved from: https://doi.org/10.2307/2110900

Galen, R. (2018, November 5). "How Republicans and Democrats Prevent Independent Candidates from Getting on the Ballot." *NBC News.* Retrieved from: www.nbcnews.com/think/opinion/how-republicans-democrats-prevent-independent-candidates-getting-ballot-ncna866466

Gallup, Inc. (2021, August 13). Party Affiliation | Gallup Historical Trends. *Gallup.* Retrieved from: https://news.gallup.com/poll/15370/party-affiliation.aspx

Hankin, S. (2014, October). "The Myth of the 'Independent' Voter." *Republic 3.0.*

Holland, J. (2016, May 18). "What Everyone Gets Wrong About Independent Voters." *The Nation.* Retrieved from: www.thenation.com/article/archive/what-everyone-gets-wrong-about-independent-voters/

Jacobs, T. (2017, May 3). "'Independent' Voters Are Generally Not." *Pacific Standard.* Retrieved from: https://psmag.com/news/independent-voters-are-generally-not-3560

Jennings, M. K., & Markus, G. B. (1984). "Partisan Orientations over the Long Haul: Results from the Three-Wave Political Socialization Panel Study." *American Political Science Review*, 78(4), pp. 1000–1018. Retrieved from: https://doi.org/10.2307/1955804

Kane, P. (2021, October 23). "Democrats' Problem is Not Focusing on Issues Most Important to Independents." *The Washington Post.* Retrieved from: www.washingtonpost.com/powerpost/democrats-midterm-independents/2021/10/23/4271ad96-335f-11ec-a1e5-07223c50280a_story.html

Keith, B. E., Magleby, D. B., Nelson, C. J., Orr, E., Westlye, M. C., & Wolfinger, R. E. (1992). *The Myth of the Independent Voter.* Berkeley and Los Angeles, CA: University of California Press.

Killian, L. (2012). *The Swing Vote: The Untapped Power of Independents.* New York, NY: St. Martin's Press.

Klar, S. (2014, July 1). "Partisanship in a Social Setting." *American Journal of Political Science*, 58(3), pp. 687–704. Retrieved from: https://doi.org/10.1111/ajps.12087

Klar, S., & Krupnikov, Y. (2016a). *Independent Politics: How American Disdain for Parties Leads to Political Inaction.* Boston, MA: Cambridge University Press.

Klar, S., & Krupnikov, Y. (2016b, January 22). "9 Media Myths about Independent Voters, Debunked." *Vox.* Retrieved from: www.vox.com/2016/1/22/10814522/independents-voters-facts-myths

Levendusky, M. S., & Malhotra, N. (2015). "(Mis)perceptions of Partisan Polarization in the American Public." *Public Opinion Quarterly*, 80(1), pp. 378–391. Retrieved from: https://doi.org/10.1093/poq/nfv045

Lewis-Beck, M., Jacoby, W., Norpoth, H., and Weisberg, H. (2008). *The American Voter Revisited.* Ann Arbor, MI: University of Michigan Press.

Malone, C. (2016, March 4). New Hampshire's Independent Voter Myth. *FiveThirtyEight.* Retrieved from: https://fivethirtyeight.com/features/new-hampshires-independent-voter-myth/

Mayer, W. G. (2008). *The Swing Voter in American Politics*. Washington, DC: Brookings Institution Press.

McFadden, E. S., Daugherty, D., Hedberg, E., and Garcia, J. (2015). *Who is Arizona's Independent Voter?* Phoenix, AZ: Morrison Institute for Public Policy and Arizona State University.

Miller, W. E. (1991). "Party Identification, Realignment, and Party Voting: Back to the Basics." *American Political Science Review*, 85(2), pp. 557–568. Retrieved from: https://doi.org/10.2307/1963175

Milligan, S. (2021, May 21). "Independents Exercise Increasing Control Over Democratic, Republican Candidates." *USNews*. Retrieved from: www.usnews.com/news/the-report/articles/2021-05-21/independents-exercise-increasing-control-over-democratic-republican-candidates

Niedzwiadek, N. (2021, August 25). "Florida Poll: 53 Percent Disapprove of Biden's Job Performance." *Politico PRO*. Retrieved from: www.politico.com/states/florida/story/2021/08/25/florida-poll-53-percent-disapprove-of-bidens-job-performance-1390479

Petrocik, J. R. (2009). "Measuring Party Support: Leaners are Not Independents." *Electoral Studies*, 28(4), pp. 562–572. Retrieved from: https://doi.org/10.1016/j.electstud.2009.05.022

Pew Research Center. (2014, June 12). "Political Polarization in the American Public." *Pew Research Center*. Retrieved from: www.pewresearch.org/politics/2014/06/12/political-polarization-in-the-american-public/

Pew Research Center. (2019, December 31). "Political Independents: Who They Are, What They Think." *Pew Research Center*. Retrieved from: www.pewresearch.org/politics/2019/03/14/political-independents-who-they-are-what-they-think/.

Reilly, T., Whitsett, A., Garcia, J., Hart, W, McWhorter, P., Reiss, B., Grose, C., Cornelius, M., & Giamaros, S. (2017). "Gamechangers: Independents Voters may Rewrite the Political Playbook." *Morrison Institute*. Retrieved from: https://morrisoninstitute.asu.edu/sites/default/files/gamechangers.pdf

Sabato, L. (2009). *The Myth of the Independent Voter Revisited*. Charolttsville, VA: Center for Politics.

Salit, J., & Reilly, T. (2020). "Can Independent Voters Save American Democracy? Why 42 percent of American voters are Independent and How They Can Transform our Political System" In David W. Orr, Andrew Gumbel, Bakari Kitwana and William S. Becker, (Eds), *Democracy Unchained: How to Rebuild Government for the People*. New York: The New Press. pp. 323–335.

Sides, J. (2013, October 16). "Three Myths about Political Independents." *The Monkey Cage*. Retrieved from: https://themonkeycage.org/2009/12/three_myths_about_political_in/

Sommers, S. (2012, December 7). "Just How Independent Are Independent Voters?." *Huff Post*. Retrieved from: www.huffpost.com/entry/just-how-independent-are-_b_1777512

Teixiera, R. (2012, March 7). "The Great Illusion." *The New Republic*. Retrieved from: https://newrepublic.com/article/100799/swing-vote-untapped-power-independents-linda-killian

Todd, C., Murray, M., & Kamisar, B. (2021, August 23). "Biden's silver lining amid poll slide: Time is still on his side." *NBC News*. Retrieved from: www.nbcnews.com/politics/meet-the-press/biden-s-silver-lining-amid-poll-slide-time-still-his-n1277430

Trounstine, P., & Roberts, J. (2011, May 25). "Why Indie Voters Don't Make California Purple." *HuffPost*. Retrieved from: www.huffpost.com/entry/why-indie-voters-dont-mak_b_255393

van Boven, L., Judd, C. M., & Sherman, D. K. (2012). "Political Polarization Projection: Social Projection of Partisan Attitude Extremity and Attitudinal Processes." *Journal of Personality and Social Psychology*, 103(1), pp. 84–100. Retrieved from: https://doi.org/10.1037/a0028145.

Vedantem, S. (2011, February 2). "Partisanship Is the New Racism." *Psychology Today*. Retrieved from: www.psychologytoday.com/us/blog/the-hidden-brain/201102/partisanship-is-the-new-racism

Walter, A. (2014, January 15). "The Myth of the Independent Voter." *The Cook Political Report*.

Weisberg, H. F. (1980). "A Multidimensional Conceptualization of Party Identification." *Political Behavior*, 2(1), pp. 33–60. Retrieved from: https://doi.org/10.1007/bf00989755

Weisberg, H. F. (1993). "Review of 'The Myth of the Independent Voter.'" *The Public Opinion Quarterly*, 57(3), pp. 428–430. Retrieved from: www.jstor.org/stable/2749100

Wikipedia Contributors. (2021a, July 6). Endogeneity (econometrics). *Wikipedia*. Retrieved from: https://en.wikipedia.org/wiki/Endogeneity_(econometrics)

Wikipedia Contributors. (2021b, August 16). Retrocausality. *Wikipedia*. Retrieved from: https://en.wikipedia.org/wiki/Retrocausality

Chapter 4

Caddell, P. (2016, November 7). "The Real Election Surprise? The Uprising of the American People." *Fox News*. Retrieved from: www.foxnews.com/opinion/patrick-caddell-the-real-election-surprise-the-uprising-of-the-american-people

CNN. (2016a). "2016 Michigan Presidential Primary Election Results." *CNN*. Retrieved from: www.cnn.com/election/2016/primaries/polls/mi/Dem

CNN. (2016b). "2016 National Presidential Primary Election Results." *CNN*. Retrieved from: www.cnn.com/election/2016/results/exit-polls

CNN. (2016c). "2016 Pennsylvania Presidential Primary Election Results." *CNN*. Retrieved from: www.cnn.com/election/2016/primaries/polls/pa/Dem

CNN. (2016d). "2016 Wisconsin Presidential Primary Election Results." *CNN*. Retrieved from: www.cnn.com/election/2016/primaries/polls/WI/Dem

Cockburn, A., and Kopkind, A. (1992). "The Democrats, Perot, and the Left." *The Nation Magazine*.

CSPAN. (1993, July 7). "Ross Perot Voter Survey." *CSPAN*. Retrieved from: www.cspan.org/video/?44509-1/ross-perot-voter-survey

Exit Polls. (2020). "CNN, 2020 Presidential Race, General Election." *Exit Polls*. Retrieved from: www.cnn.com/election/2020/exit-polls/president/national-results

From, A., and Marshall, W. (1993). "The Road to Realignment: Democrats and Perot Voters." *Democratic Leadership Council*.

History Channel. (2018). "Great Society." *History Channel*. Retrieved from: www.history.com/topics/1960s/great-society

Independent Voting. (2020). "Confronting a New Reality: Independents Speak Out." *Independent Voting*. Retrieved from: www.independentvoting.org

Initiative and Referendum Institute. (n.d.). "Statewide Initiative Usage." *Initiative and Referendum Institute*. University of Southern California. Retrieved from: www.iandrinstitute.org/docs/Colorado.pdf

Merline, J. (2016, October 19). "Trump Leads Clinton by One Point Going into Debate in IBDTIPP Tracking Poll." *Investors.com*. Retrieved from: www.investors.com/politics/trump-leads-clinton-by-one-point-going-into-debate-in-ibdtipp-tracking-poll/

Merry, R. (2017, May 18) "Removing Trump Won't Solve America's Crisis." *The American Conservative*. Retrieved from: www.theamericanconservative.com/articles/removing-trump-wont-solve-americas-crisis/

New York City Board of Elections. (2001, November 6). "2001 New York General Election Vote for Mayor Results." *New York City Board of Elections*. Retrieved from: https://vote.nyc/sites/default/files/downloads/pdf/results/2001/generalelection/general2001.pdf

Phillips, K. P. (1995). *Arrogant Capital: Washington, Wall Street, and the Frustration of American Politics*. Paris: Hachette. pp. XVI.

Reform Party's Black Reformers Network. (1997, October 31). "Unity and Diversity." *Reform Party's Black Reformers Network*. Kansas City, Missouri. Retrieved from: www.youtube.com/watch?v=zwSHPZJlrxg

Roberts, S. (2014, December 15). "David Garth, 84, Dies; Consultant Was an Innovator of Political TV Ads." *The New York Times*. Retrieved from: https://www.nytimes.com/2014/12/16/nyregion/david-garth-pioneer-of-the-political-ad-dies-at-84.html

Stein, J. (2017, August 24). "The Bernie Voters who Defected to Trump, Explained by a Political Scientist." *Vox*. Retrieved from: www.vox.com/policy-and-politics/2017/8/24/16194086/bernie-trump-voters-study

Supreme Court of the United States. (1995, May 22). "U.S. Term Limits, Inc. v. Thornton." *Supreme Court of the United States*. Retrieved from: https://supreme.justia.com/cases/federal/us/514/779/

Tomasky, M. (1992, May 26). "The Village Voice." *Texas Monthly*. Retrieved from: https://www.texasmonthly.com/issue/may-1992/

YouTube. (2020, August 31). "Interview with Bilal Qureshi at the Edinburgh International Book Festival." *YouTube*. Retrieved from: www.youtube.com/watch?v=iOcRil4AjeQ

Chapter 5

Abramowitz, A. I., & Saunders, K. L. (2008). "Is Polarization a Myth?" *The Journal of Politics*, 70(2), pp. 542–555. Retrieved from: https://doi.org/10.1017/s0022381608080493

Alashri, S., Kandala, S. S., Bajaj, V., Ravi, R., Smith, K. L., & Desouza, K. C. (2016). "An Analysis of Sentiments on Facebook During the 2016 U.S. Presidential Election." *Institute of Electrical and Electronics Engineers Inc.* Retrieved from: https://doi.org/10.1109/ASONAM.2016.7752329

Alvarez, R. M. (1990). "The Puzzle of Party Identification." *American Politics Quarterly*, 18(4), pp. 476–491. Retrieved form: https://doi.org/10.1177/1532673x9001800405.

Anderson, C. (2007). *The Long Tail: How Endless Choice is Creating Unlimited Demand*. London, UK: Business Books.

ANES Guide. (2021, August 20). American National Election Studies. Retrieved from: www.electionstudies.org/resources/anes-guide/

Ayala, L. J. (2000). "Trained for Democracy: The Differing Effects of Voluntary and Involuntary Organizations on Political Participation." *Political Research Quarterly*, 53(1), pp. 99. Retrieved from: https://doi.org/10.2307/449248.

Baker, K. J. (2016, November 9). "Why People Are Unfriending Newly Public Trump Supporters." *BuzzFeed News*. Retrieved from: www.buzzfeednews.com/article/katie-jmbaker/why-people-are-unfriending-newly-public-trump-supporters?utm_term=.gvae03pRA#.hgGm5WXQw

Barnidge, M., Gunther, A. C., Kim, J., Hong, Y., Perryman, M., Tay, S. K., & Knisely, S. (2020). "Politically Motivated Selective Exposure and Perceived Media

Bias." *Communication Research*, 47(1), pp. 82–103. Retrieved from: https://doi. org/10.1177/0093650217713066.

Barnidge, M., & Peacock, C. (2019). "A Third Wave of Selective Exposure Research? The Challenges Posed by Hyperpartisan News on Social Media." *Media and Communication*, 7(3), pp. 4–7. Cogitatio. Retrieved from: https://doi.org/10.17645/mac. v7i3.2257

Baron, D. P. (2006). "Persistent Media Bias." *Journal of Public Economics*, 90(1–2), pp. 1–36. Retrieved from: https://doi.org/10.1016/j.jpubeco.2004.10.006

Barthel, M. (2016, May 12). "Liberal Democrats Most Likely to Have Learned About Election from Facebook." *Pew Research Center*. Retrieved from: www.pewresearch. org/fact-tank/2016/05/12/liberal-democrats-most-likely-to-have-learned-about-election-from-facebook/

Beck, P. A., Dalton, R. J., Greene, S., & Huckfeldt, R. (2002). "The Social Calculus of Voting: Interpersonal, Media, and Organizational Influences on Presidential Choices." *American Political Science Review*, 96(1), pp. 57–73. Retrieved from: https://doi. org/10.1017/s0003055402004239

Bennett, W. L. (2004). *News: The Politics of Illusion*. London, UK: Pearson/Longman.

Bovet, A., Morone, F., & Makse, H. A. (2016, October 5). Validation of Twitter Opinion Trends with National Polling. *ArXiv*. Retrieved from: https://arxiv.org/abs/1610.01587

Burt, R. (2004). "Structural Holes and Good Ideas." *American Journal of Sociology*, 110(2), pp. 349–399. Retrieved from: https://doi.org/10.1086/421787.

Burt, R. S. (1984). "Network Items and the General Social Survey." *Social Networks*, 6(4), pp. 293–339. Retrieved from: https://doi.org/10.1016/0378-8733(84)90007-8

Chin, C. (2021). "Social Media and Political Campaigns." *Georgetown Public Policy Review*. Retrieved from: www.gpprspring.com/social-media-political-campaigns#test-copy-of-retweets-hashtags-and-political-campaigns

Cline, A. R. (2009). "Bias." In *21st Century Communications*. SAGE. pp. 479–486.

Easley, J. (2016, November 9). "Here's The Proof That Jill Stein and Gary Johnson Cost Hillary Clinton The Election." *PoliticusUSA*. Retrieved from: www.politicususa. com/2016/11/09/proof-jill-stein-gary-johnson-cost-hillary-clinton-election.html

Eberl, J. M., Boomgaarden, H. G., & Wagner, M. (2017). "One Bias Fits All? Three Types of Media Bias and Their Effects on Party Preferences." *Communication Research*, 44(8), pp. 1125–1148. Retrieved from: https://doi.org/10.1177/0093650215614364

Ekstrom, P. D., Smith, B. A., Williams, A. L., & Kim, H. (2020). "Social Network Disagreement and Reasoned Candidate Preferences." *American Politics Research*, 48(1), pp. 132–154. Retrieved from: https://doi.org/10.1177/1532673x19858343

Entman, R. M. (2007). "Framing Bias: Media in the Distribution of Power." *Journal of Communication*, 57(1), pp. 163–173. Retrieved from: https://doi. org/10.1111/j.1460-2466.2006.00336.x

Fingas, J. (2021). "Engadget Is Now a Part of Verizon Media." *Engaget*. Retrieved from: www.engadget.com/donald-trump-social-network-211532975.html

Fiorina, P. M., Abrams, S. J., & Pope, J. (2005). *Culture War?: The Myth of a Polarized America*. London, UK: Pearson Longman.

Foos, F., & de Rooij, E. A. (2016). "All in the Family: Partisan Disagreement and Electoral Mobilization in Intimate Networks—A Spillover Experiment." *American Journal of Political Science*, 61(2), pp. 289–304. Retrieved from: https://doi.org/10.1111/ajps.12270

Friedkin, N. E., & Johnsen, E. C. (1990). "Social Influence and Opinions." *The Journal of Mathematical Sociology*, 15(3–4), pp. 193–206. Retrieved from: https://doi.org/10.108 0/0022250x.1990.9990069

Fuchs, C. (2009). "Information and Communication Technologies and Society." *European Journal of Communication*, 24(1), pp. 69–87. Retrieved from: https://doi.org/10.1177/0267323108098947

Gans, H. (1980). *Deciding What's the News*. New York, NY: Vintage Books.

Garrett, R. K., Weeks, B. E., & Neo, R. L. (2016). "Driving a Wedge Between Evidence and Beliefs: How Online Ideological News Exposure Promotes Political Misperceptions." *Journal of Computer-Mediated Communication*, 21(5), pp. 331–348. Retrieved from: https://doi.org/10.1111/jcc4.12164

Gentzkow, M. A., & Shapiro, J. M. (2008). "Competition and Truth in the Market for News." *SSRN Electronic Journal*. Retrieved from: https://doi.org/10.2139/ssrn.1269545

Gerber, A. S., Green, D. P., & Larimer, C. W. (2008). "Social Pressure and Voter Turnout: Evidence from a Large-Scale Field Experiment." *American Political Science Review*, 102(1), pp. 33–48. Retrieved from: https://doi.org/10.1017/s000305540808009x

Gerber, A. S., Karlan, D., & Bergan, D. (2009). "Does the Media Matter? A Field Experiment Measuring the Effect of Newspapers on Voting Behavior and Political Opinions." *American Economic Journal: Applied Economics*, 1(2), pp. 35–52. Retrieved from: https://doi.org/10.1257/app.1.2.35

Gottfried, J., Barthel, M., Shearer, E., & Mitchell, A. (2016, February 4). "The 2016 Presidential Campaign—A News Event That's Hard to Miss." *Pew Research Center*. Retrieved from: www.pewresearch.org/journalism/2016/02/04/the-2016-presidential-campaign-a-news-event-thats-hard-to-miss/

Gottfried, J., & Shearer, E. (2016, May 26). "News Use Across Social Media Platforms 2016." *Pew Research Center*. Retrieved from: www.pewresearch.org/journalism/2016/05/26/news-use-across-social-media-platforms-2016/

Greene, S. (2004). "Social Identity Theory and Party Identification." *Social Science Quarterly*, 85(1), pp. 136–153. Retrieved from: https://doi.org/10.1111/j.0038-4941.2004.08501010.x

Groseclose, T. (2011). *Left Turn: How Media Bias Distorts the American Mind*. New York, NY: St. Martin's Press.

Gunther, R., Beck, P. A., & Nisbet, E. C. (2019). "'Fake News' and the Defection of 2012 Obama Voters in the 2016 Presidential Election." *Electoral Studies*. Retrieved from: https://doi.org/10.1016/j.electstud.2019.03.006

Hall, T. & Phillips, J. C., (2011). "The Fairness Doctrine in Light of Hostile Media Perception." *Journal of Communications Law and Policy*, 19(2), pp. 395–422.

Hanson, K., O'Dwyer, E., & Lyons, E. (2019). "The Individual and the Nation: A Qualitative Analysis of US Liberal and Conservative Identity Content." *Journal of Social and Political Psychology*, 7(1), pp. 378–401. Retrieved from: https://doi.org/10.5964/jspp.v7i1.1062

Hasell, A., & Weeks, B. E. (2016). "Partisan Provocation: The Role of Partisan News Use and Emotional Responses in Political Information Sharing in Social Media." *Human Communication Research*, 42(4), pp. 641–661. Retrieved from: https://doi.org/10.1111/hcre.12092

Hedberg, E., Reilly, T., Daugherty, D., & Garcia, J (2017). *Voters, Media & Social Networks*. Phoenix, AZ: Morrison Institute for Public Policy, Arizona State University.

Heidhues, P., & Kőszegi, B. (2016). "Naïveté-Based Discrimination." *The Quarterly Journal of Economics*, 132(2), pp. 1019–1054. Retrieved from: https://doi.org/10.1093/qje/qjw042

Hoffmann, F., Inderst, R., & Ottaviani, M. (2014). "Hypertargeting, Limited Attention, and Privacy: Implications for Marketing and Campaigning" Retrieved from: www.novasbe. unl.pt/images/novasbe/files/INOVA_Seminars/Roman_inderst.PDF

Huckfeldt, R., & Sprague, J. (1987). "Networks in Context: The Social Flow of Political Information." *American Political Science Review*, 81(4), pp. 1197–1216. Retrieved from: https://doi.org/10.2307/1962585

Huckfeldt, R., & Sprague, J. (1991). "Discussant Effects on Vote Choice: Intimacy, Structure, and Interdependence." *The Journal of Politics*, 53(1), pp. 122–158. Retrieved from: https://doi.org/10.2307/2131724

Ioanides, Y. M. (2013). *From Neighborhoods to Nations: The Economics of Social Interaction.* Princeton, NJ: Princeton University Press.

Jones, J., & Trice, M. (2020). "Social Media Effects: Hijacking Democracy and Civility in Civic Engagement." *PubMed Central.* Retrieved from: www.ncbi.nlm.nih.gov/pmc/articles/PMC7343248/

Kalla, J. L., & Broockman, D. E. (2017). "The Minimal Persuasive Effects of Campaign Contact in General Elections: Evidence from 49 Field Experiments." *American Political Science Review*, 112(1), pp. 148–166. Retrieved from: https://doi.org/10.1017/s0003055417000363

Kamieniecki, S. (1988). "The Dimensionality of Partisan Strength and Political Independence." *Political Behavior*, 10(4), pp. 364–376. Retrieved from: https://doi.org/10.1007/bf00990809

Keith, B. E., Magelby, D. B., Nelson, C. J., Orr, E. A., Westlye, M. C., & Wolfinger, R. E. (1992). *The Myth of the Independent Voter.* Berkeley, CA: University of California Press.

Klar, S. (2014). "Partisanship in a Social Setting." *American Journal of Political Science*, 58(3), pp. 687–704. Retrieved from: https://doi.org/10.1111/ajps.12087

Klar, S. (2016). *Independent Politics: How American Disdain for Parties Leads to Political Inaction.* Cambridge: Cambridge University Press.

Knobloch-Westerwick, S., & Jingbo, M. (2009). "Looking the Other Way: Selective Exposure to Attitude-Consistent and Counterattitudinal Political Information." *Communication Research*, 36(3), pp. 426–448. Retrieved from: https://doi.org/10.1177/0093650209333030

Kulshrestha, J., Eslami, M., Messias, J., Zafar, M. B., Ghosh, S., Gummadi, K. P., & Karahalios, K. (2017). "Quantifying Search Bias: Investigating Sources of Bias for Political Searches in Social Media." In *Proceedings of the 2017 ACM Conference on Computer Supported Cooperative Work and Social Computing.* pp. 417–432. Retrieved from: https://doi.org/10.1145/2998181.2998321

Lee, B., & Bearman, P. (2017). "Important Matters in Political Context." *Sociological Science*, 4, pp. 1–30. Retrieved from: https://doi.org/10.15195/v4.a1

Lee, J., & Lim, Y. S. (2016). "Gendered Campaign Tweets: The Cases of Hillary Clinton and Donald Trump." *Public Relations Review*, 42(5), pp. 849–855. Retrieved from: https://doi.org/10.1016/j.pubrev.2016.07.004

Levendusky, M. S., & Malhotra, N. (2016). "(Mis)perceptions of Partisan Polarization in the American Public." *Public Opinion Quarterly*, 80(1), pp. 378–391. Retrieved from: https://doi.org/10.1093/poq/nfv045

Lockhart, M., Hill, S. J., Merolla, J., Romero, M., & Kousser, T. (2020). "America's Electorate is Increasingly Polarized Along Partisan Lines about Voting by Mail During the COVID-19 Crisis." *Proceedings of the National Academy of Sciences*, 117(40), pp. 24640–24642. Retrieved from: https://doi.org/10.1073/pnas.2008023117

McClurg, S. D. (2003). "Social Networks and Political Participation: The Role of Social Interaction in Explaining Political Participation." *Political Research Quarterly*, 56(4), pp. 449. Retrieved from: https://doi.org/10.2307/3219806

McGraw, M., Nguyen, T., & Lima, C. (2021, July 1). "Team Trump Quietly Launches New Social Media Platform." *Politico*. Retrieved from: www.politico.com/news/2021/07/01/gettr-trump-social-media-platform-497606

Meraz, S. (2012). "The Democratic Contribution of Weakly Tied Political Networks." *Social Science Computer Review*, 31(2), pp. 191–207. Retrieved from: https://doi.org/10.1177/0894439312451879

Mitchell, A., Gottfried, J., Barthel, M., & Shearer, E. (2016, July 7). "The Modern News Consumer." *Pew Research Center*. Retrieved from: www.pewresearch.org/journalism/2016/07/07/the-modern-news-consumer/

Mitchell, A., Gottfried, J., Kiley, J., & Matsa, K. E. (2014, October 21). "Political Polarization & Media Habits." *Pew Research Center*. Retrieved from: www.pewresearch.org/journalism/2014/10/21/political-polarization-media-habits/

Mitchell, A., Jurkowitz, M., Oliphant, J. B., & Shearer, E. (2020). "How Americans Navigated the News in 2020." *Pew Research Center*. Retrieved from www.pewresearch.org/topic/news-habits-media/media-society/american-news-pathways-2020-project/

Montanaro, D. (2021, March 24). "NPR Cookie Consent and Choices." *NPR*. Retrieved from: https://choice.npr.org/index.html?origin=www.npr.org/2021/03/24/980436658/trump-teases-starting-his-own-social-media-platform-heres-why-itd-be-tough

Mullainathan, S., & Shleifer, A. (2005). "The Market for News." *American Economic Review*, 95(4), pp. 1031–1053. Retrieved from: https://doi.org/10.1257/0002828054825619

Mutz, D. C. (2002). "Cross-cutting Social Networks: Testing Democratic Theory in Practice." *American Political Science Review*, 96(1), pp. 111–126. Retrieved from: https://doi.org/10.1017/s0003055402004264

Oates, S. (2016, August 25). "Donald Trump and the "Oxygen of Publicity": Branding, Social Media, and Mass Media in the 2016 Presidential Primary Elections." *SSRN*. Retrieved from: https://papers.ssrn.com/sol3/papers.cfm?abstract_id=2830195

Osmundsen, M., Petersen, M. B., & Bor, A. (2021, May 13). "How Partisan Polarization Drives the Spread of Fake News." *Brookings*. Retrieved from: www.brookings.edu/techstream/how-partisan-polarization-drives-the-spread-of-fake-news/

Pattie, C. J., & Johnston, R. J. (2008). "It's Good To Talk: Talk, Disagreement and Tolerance." *British Journal of Political Science*, 38(4), pp. 677–698. Retrieved from: https://doi.org/10.1017/s0007123408000331

Prior, M. (2005). "News vs. Entertainment: How Increasing Media Choice Widens Gaps in Political Knowledge and Turnout." *American Journal of Political Science*, 49(3), pp. 577–592. Retrieved from: https://doi.org/10.1111/j.1540-5907.2005.00143.x

Rainie, L., Smith, A., Schlozman, K. L., Brady, H., & Verba, S. (2012, October 19). "Social Media and Political Engagement." *Pew Research Center*. Retrieved from: www.pewresearch.org/internet/2012/10/19/social-media-and-political-engagement/

Reedy, J., Wells, C., & Gastil, J. (2014). "How Voters Become Misinformed: An Investigation of the Emergence and Consequences of False Factual Beliefs." *Social Science Quarterly*, 95(5), pp. 1399–1418. Retrieved from: https://doi.org/10.1111/ssqu.12102

Reilly, T., & Hedberg, E. (2022). "Social Networks of Independents and Partisans: Are Independents a Moderating Force?" *Politics & Policy*, 50(2), pp. 225–243.

Rothman, S. (1992). *The Mass Media in Liberal Democratic Societies*. Bangkok: Paragon House.

Russel, A. (2014). *U. S. Senators on Twitter: Party Polarization in 140 Characters (Doctoral dissertation)*. Austin: UT Electronic Theses and Dissertations. Retrieved from: http://hdl.handle.net.ezproxy1.lib.asu.edu/2152/28543

Settle, J. E., & Carlson, T. N. (2019). "Opting Out of Political Discussions." *Political Communication*, 36(3), pp. 476–496. Retrieved from: https://doi.org/10.1080/10584609.2018.1561563

Siegel, D. A. (2009). "Social Networks and Collective Action." *American Journal of Political Science*, 53(1), pp. 122–138. Retrieved from: https://doi.org/10.1111/j.1540-5907.2008.00361.x

Smith, A. E. (2015). "The Diverse Impacts of Politically Diverse Networks: Party Systems, Political Disagreement, and the Timing of Vote Decisions." *International Journal of Public Opinion Research*. Retrieved from: https://doi.org/10.1093/ijpor/edv018

Starr, P. (2005). *The Creation of the Media: Political Origins of Modern Communications*. New York, NY: Basic Books.

Swan, J., & Fischer, S. (2021, March 24). "Scoop: Trump in Talks with Upstart Apps About New Social Network." *Axios*. Retrieved from: www.axios.com/trump-social-media-platform-freespace-a77d7dfc-3288-48bf-bc7e-8942da24bdbd.html

Vaccari, C. (2012). "From Echo Chamber to Persuasive Device? Rethinking the Role of the Internet in Campaigns." *New Media & Society*, 15(1), pp. 109–127. Retrieved from: https://doi.org/10.1177/1461444812457336

Verba, S., Schlozman, K. L., & Brady, H. E. (1995). *Voice and Equality: Civic Voluntarism in American Politics*. Cambridge, MA: Harvard University Press.

Webster, J. G., & Ksiazek, T. B. (2012). "The Dynamics of Audience Fragmentation: Public Attention in an Age of Digital Media." *Journal of Communication*, 62(1), pp. 39–56. Retrieved from: https://doi.org/10.1111/j.1460-2466.2011.01616.x

Weisberg, H. F. (1980). "A Multidimensional Conceptualization of Party Identification." *Political Behavior*, 2(1), pp. 33–60. Retrieved from: https://doi.org/10.1007/bf00989755

Wikipedia Contributors. (2021, September 30). "FCC Fairness Doctrine." *Wikipedia*. Retrieved from: https://en.wikipedia.org/wiki/FCC_fairness_doctrine

Xiang, Y., & Sarvary, M. (2007). "News Consumption and Media Bias." *Marketing Science*, 26(5), pp. 611–628. Retrieved from: https://doi.org/10.1287/mksc.1070.0279

Zschirnt, S. (2011). "The Origins & Meaning of Liberal/Conservative Self-Identifications Revisited." *Political Behavior*, 33(4), pp. 685–701. Retrieved from: https://doi.org/10.1007/s11109-010-9145-6

Chapter 6

Ackerman, P., and Shapiro, A. (2017, February 12). "A Victory in the Battle to Open Presidential Elections." Retrieved from: www.realclearpolitics.com/articles/2017/02/12/a_victory_in_the_battle_to_open_presidential_elections_133060.html

Ballot Access News. (1988, May 23). "'Florida' and 'Texas.'" *Ballot Access News*, 3(11), pp. 1, 3. Retrieved from: www.ballot-access.org/1988/BAN.1988.05-23-88.pdf

Ballot Access News. (1988, July 8). "Michigan." *Ballot Access News*, 4(1), pp. 1. Retrieved from: www.ballot-access.org/1988/BAN.1988.07-08-88.pdf

Ballot Access News. (1988, August 1). "Nebraska." *Ballot Access News*, 4(1), pp. 1. Retrieved from: www.ballot-access.org/1988/BAN.1988.08-01-88.pdf

Ballot Access News. (1988, August 27). "Five Victories." *Ballot Access News*, 4(3), pp. 1. Retrieved from: www.ballot-access.org/1988/BAN.1988.08-27-88.pdf

Ballot Access News. (1988, September 16). "Peace & Freedom Party." *Ballot Access News*, 4(4), pp. 2. Retrieved from: www.ballot-access.org/1988/BAN.1988.09-16-88.pdf

Ballot Access News. (1988, October 12). "Arizona." *Ballot Access News*, 4(5), pp. 2. Retrieved from: www.ballot-access.org/1988/BAN.1988.10-12-88.pdf

Ballot Action News. (1987, November 19). "Settlement in New York City." *Ballot Action News*, 3(5), pp. 4. Retrieved from: www.ballot-access.org/1987/BAN.1987.11-19-87.pdf

Ballot Action News. (1988, January 20). "West Virginia." *Ballot Action News*, 3(7), pp. 5. Retrieved from: www.ballot-access.org/1988/BAN.1988.01-20-88.pdf

Ballot Action News. (1988, April 19). "'North Carolina Victory' and 'New Lawsuits Filed.'" *Ballot Action News*, 3(10), pp. 1, 4. Retrieved from: www.ballot-access.org/1988/BAN.1988.04-19-88.pdf

Ballotpedia. (2020). "Florida Amendment 3, Top-Two Open Primaries for State Offices Initiative." *Ballotpedia*. Retrieved from: https://ballotpedia.org/Florida_Amendment_3,_Top-Two_Open_Primaries_for_State_Offices_Initiative_(2020)

Ballotpedia. (n.d.). "Partisan Election of Judges." *Ballotpedia*. Retrieved from: https://ballotpedia.org/Partisan_election_of_judges

Ballotpedia. (n.d.). "Fusion Voting." *Ballotpedia*. Retrieved from: https://ballotpedia.org/Fusion_voting

Costa, R. J. (1988). *Eligibility of Lenora B. Fulani to Receive Primary Matching Funds* [Memorandum]. Washington, DC: Federal Election Commission.

Diamond, L. (2015, May 8). "Ending the Presidential-Debate Duopoly." *The Atlantic*. Retrieved from: www.theatlantic.com/politics/archive/2015/05/ending-the-presidential-debate-duopoly/392480/

Fulani, L. (2000, January 12). *Campaign Launched to Change the Commission on Presidential Debates Polling Question*. CUIP Press Release.

Gailey, P. (1987, February 19). "Democrats and Republicans Form Panel to Hold Presidential Debates." *The New York Times*. Retrieved from: www.nytimes.com/1987/02/19/us/democrats-and-republicans-form-panel-to-hold-presidential-debates.html?pagewanted=1

Hofstadter, R. (1955). *The Age of Reform*. New York, NY: Vintage. pp. 97.

Juffer, A. J. (2007, December 13). "Living in a Party World: Respecting the Role of Third Party and Independent Candidates in the Equal Protection Analysis of Ballot Access Cases." *Drake Law Review*, 56.

Justia.com. (n.d.) *William v. Rhodes* (1968); *Illinois v. Socialist Workers Party* (1979); *Anderson v. Celebrezze* (1983); *Jenness v. Fortson* (1971); *American Party of Texas v. White* (1974); *Bullock v. Carter* (1972); *Lubin v. Panish* (1974); *Communist Party of Indiana v. Whitcomb* (1974); *Storer v. Brown* (1974). *Justia.com*. Retrieved from *Justia.com*, https://supreme.justia.com/cases/federal/us/393/23/, https://supreme.justia.com/cases/federal/us/440/173/, https://supreme.justia.com/cases/federal/us/460/780/, https://supreme.justia.com/cases/federal/us/403/431/, https://supreme.justia.com/cases/federal/us/415/767/,https://supreme.justia.com/cases/federal/us/405/134/,https://supreme.justia.com/cases/federal/us/415/709/, https://supreme.justia.com/cases/federal/us/414/441/, https://supreme.justia.com/cases/federal/us/415/724/.

League of Women Voters. (1988, October 3). "League Refuses to 'Help Perpetuate a Fraud." *League of Women Voters*. Retrieved from: www.lwv.org/newsroom/press-releases/league-refuses-help-perpetrate-fraud

Libertarian Party. (2021, August 26). "The Sinister Attack on Ballot Access in New York." *Libertarian Party*. Retrieved from: www.lp.org/the-sinister-attack-on-ballot-access-in-new-york/

Lowi, T. (1992). "The Party Crasher." *The New York Times*. Retrieved from: www.nytimes.com/1992/08/23/magazine/the-party-crasher.html?searchResultPosition=4

Michele L. TIMMONS, v. TWIN CITIES AREA NEW PARTY. (1997). 520 U.S. 351. pp. Syllabus, II(43), III(46). Retrieved from: www.law.cornell.edu/supremecourt/text/520/351

Mikva, A. (1991). *FULANI v BRADY*. 935 F.2d 1324. Part IV. Retrieved from: https://casetext.com/case/fulani-v-brady

Muller, T. (2021, September 17). "Manchin Offers a Path Forward on Voting Rights With Compromise Bill." *Democracy Docket*. Retrieved from: www.democracydocket.com/news/manchin-offers-a-path-forward-on-voting-rights-with-compromise-bill

Noble, L., M. (1987). *Threshold Submission and Letter of Candidate Certifications and Agreements* [Memorandum]. Washington, DC: Federal Election Commission.

PBS NewsHour. (1992). "Interview with Judy Woodruff." *PBS NewsHour*. Retrieved from: www.youtube.com/watch?v=YpeYCvPQPn4

Ryan, T. (2020, June 12). "Court Rejects Push to Have Debates Welcome 3rd Party Candidates." *Courthouse News*. Retrieved from: www.courthousenews.com/court-rejects-push-to-have-debates-welcome-3rd-party-candidates/

Stevens, J. (2010). *CITIZENS UNITED v. FEDERAL ELECTION COMM'N*. 558 U.S. 310. Part V. Retrieved from: www.law.cornell.edu/supct/html/08-205.ZX.html.

The Hill. (2015, March 17). "Adding Independent Voices to the Debate." *The Hill*. Retrieved from: https://thehill.com/homenews/campaign/236046-adding-independent-voices-to-the-debate/.

Washington, G. (1769). "George Washington's Farewell Address." *Independent Chronicle*. Retrieved from: https://avalon.law.yale.edu/18th_century/washing.asp

Weiner, D., I. (2019) "Fixing the FEC: An Agenda for Reform." *Brennan Center for Justice*. pp. 11–12, endnote #27.

Wikipedia. (n.d.). "List of United States Presidential Candidates." *Wikipedia*. Retrieved from: https://en.wikipedia.org/wiki/List_of_United_States_presidential_candidates

Wikipedia. (n.d.). "1984 United States Presidential Election." *Wikipedia*. Retrieved from: https://en.wikipedia.org/wiki/1984_United_States_presidential_election

Chapter 7

McFadden, E., Daugherty, D., Hedberg, E., & Garcia, J. (2015). "Who is Arizona's Independent Voter?" *Morrison Institute for Public Policy*. Arizona State University. pp. 10. Retrieved from: https://morrisoninstitute.asu.edu/node/179

Chapter 8

Bradley, B. (2012, May 8). "Bill Bradley." Interview by C. Rose. Retrieved from: https://charlierose.com/videos/23653.

Choate, P. (2009). *Saving Capitalism: Keeping America Strong*. New York, NY: Vintage Books, pp. xiv.

Hedberg, E., Reilly, T., Daugherty, D., Garcia, J. (2017, April). "Voters, Media and Social Networks." *Morrison Institute for Public Policy*. Arizona State University. pp. 2.

Independent Voting. (2020). "Confronting a New Reality." *Independent Voting*. Retrieved from: https://independentvoting.org/survey-report/

Klar, S., and Krupnikov, Y. (2016) *Independent Politics*. Cambridge, UK: Cambridge University Press.

Pew Research Center. (2019, March 14). "Political Independents: Who They Are, What They Think." *Pew Research Center*. Retrieved from: https://www.pewresearch.org/politics/2019/03/14/political-independents-who-they-are-what-they-think/.

Roy, A. (2020, April 3). "The Pandemic is a Portal." *Financial Times*. Retrieved from: www.ft.com/content/10d8f5e8-74eb-11ea-95fe-fcd274e920ca

Sheffield, M. (2019, January 25). "Most Favor Policies to Improve Environment, But Are Divided Over Paying for it." *The Hill*. Retrieved from: www.ft.com/content/10d8f5e8-74eb-11ea-95fe-fcd274e920ca.

Skelley, G. (2017, June, 1). "Just How Many Obama 2012-Trump 2016 Voters Were There?." *Center for Politics*. Retrieved from: https://centerforpolitics.org/crystalball/articles/just-how-many-obama-2012-trump-2016-voters-were-there/

Skelley, G. (2021, April 15). "Few Americans who Identify as Independent are Actually Independent. That's Really Bad for Politics." *FiveThirtyEight*. Retrieved from: https://fivethirtyeight.com/features/few-americans-who-identify-as-independent-are-actually-independent-thats-really-bad-for-politics/

Yourdictionary.com. (n.d.). "Soup-sandwich." *Yourdictionary.com*. Retrieved from: www.yourdictionary.com/soup-sandwich

Chapter 9

About ALEC. (n.d.). American Legislative Exchange Council. Retrieved from: www.alec.org/about/

Altic, J., & Pallay, G. (2016, August 31). "Opinion | Ballot Measures: American Direct Democracy at Work." *The New York Times*. Retrieved from: www.nytimes.com/2016/08/31/opinion/campaign-stops/ballot-measures-american-direct-democracy-at-work.html

Altman, D., Flavin, P., & Radcliff, B. (2017). "Democratic Institutions and Subjective Well-Being." *Political Studies*, 65(3), pp. 685–704. Retrieved from: https://doi.org/10.1177/0032321716683203

Anthony, G., & Carl, A. (2019). "Two-Party System: A Case Study of United States of America." *Journal of Communication and English*, 4(1), pp. 18–26. Retrieved from: www.idosr.org/wp-content/uploads/2019/10/IDOSR-JCE-41-18-26-2019.pdf

AP NEWS. (2016, May 31). "AP-NORC Poll: Americans Want Nomination System Changed." *AP NEWS*. Retrieved from: https://apnews.com/article/f5821f2774c14c39ad00c1777f9ec6ea

Ballot Access News. (2020, March 1). "Volume 25, Number 10." *Ballot Access News*. Retrieved from: https://apnews.com/article/f5821f2774c14c39ad00c1777f9ec6ea.

Ballotpedia. (n.d.). "State-by-State Redistricting Procedures." *Ballotpedia*. Retrieved from: https://ballotpedia.org/State-by-state_redistricting_procedures

Ballotpedia. (n.d.). "Forms of Direct Democracy in the American States." *Ballotpedia*. Retrieved from: https://ballotpedia.org/Forms_of_direct_democracy_in_the_American_states

Ballotpedia. (n.d.). "Top-two Primary." *Ballotpedia*. Retrieved from: https://ballotpedia.org/Top-two_primary

Blais, A., & Dobrzynska, A. (1998). "Turnout in Electoral Democracies." *European Journal of Political Research*, 33(2), pp. 239–261. Retrieved from: https://doi.org/10.1111/1475-6765.00382

Boix, C., Miller, M., & Rosato, S. (2013). "A Complete Data Set of Political Regimes, 1800–2007." *Comparative Political Studies*, 46(12), pp. 1523–1554. Retrieved from: https://doi.org/10.1177/0010414012463905

Brooks, A. (2020, October 14). "'A Greater Choice' or 'Confusing': Arguments for and Against Ranked Choice Voting In WBUR Debate." *WBUR*. Retrieved from: www.wbur.org/news/2020/10/14/wbur-debate-question-2-ranked-choice-voting

Campaign Legal Center. (2019). "Bipartisan Poll Shows Strong Support for Redistricting Reform." *Campaign Legal Center*. Retrieved from: https://campaignlegal.org/update/bipartisan-poll-shows-strong-support-redistricting-reform

Campaign Legal Center. (2019, January 28). "New National Bipartisan Redistricting Poll." *Campaign Legal Center*. Retrieved from: https://campaignlegal.org/document/new-national-bipartisan-redistricting-poll

Centeno, R., Grose, C. R., Hernandez, N., & Wolf, K. (2021). *"The Demobilizing Effect of Primary Electoral Institutions on Voters of Color."* Presented at 2021 Midwest Political Science Association, Chicago, IL.

Chernow, R. (2004). *Alexander Hamilton*. London, UK: Penguin Books.

Chervinsky, L. (2021, December 8). "The History of Fake News from George Washington to Donald Trump." *Governing*. Retrieved from: www.governing.com/context/the-history-of-fake-news-from-george-washington-to-donald-trump

Comparative Data. (n.d.). AceProject.Org. Retrieved from: https://aceproject.org/epic-en

Croly, H. D. (1914). *Progressive Democracy*. New York, NY: Macmillan Co.

Crosson, J. (2018). "Extreme Districts, Moderate Winners: Same Party Challenges, and Deterrence in Top-two Primaries" *Political Science Research and Methods*. pp 1–17.

Cunningham, M. (2017). "Gerrymandering and Conceit: The Supreme Court's Conflict With Itself." *SSRN Electronic Journal*. Retrieved from: https://doi.org/10.2139/ssrn.2989985

De Leon, R. E. (2005). "San Francisco and Instant Runoff Voting: An Analysis of the SFSU/PRI Exit Poll Data Assessing Voter Opinions About Ranked Choice Voting in the November 2004 Board of Supervisors elections." San Francisco, CA. Retrieved from: http://archive.fairvote.org/media/irv/deleon2004_sanfran.pdf

de Tocqueville, A. (1948). *Democracy in America* (Vintage Books ed., Vol. 1). New York, NY: Vintage Books.

Drutman, L. (2020a). *Breaking the Two-Party Doom Loop: The Case for Multiparty Democracy in America*. Oxford, UK: Oxford University Press.

Drutman, L. (2020b, January 2). "The Two-Party System Broke the Constitution." *The Atlantic*. Retrieved from: www.theatlantic.com/ideas/archive/2020/01/two-party-system-broke-constitution/604213/

DuBois, W., E., B. (1956). "Why I Won't Vote." *The Nation Magazine*. Retrieved from: https://pisbpublications.wordpress.com/2016/07/31/why-i-wont-vote-by-w-e-b-dubois-published-in-the-nation-magazine-1956/

Eldersveld, S. J. (2000). "The American Party System: Origins and Development." In H. Walton Jr. (Ed.), *Political Parties in American Society* (pp. 43–65). London, UK: Palgrave Macmillan. Retrieved from: https://doi.org/10.1007/978-1-137-11290-3_3

Election Reformers Network. (n.d.). Supporting Ranked Choice Voting. *Election Reformers Network*. Retrieved from: https://electionreformers.org/supporting-ranked-choice-voting/

Elmelund, Præstekær, C. (2008). "Negative Campaigning in a Multiparty System." *Representation*, 44(1), pp. 27–39. Retrieved from: https://doi.org/10.1080/00344890701869082

FairVote. (n.d.). "Proportional Ranked Choice Voting." *FairVote*. Retrieved from: www.fairvote.org/prcv#how_prcv_works

FairVote.org. (2021). "Ranked Choice Voting/Instant Runoff." *FairVote*. Retrieved from: www.fairvote.org/rcv#where_is_ranked_choice_voting_used

Florida Poll. (n.d.). "Open Primaries." *Florida Poll*. Retrieved from: www.openprimaries. org/florida_poll

Gagnon, M. O. C. (2020, August 5). "Ranked-choice Voting Makes Elections Unnecessarily Complex and Confusing." *Bangor Daily News*. Retrieved from: https:// bangordailynews.com/2020/08/05/opinion/ranked-choice-voting-makes-elections-unnecessarily-complex-and-confusing-2/

Gehl, K. B. O. M. (2021, March 12). "Opinion: It's Time to Get Rid of Party Primaries." *CNN*. Retrieved from: https://edition.cnn.com/2021/03/12/opinions/reform-american-political-primaries-gehl/index.html

Gehl, K. M., & Porter, M. E. (2020). *The Politics Industry: How Political Innovation Can Break Partisan Gridlock and Save Our Democracy*. Cambridge, MA: Harvard Business Review Press.

Graham, M. H., & Svolik, M. W. (2020). "Democracy in America? Partisanship, Polarization, and the Robustness of Support for Democracy in the United States." *American Political Science Review*, 114(2), pp. 392–409. Retrieved from: https://doi.org/10.1017/s0003055420000052

Greenblatt, A., (2021, December 3). "Redistricting Reform is Easier Said than Done." *Governing*. Retrieved from: www.governing.com/now/redistricting-reform-is-easier-said-than-done

Grose, C. R. (2020). "Reducing Legislative Polarization: Top-Two and Open Primaries Are Associated with More Moderate Legislators." *Journal of Political Institutions and Political Economy*. pp. 267–287.

Gruber, J, Hardy, M., A., & Kresky, H. (2019). "Let All Voters Vote: Independents and the Expansion of Voting Rights in the United States." *Touro Law Review*, 35(2), pp. 652. Touro Law.

Hasan, M. (2021, September 3). "Eight Simple Steps to Fix American Democracy." *New Statesman*. Retrieved from: www.newstatesman.com/world/americas/north-america/2018/11/eight-simple-steps-fix-american-democracy

Hofstadter, R. (1968). *The Idea of a Party System* (First Ed.). Berkeley, CA: University of California Press.

Indivisible. (2021, July 16). "Fighting Gerrymandering in the States." *Indivisible*. Retrieved from: https://indivisible.org/resource/fighting-gerrymandering-states

Kambhampaty, A. P. (2019, November 6). "New York City Voters Just Adopted Ranked-Choice Voting in Elections. Here's How It Works." *Time*. Retrieved from: https://time.com/5718941/ranked-choice-voting/

Kruzel, J. (2021a, August 4). "American Voters Largely United Against Partisan Gerrymandering, Polling Shows." *The Hill*. Retrieved from: https://thehill.com/homenews/state-watch/566327-american-voters-largely-united-against-partisan-gerrymandering-polling

Kruzel, J. (2021b, August 8). "Supreme Court Decision Could Set Off Gerrymandering 'Arms Race.'" *The Hill*. Retrieved from: https://thehill.com/regulation/court-battles/566631-supreme-court-decision-could-set-off-gerrymandering-arms-race

Legal Information Institute. (n.d.). "One-person, One-vote Rule." *Legal Information Institute*. Retrieved from: www.law.cornell.edu/wex/one-person_one-vote_rule

Lijphart, A. (2007). *Thinking about Democracy*. Abingdon, UK: Routledge.

Lumen Learning. (n.d.). "The Two-Party System." *Lumen Learning*. Retrieved from: https://courses.lumenlearning.com/boundless-politicalscience/chapter/the-two-party-system/

McGhee, E., & Shor, B. (2017). "Has the Top Two Primary Elected More Moderates?" *Perspectives on Politics*, 15(4), pp. 1053–1066. Retrieved from: https://doi.org/10.1017/S1537592717002158

Miller, J. (2020, May 21). "Top-two and Open Primary Elections Produce Less Extreme Lawmakers." *USC News*. Retrieved from: https://news.usc.edu/170366/top-two-open-primary-elections-less-extreme-lawmakers-usc-study/

Mulroy, S. (2020). *Rethinking US Election Law: Unskewing the System (Rethinking Law)*. Cheltenham: Edward Elgar Pub.

NCSL.Org. (2021). "Initiative and Referendum Processes." *NCSL.Org*. Retrieved from: www.ncsl.org/research/elections-and-campaigns/initiative-and-referendum-processes.aspx#/

Negri, M. (2014). *Minority Representation in Proportional Representation Systems (Unpublished manuscript)*. St Andrews, UK: University of St. Andrews.

Open Primaries. (n.d.). "Myths and Facts." *Open Primaries*. Retrieved from: www.openprimaries.org/myths_and_facts

OpenSecrets. (n.d.) "Reelection Rates Over the Years." *OpenSecrets*. Retrieved from: www.opensecrets.org/elections-overview/reelection-rates

Oxford University Press. (2020, October 28). "Is Gerrymandering 'Poisoning the Well' of Democracy?" *OUP Blog*. Retrieved from: https://blog.oup.com/2020/10/is-gerrymandering-poisoning-the-well-of-democracy/

Pierce, R. O. C. (2019, July 12). "Eliminate Primary Elections to Restore Our Strong Democracy." *The Hill*. Retrieved from: https://thehill.com/opinion/campaign/452844-eliminate-primary-elections-to-restore-our-strong-democracy

Pierson, G. W. (1938). *Tocqueville and Beaumont in America* (First Ed.). Oxford, UK: Oxford University Press.

Pildes, R. H. (2011). "Why the Center Does Not Hold: The Causes of Hyperpolarized Democracy in America." *California Law Review*, 99(2), pp. 273–333. Retrieved from: www.jstor.org/stable/23018603

Postell, J. (2018). "The Rise and Fall of Political Parties in America." *The Heritage Foundation*. Retrieved from: www.heritage.org/political-process/report/the-rise-and-fall-political-parties-america

Radcliff, B. (2013). *The Political Economy of Human Happiness: How Voters' Choices Determine the Quality of Life*. Cambridge, UK: Cambridge University Press.

Reilly, T. (2014). *Rethinking Public Sector Compensation*. Abingdon, UK: Routledge.

Rubinstein, D., Mays, J. C., & Fitzsimmons, E. G. (2021, June 30). "Why Some N.Y.C. Lawmakers Want to Rethink Ranked-Choice Voting." *The New York Times*. Retrieved from: www.nytimes.com/2020/12/09/nyregion/ranked-choice-lawsuit-voting.html

RUCHO v. COMMON CAUSE. (2019, June 27). No. 18–422. Retrieved from: www.law.cornell.edu/supremecourt/text/18-422#writing-18-422_SYLLABUS

"S. Doc No. 106–21." (2000). Retrieved from: www.govinfo.gov/content/pkg/GPO-CDOC-106sdoc21/pdf/GPO-CDOC-106sdoc21.pdf

Selb, P. (2008). "A Deeper Look at the Proportionality—Turnout Nexus." *Comparative Political Studies*, 42(4), pp. 527–548. Retrieved from: https://doi.org/10.1177/0010414008327427

The Democracy Amendments. (2021, April 29). "The Democracy Amendments." *Free Speech For People.* Retrieved from: https://freespeechforpeople.org/democracy-amendments/

Time. (2016, December 2). "5 Radical Solutions to Fix Our Busted Government." *Time.* Retrieved from: https://time.com/4585012/technocracy-how-to-fix-government/

Trickey, E. (2017, July 20). "Where Did the Term 'Gerrymander' Come From?" *Smithsonian Magazine.* Retrieved from: www.smithsonianmag.com/history/where-did-term-gerrymander-come-180964118/

Troiano, N. (2021, March 30). "Party Primaries Must Go." *The Atlantic.* Retrieved from: www.theatlantic.com/ideas/archive/2021/03/party-primaries-must-go/618428/

Tyson, R. (2021). "National Electoral Reforms Survey." *R Street Institute.* Retrieved from: www.rstreet.org/wp-content/uploads/2021/02/National-Survey-Memo_2-8-21.pdf

University of Virginia Press. (1780, October). "Founders Online: From John Adams to Jonathan Jackson." *FoundersArchives.Gov.* Retrieved from: https://founders.archives.gov/documents/Adams/06-10-02-0113

Vasilogambros, M. (2021, March 12). "Ranked-Choice Voting Gains Momentum Nationwide." *The Pew Charitable Trusts.* Retrieved from: www.pewtrusts.org/en/research-and-analysis/blogs/stateline/2021/03/12/ranked-choice-voting-gains-momentum-nationwide

Wikipedia Contributors. (2021, November 24). "Proportional Representation." *Wikipedia.* Retrieved from: https://en.wikipedia.org/wiki/Proportional_representation

Williamson, R. D. (2019). "Examining the Effects of Partisan Redistricting on Candidate Entry Decisions." *Election Law Journal*, 18(3), pp. 214–226. Retrieved from: https://doi.org/10.1089/elj.2018.0505

Chapter 10

Adams, B., Lascher, E., & Martin, D. (2020). *Ballot Cues, Business Candidates, and Voter Choices in Local Elections.* American Political Research.

Ballotpedia. (2017). "Partisanship in United States Municipal Elections, 2017." *Ballotpedia.* Retrieved from: https://ballotpedia.org/Partisanship_in_United_States_municipal_elections,_2017#History_of_local_nonpartisanship

Ballotpedia. (2020). "Unicameralism." *Ballotpedia.* Retrieved from: https://ballotpedia.org/Unicameralism

Ballotpedia. (n.d.). "Nonpartisan Election of Judges." *Ballotpedia.* Retrieved from: https://ballotpedia.org/Nonpartisan_election_of_judges

Ballotpedia. (n.d.). "Nonpartisan." *Ballotpedia.* Retrieved from https://ballotpedia.org/Nonpartisan

Bonneau, C. W., & Cann, D. M. (2015). "Party Identification and Vote Choice in Partisan and Nonpartisan Elections." *Political Behavior*, 37(1), pp. 43–66. Springer.

Campbell, A. (1960). *The American Voter.* Hoboken, NJ: John Wiley & Sons.

Croly, H. (1914). *Progressive Democracy.* New York: The Macmillan Company. p. 341.

Diamond, L., Johnson, K., & Rapoport, M. (2021, April 4). "The Time Has Come for Nonpartisan State Election Leadership." *The Hill.* Retrieved from: https://thehill.com/opinion/campaign/546307-the-time-has-come-for-nonpartisan-state-election-leadership.

Douglass, F. (1863, January). "Douglass' Monthly." Retrieved from: https://transcription.si.edu/view/13223/ACM-2007.19.27_02.

Fiorina, M. P. (2017). *Unstable Majorities, Polarization, Party Sorting & Political Stalemate.* Stanford, CA: Hoover Institution Press. pp. 218–219.

Freedom House. (n.d.). "United States: Freedom in the World 2021 Country Report." *Freedom House.* Retrieved from: https://freedomhouse.org/country/united-states/freedom-world/2021

Friedman, T. (2018, October 2). "The American Civil War, Part II." *The New York Times.* Retrieved from: www.nytimes.com/2018/10/02/opinion/the-american-civil-war-part-ii.html.

Gruber, J. (2015). "The Myth of the Red State." *Open Primaries.* Retrieved from: www.openprimaries.org/research_nebraska

Guelzo, A. (2006). *Lincoln's Emancipation Proclamation: The End of Slavery in America.* New York, NY: Simon & Schuster. pp. 178–179.

Hawley, W. D. (1973). *Nonpartisan Elections and the Case for Party Politics.* New York, NY: John Wiley.

Homans, C. (2021). "Trump Loyalists Speed Into Jobs Overseeing Votes." *The New York Times.* Retrieved from: https://www.nytimes.com/2021/12/11/us/politics/trust-in-elections-trump-democracy.html.

Jacobson, G. C. (1997). *The Politics of Congressional Elections* (Fourth Ed.). New York, NY: Longman.

Jewell, M. E., & Breaux, D. (1988). "The Effect of Incumbency on State Legislative Elections." *Legislative Studies Quarterly*, 13, pp. 495–514.

Kirkland, P. A., & Coppock, A. (2018). "Candidate Choice Without Party Labels." *Political Behavior*, 40, pp. 571–591. Springer.

Lascher, E. (1991). "The Case of the Missing Democrats: Reexamining the Republican Advantage in Nonpartisan Elections." *Western Political Quarterly*, 44, pp. 656–75.

Lee, E. C. (1960). *The Politics of Nonpartisanship: A Study of California City Elections.* Berkeley, CA: University of California Press.

Matson, M., & Fine, T. (2006). "Gender, Ethnicity, and Ballot Information: Ballot Cues in Low-information Elections." *State Politics and Policy Quarterly*, 6, pp. 49–72.

National League of Cities. (2020, October 23). "Cities 101—Partisan and Non-Partisan Elections." *National League of Cities.* Retrieved from: www.nlc.org/resource/cities-101-partisan-and-non-partisan-elections/

Nebraska Legislature. (n.d.). "Nebraska Legislature—History of the Unicameral." *Nebraska Legislature.* Retrieved from: https://nebraskalegislature.gov/about/history_unicameral.php

Reilly, T. (2016) *The Failure of Governance in Bell, California.* Lanham, MD: Lexington Books.

Schaffner, B. F., Streb, M., & Wright, G. (2001). "Teams without Uniforms: The Nonpartisan Ballot in State and Local Elections." *Political Research Quarterly*, 54(1), pp. 7–30.

Schaffner, B. F., Streb, M., & Wright, G. (2007). "A New Look at the Republican Advantage in Nonpartisan Elections." *Political Science Quarterly*, 54, pp. 7–30.

Schattschneider, E. (1942). *Party Government.* New York: Farrar & Rinehart, pp. 1.

Smith, R., & Squire, P. (1990). "The Effects of Prestige Names in Question Wording." *Public Opinion Quarterly*, 54, pp. 97–116.

Squire, P., & Smith, R. (1988). "The Effect of Partisan Information on Voters in Nonpartisan Elections." *Journal of Politics*, 50, pp. 169–179.

Walter, B. (2022). *How Civil War Starts: And How to Stop Them.* New York, NY: Crown Publishing.

Wikimedia Foundation. (2021, December 5). "United States Secretary of State." *Wikipedia*. Retrieved from: https://en.wikipedia.org/wiki/United_States_Secretary_of_State

Wikimedia Foundation. (2021, November 15). "Federal Election Commission." *Wikipedia*. Retrieved from: https://en.wikipedia.org/wiki/Federal_Election_Commission

Wright, G. (2008). "Charles Adrian and the Study of Nonpartisan Elections." *Political Research Quarterly*, 61(1), 13–16. Retrieved from: https://doi.org/10.1177/1065912907311743.

Afterword

Ali, O. (2020). *In the Balance of Power Independent Black Politics and Third Party Movements in the United States*. Athens, OH: Ohio University Press. pp. 14–17.

Ferreira da Silva, D. (2016). *On Difference Without Separability*. São Paulo: Fundaca Bienal de Sao Paulo. pp. 57–65.

Ortiz, P. (2018). *An African American and Latinx History of the United States*. Boston, MA: Beacon Press. pp. 14–18.

INDEX

Communist Party of Indiana v. Whitcomb
(US Supreme Court 1974) 81
Congress for Racial Equality 23
Constitution Party 26
Constitutional Convention (1787) 113
Conyers, John 80
Cook Political Report 6
Cooper, Christopher 39
corruption, two-partyism and 114–16
COVID-19 7, 79, 95, 147
Croly, Herbert D. 115, 117, 119, 126, 133
Crosson, Jesse 123
Cunningham, McKay 119
Cuomo, Andrew 79

Dahl, Robert A. 20
Davis, Angela 25
Dawkins, Andy 82
De Tocqueville, Alexis 114
Dean, Howard 146
Debs, Eugene V. 22, 143
Declaration of Independence 120, 142
Delaney, John 80
On Democracy (Dahl, R.) 20
Democracy in America (De Tocqueville, A.)
114
Democratic Leadership Council (DLC)
9; power, independent voters and their
uses of 48, 49, 54
Democratic National Committee (DNC)
6, 54, 146
Democratic Party 4–5, 6, 9, 10, 34,
35–6, 108, 110, 142–7; concessions
made to labor movement by (1935)
143; dilemma for democracy 114–15;
historical perspective 18, 19–20, 21,
22–4, 25, 26–8; inability to fulfill
promise of Great Society 46; legal
barriers and biases against independents
76, 79; power (and uses of) 46, 48, 49,
51–2, 53–4, 55; reaction to the Black
and independent alliance 20; violence
and divisive tactics employed by 19;
white supremacy and 18
development of democracy: anti-
fusion laws 136; bipartisan systems,
nonpartisan arrangements and 136;
Civil War (1861–5) 132; elections,
decline of democracy and 134–5;
Emancipation Proclamation (1863)
131–2; Federal Election Commission
(FEC) 134, 135; *How Civil War Starts*
(Walter, B. F.) 132; independent voters,

American people and saving democracy
136; institutions of government,
separation between functions of political
parties and 136; Nebraska, democracy
reforms in 135–6; nonpartisan ballot,
expansion of 133–5; partisan contests
for election officials 135; party
allegiance 132–3; *Party Government*
(Schattschneider, E. E.) 134; party
identification, voter decision-making
and 134; Reconstruction (1863–7)
132; socioeconomic transformation,
party creativity and 132; transformative
reform 133; tribal worlds, power in 132
Diamond, Larry 84
dilemma for democracy 113–26; bipartisan
government, limitations of 116–18;
bipartisan government, Washington's
warning against 113; *Breaking the
Two-Party Doom Loop: The Case
for Multiparty Democracy in America*
(Drutman, L.) 118; civil discourse,
party division and decline in 116–17;
Constitutional Convention (1787)
113; corruption, two-partyism and
114–16; *Democracy in America* (De
Tocqueville, A.) 114; gerrymandering
119–20; good government groups 121;
Louisiana, general elections in 123;
multiparty system 118–19; National
Association for the Advancement
of Colored People (NAACP) 115;
nonpartisan primaries, general elections
and 122–4; nonpartisan redistricting
119–21; open primaries 121–2; open
primaries, moderating potential of 122;
partisan gerrymandering, overwhelming
opposition to 121; partisanship,
assessment of reform in conditions of
126; political parties, De Tocqueville's
concerns about dangers of 114; political
patronage, spoils system and 114–15;
*The Politics Industry: How Political
Innovation Can Break Partisan Gridlock
and Save Our Democracy* (Gehl, K., &
Porter, M.) 116–17; primary elections,
creation of 121–2; propaganda and
political disinformation, Washington's
warning against 114; proportional
representation 118–19; ranked-choice
voting (RCV) 123–4, 125; *Rucho v.
Common Cause* (US Supreme Court
2019) 120, 147; state legislatures,